AF478933

THE MERLIN YEARS
The Art of Team Macho II

Copyright 2012 Magic Pony
All rights reserved. First Edition.
ISBN 978-0-9783568-5-9

Designed by Steve Cober.
Photography by Richelle Forsey, Steve Cober, Kristin Weckworth, Desiree Beaubien and Team Macho.
Printed in Canada.

MAGIC PONY
680 Queen St West Toronto ON Canada M6J 1E5
www.magic-pony.com
www.narwhalprojects.com

Other Publications by Magic Pony & Narwhal Projects

MY MANIA: THE ART OF DERRICK HODGSON
ISBN: 978-0-9783568-1-1

FANCY ACTION NOW: THE ART OF TEAM MACHO
ISBN: 978-0-9783568-0-4

THE UNKNOWN PORTRAITS by KOZYNDAN
ISBN: 978-0-9783568-2-8

THE TAXALI 300 by GARY TAXALI
ISBN: 978-0-9783568-3-5

THE DAZZLE : A Cabinet of Wonder
ISBN: 978-0-9783568-4-2

Original artwork is available through Narwhal Projects.
www.narwhalprojects.com

TEAM MACHO

THE
MERLIN
YEARS

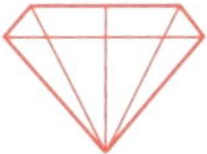

NARWHAL

BEING MACHO

by A. James Bradley

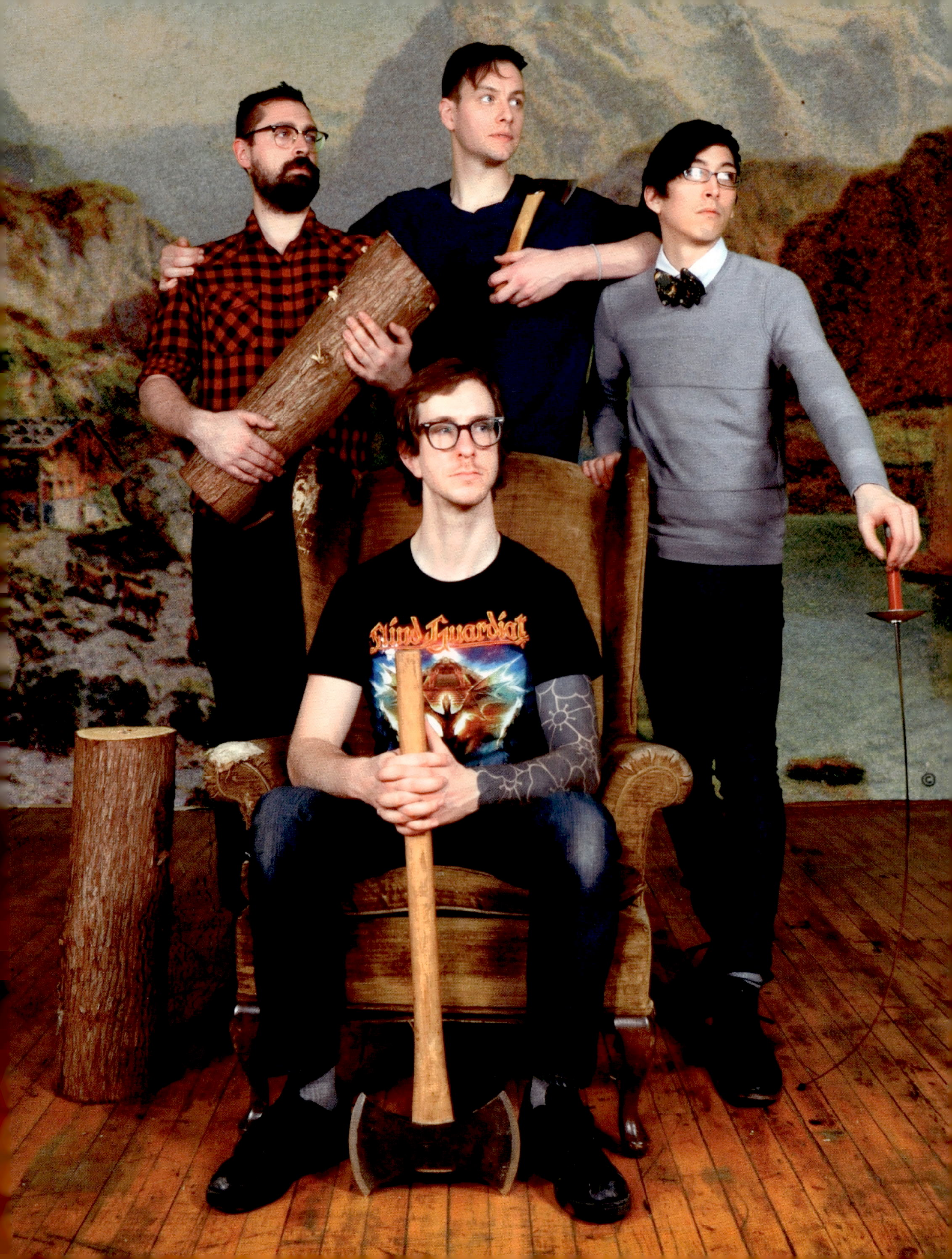

Blind Guardian

BEING MACHO

A. James Bradley

On the eve of Team Macho's first show at the AGO, I sit in the basement of the gallery watching the creation of their large-scale installation and wonder, how do four art-school kids end up here in this space that also houses Reubens's *"Massacre of the Innocents"*? How did they get here? During a walking tour of the gallery one of the guys is quick to point out how "fucking good" a set of paintings by Clarence Gagnon (a relatively unknown French Canadian impressionist) are, citing details about the technical virtuosity involved in creating his landscapes. Forever concerned with the process of art, their jaunts around the gallery are not meant to be leisurely. They may move slowly through the salons but their engagement with the art on the walls is frenetic; they hone their craft by consuming things like the variations in color-use and consistency of the brushstrokes of the gallery's artists. For Team Macho this is serious study and they deconstruct paintings in much the same way that a musician separates instruments in a radio mix: piece-by-piece and moment-by-moment.

Team Macho is rarely labeled serious. Read about them in any of their previous publications and you will hear about how witty and fun they are, how their work is an amalgam of illustration and painting; how they collectively undermine each other's offerings in a type of ego-destroying game, and how the everyday, when seen through their eyes, somehow becomes extraordinary. We are told this is what it means to be "Macho" in their world. This is all true. But what this description lacks is a real sense of what Team Macho does. The slapstick brushstrokes in most of their work are a challenge to the idea of what constitutes art and how it is made. Their trademark spirit of competition is present in nearly all of their work: they brainstorm with friendly disagreements about most things, including who came up with the name Team Macho.

If there were a primer on Team Macho, the first thing it would tell you is that to pigeonhole them as a certain type of art collective is simply to miss the point of their work altogether. In general, the consensus from the team is that they are always amazed by interpretations of their work because they don't know how to interpret it themselves. The second thing you should know about Team Macho is that they are working artists. Around Queen St West in Toronto, where they show their art, it may appear that everyone is making art. The streets are filled with everything from ladies on the corner hawking what seems like paint-by-number dogs to galleries selling high-priced pieces. But while most of these people call themselves artists, Team Macho make their living as artists. To understand Team Macho, you must understand that their work is their life and their living. They have dedicated themselves to performing the act of mark-making, and their collective goal is to reveal the process of this endeavour, to demystify what it means to live a life dedicated to art, and to display both their mistakes and triumphs in front of a crowd. Often charged with being funny or base, Team Macho does not present only the best of what they make, and, paradoxically, it's by overcoming their collective ego that this approach always produces their best. In general their work is not purely an exercise in aesthetics, although walking around a Team Macho show you will overhear wild interpretations claiming that it is. The Team will say outright that their work is not meant to be decoded, not intended to flummox or bamboozle their audience; they simply paint and draw, exposing what goes on inside their heads. But the public disagrees.

Team Macho have chosen to walk a different path, to live what they call the "Macho" lifestyle, which inevitably means that they are enamoured by the way other people live: things like new frying pans and home fixtures that work are simple pleasures that they have chosen to forgo to be able to get to this point in their career. In this part of their universe the word "Macho" is used ironically, inverting the expected notions of what people think they should be and how they should live. To experience this lifestyle one need only pay a visit to their downtown headquarters. Climbing through the basement window of their studio is like falling down the rabbit hole, and after five minutes among the machismo one realizes

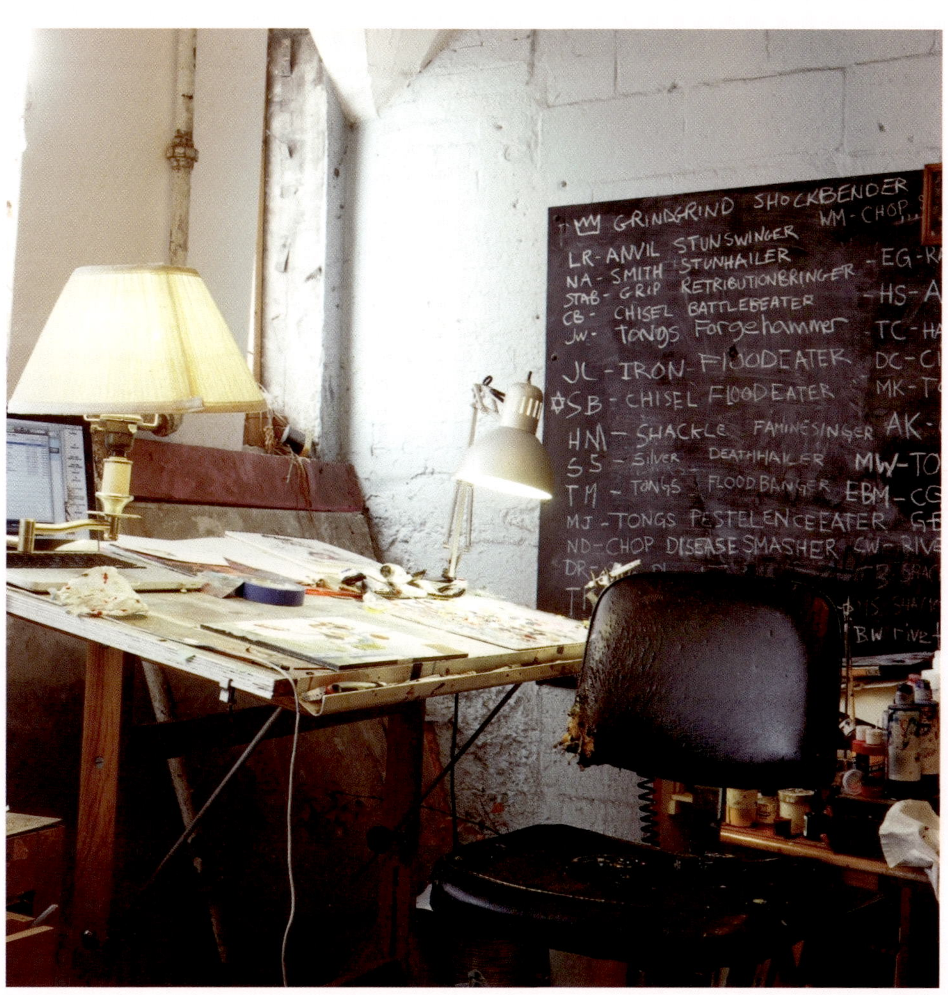
GRINDGRIND SHOCKBENDER   WM- CHOP
LR- ANVIL STUNSWINGER
NA- SMITH   STUNHAILER   EG- KA
STAB- GRIP RETRIBUTIONBRINGER   HS- A
CB- CHISEL BATTLEBEATER
JW- TONGS FORGEHAMMER   TC- HA
JL- IRON FLOODEATER   DC- CI
SB- CHISEL FLOODEATER   MK- TO
HM- SHACKLE FAMINESINGER AK-
SS- SILVER DEATHHAILER   MW- TO
TM- TONGS FLOODBANGER EBM- CG
MJ- TONGS PESTELENCEEATER GE
ND- CHOP DISEASE SMASHER GW- RIVE
DRE
BW RIVE

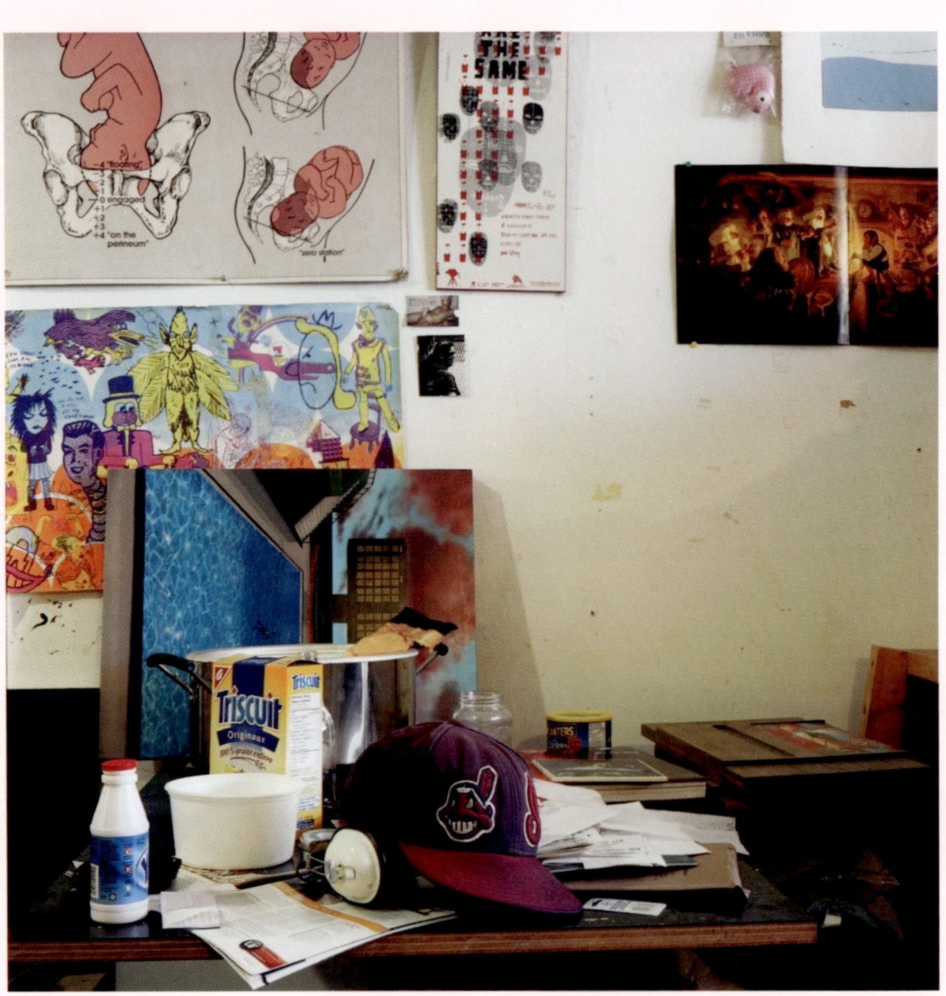

that it is not an act, that Team Macho's secret lies in their everyday belief that art is about process, about form and content, about the ego-less pursuit of the interesting. And, it is about sometimes staring at a painting to try to find out what's missing and someone crying aloud: "Lets just put some dicks in it." This is the story of being Macho.

PROCESS AS ART

In her essay *Against Interpretation,* Susan Sontag writes that "[n]one of us can ever retrieve that innocence before all theory when art knew no need to justify itself, when one did not ask of a work of art what it said because one knew (or thought one knew) what it did." If, as Sontag claims, interpretation is now inescapable, then we must conclude that the philosophy of Team Macho is based on a type of anti-art. It is an attempt to return to artistic innocence before art had to be a certain way. This is a slippery slope for the gallery goer, who wants to interpret, who feels that any picture of a baby with "Dyke" written across her forehead in big block letters must be a comment on something. But for Team Macho their art is presented without an overt message and they take great pride in the myriad of explanations they have received over the years from the gallery-going public as to what their work means. In that particular piece, one member began the process by painting a charming watercolour of a smiling infant and then passed it on to another to finish. This is when "Dyke" got scrawled across her forehead. And then they laughed. In this particular work there are subtle clues that allude to the baby identifying as gay, which are often missed because of initial outrage. The process that is demonstrated in a painting like this is both an act of creation and destruction; the only intent is to ruin what was already done and in so doing to augment what has been made. In most cases the motivation for such an addition is humour.

Team Macho shies away from posturing. Their work can be both funny and dark but it is always accessible, and their willingness to fail in public helps the viewers to make sense of what they are seeing. In another of my favourite paintings they have embedded the deliberately ungrammatical text: "Dear diary Today I ask my father where babees com form This is a drawing of his explanation." It ends up presenting an aesthetic of representation using

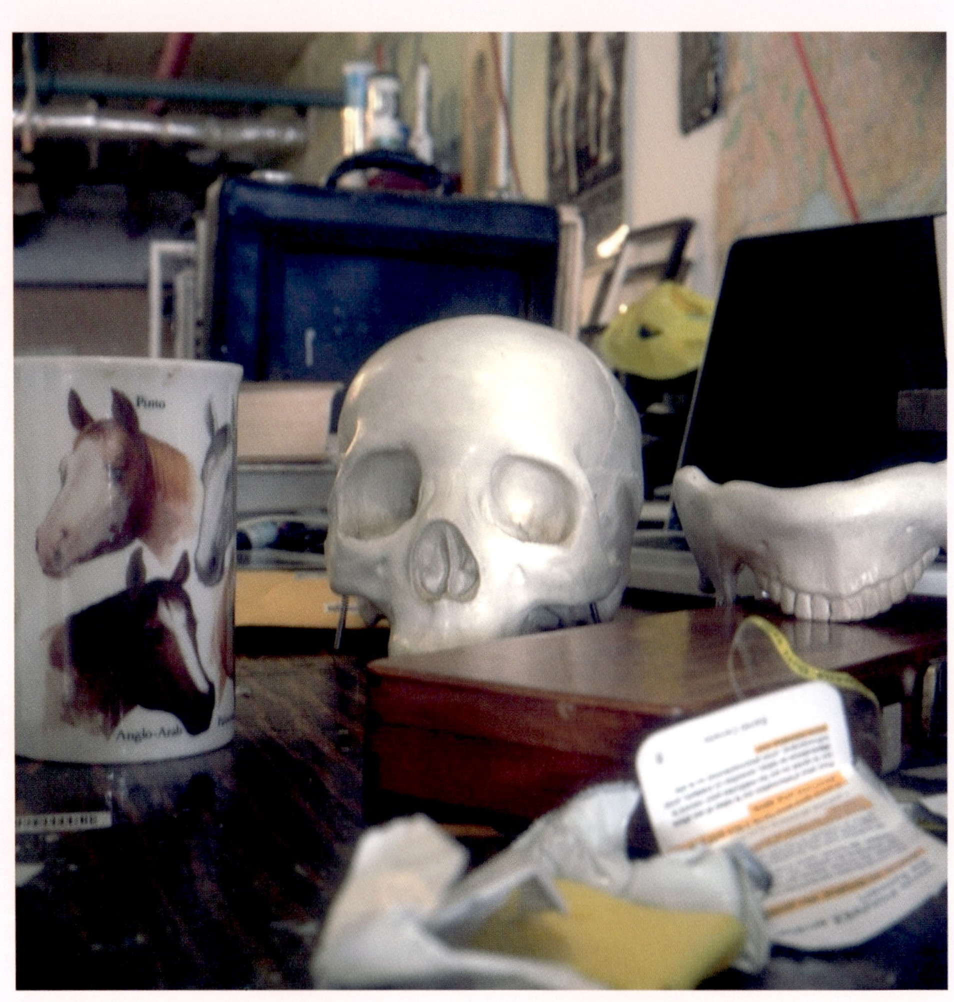

lines and text, making the actual picture secondary to the misspelled words that do not seem to match the doodle-like sketch that stands below it. Team Macho have their own language not unlike the text in the "babees" painting. After years of working in such close proximity they have a shorthand way of talking that borders on the unintelligible. Spending time with them is like being in the presence of quadruplets who speak their own brand of Pig Latin so as not to divulge their secrets to their mother. This is how they live, work and operate — collectively — and their brand of art reverberates with this fact in every piece. Their goal has always been to reveal the process, to paint in public, and to externalize the grind of making art. Spending years learning the grammar of the brush and then producing some of the finest paintings around does not mean that they must always create art using the same methods. They are constantly trying to unlearn what they know, to push the boundaries of their work, and to reclaim their innocence and playfulness in regards to art. Ruskin writes that

> *"He who has learned what is commonly considered the whole art of painting, that is, the art of representing any natural object faithfully, has as yet only learned the language by which his thoughts are to be expressed. He has done just as much toward being that which we ought to respect as a great painter, as a man who has learned how to express himself grammatically and melodiously has toward being a great poet"* (Ruskin, On Painting 40).

Team Macho believes that to be great painters their art must challenge the idea of how to unlearn what they have been taught, that the process of making art should not be privileged so as to remain hidden, and that the interpretation of all of this belongs in the hands of the viewer.

As an example, their current installation, *Axis Mundi,* has a large mural backdrop of a forest that has bright pink spots on it standing ready for analysis. These marks have a special meaning for the artists, but Team Macho simultaneously harbour excitement waiting to see what they mean to everyone else. After the process of transmission and reception concludes they always seem to find humour in how wide the spectrum of interpretation that relates to their work really is. The mythos that drives them is always private and, in an ironic twist, their art seems to charm specifically because their final products are approachable. Making the private amicable is what Team Macho does. But in this process their artistic intentions are almost always different from the meaning that the viewer extracts. This is one of the things that draw people to Team Macho; their art is so varied and seemingly disparate that publicly it is hard to dispute any interpretation. In the same essay quoted above, Sontag makes the statement that "Art is seduction, not rape." When read this statement, half of Team Macho swore that their work was the former and the other half swore it was the latter, and then they laughed, the joke being that it is probably both.

SERIOUS ART

What Team Macho understands collectively is that serious art need not be filled with serious content. They often employ traditional painterly techniques to create works of the utmost beauty and then playfully undermine the entire endeavour by including some subversive act. My favourite example is *A Fine Balance* from a recent show. It is a painting, done in oils on board, of a pyramid of acrobats, presented in painstaking detail that looks more like a renaissance piece than a contemporary offering. But, in usual Team Macho style, upon closer inspection the viewer will notice that the leotards of the acrobats are crotchless and that their acrobatic members are all hanging out. A product of the team mantra ("lets just put some dicks in it"), this painting appears to be funny —but for them it is not a joke. They want to put you in a critical space in which you are forced to question what you are looking at, and then you laugh. Because of moves like this, Team Macho are often labeled as being jokesters, but they are so much more than that. What they do with their work is create a large metaphorical gap to allow the viewers to engage with a piece of art on their own terms. This is why the interpretations of their work are so varied. The edges of their metaphors are wide —often producing a humorous response because the content borders on the absurd — but their process allows something much more important than humour. It allows room for interpretation, not solicited, rarely agreed upon, but always possible.

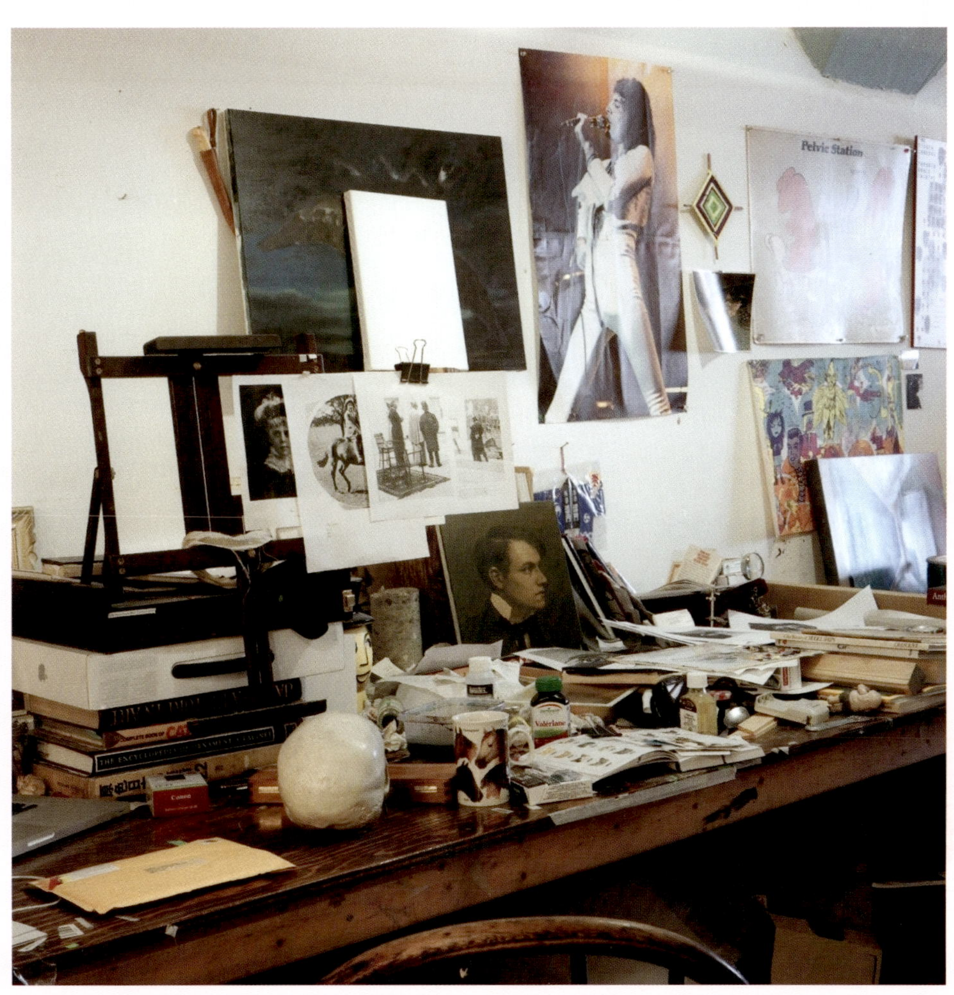

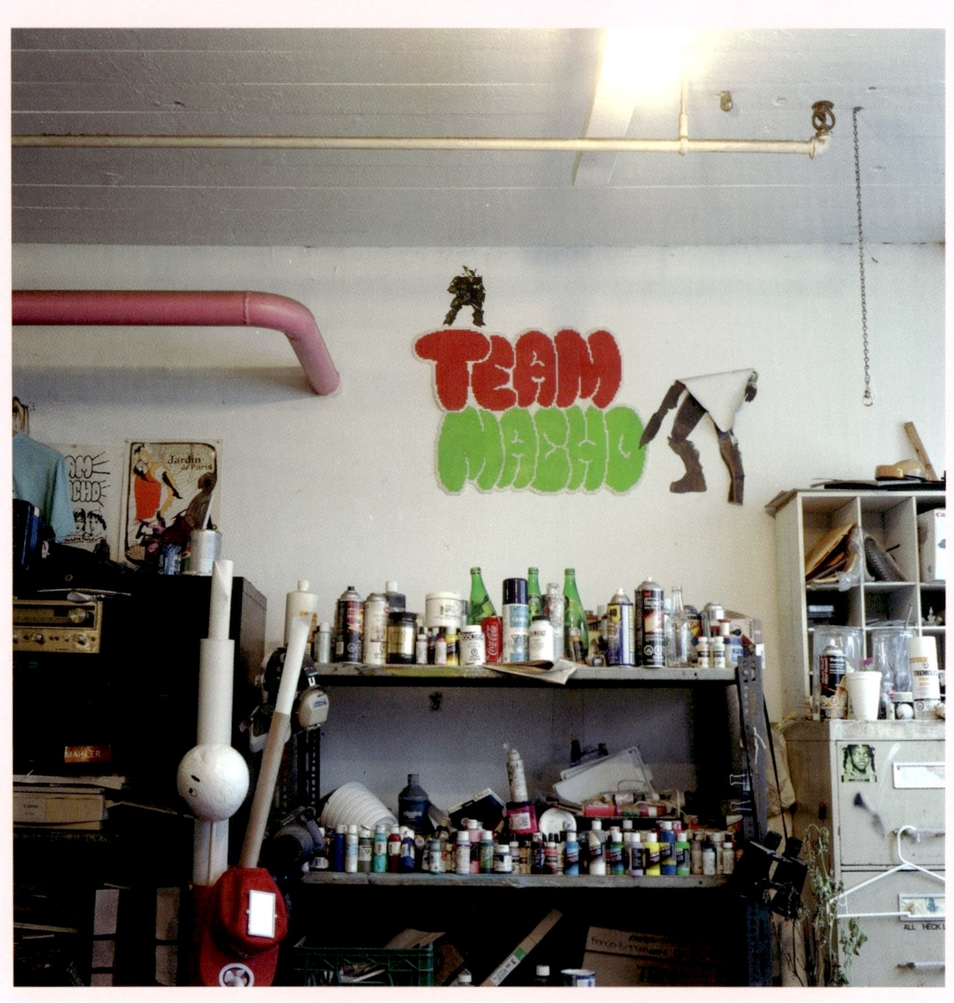

Team Macho paintings mean something different to each viewer and in this way deliver a sense of personal connection to those who seek out their work, often inverting subject and object and asking their patrons to consider that the painting may in fact be looking at them. Viewers of *A Fine Balance* engage the painting in the usual way until they realize what is happening on the canvas and their embarrassment becomes the new dialogue. In this way the painting is acting on the viewer, just as the viewer's interpretation acts on the painting.

THE MACHO INSTANT

One final thing to consider is that time as we usually experience it in art is absent in Team Macho's work. The collaborative nature of their art means that each piece and each contribution has a different axis of time, one in which every addition marks another instant of the narrative. Each work is about that exact thing at that exact instant; it does not allude to the moment before or the moment after, but is about right now. The right now may be about Siamese robots and twenty-three toed cats, but it is about those things in the moment they were imagined. Collectively they all seem to view this moment a little differently and their contributions explain this, meaning that each work of art is a collection of how they each individually see the moment, together. For Team Macho that moment is what they are trying to show you. It is a way to challenge your expectations of them, including what the word "macho" means in relation to their work. It is about being in their world and about the exposure of the process that makes these four guys, and everyone who engages in the experience of their art, Macho.

SELECTED ARTWORK

2007 - 2011

Weapon of Choice   2007

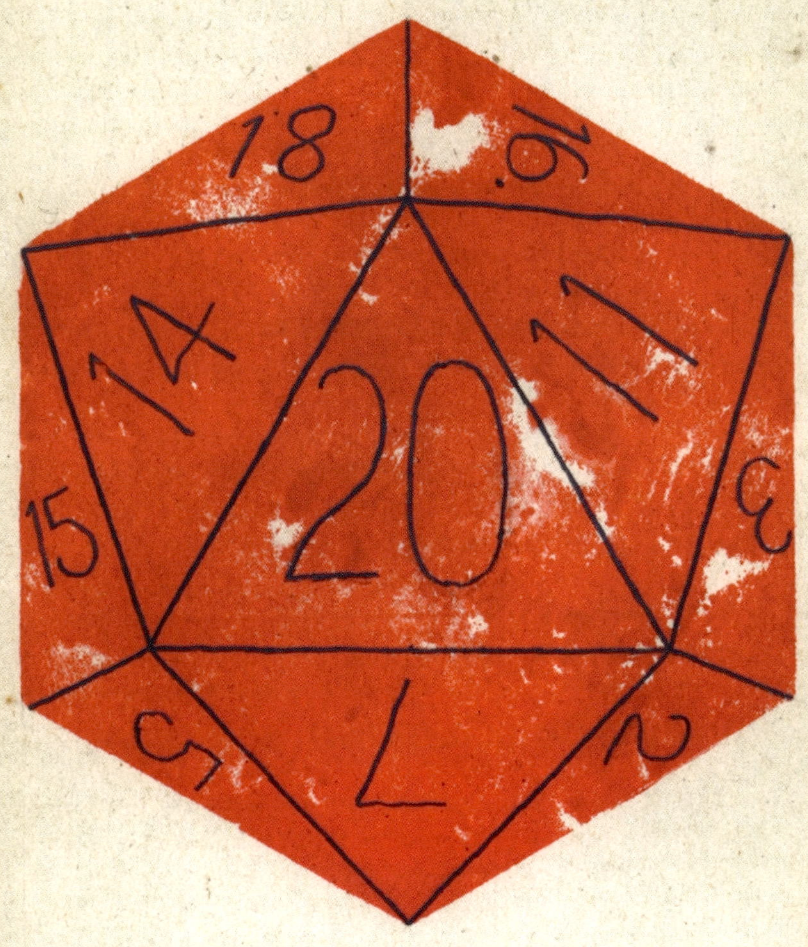

Weapon of choice

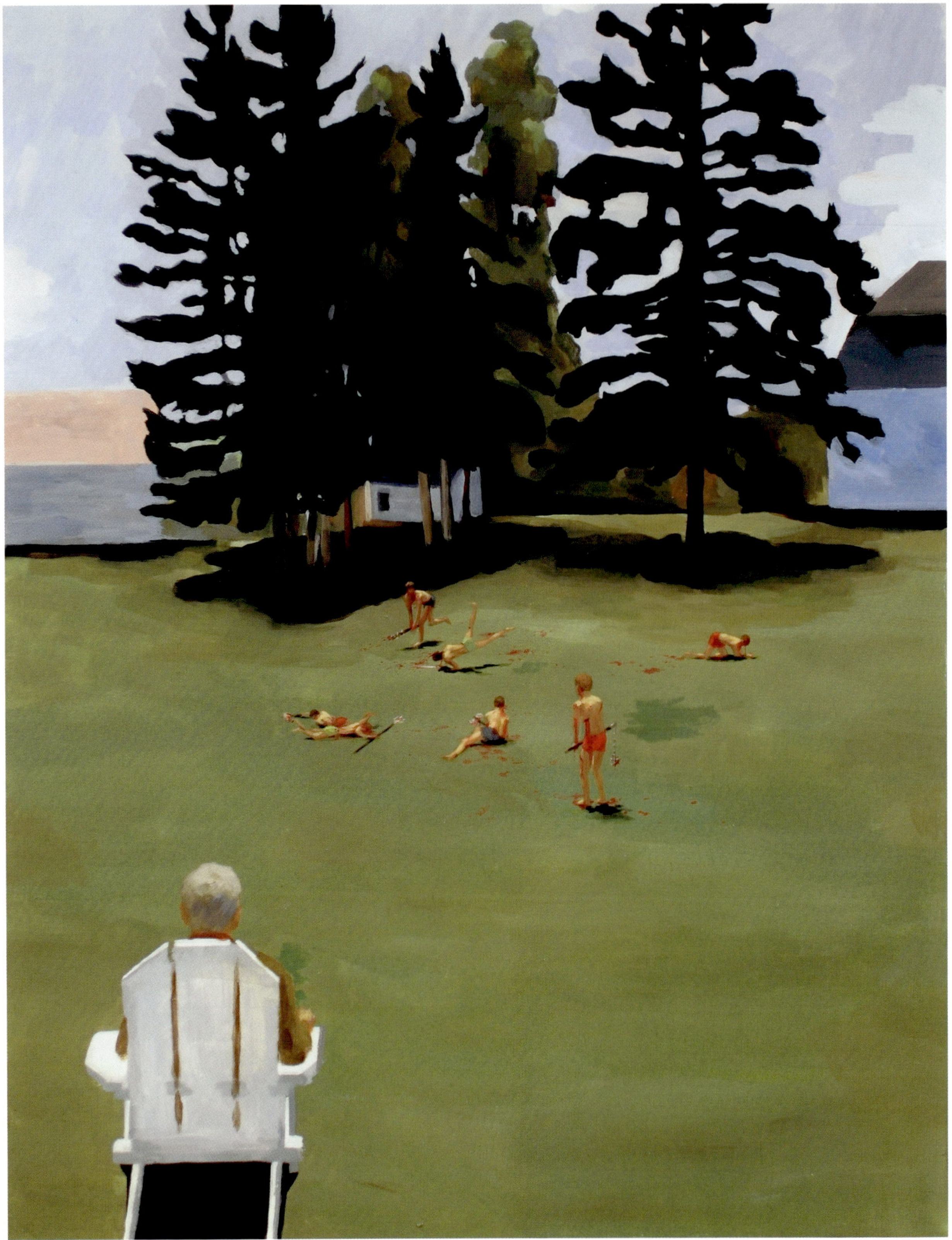

Earlier That Morning 2010

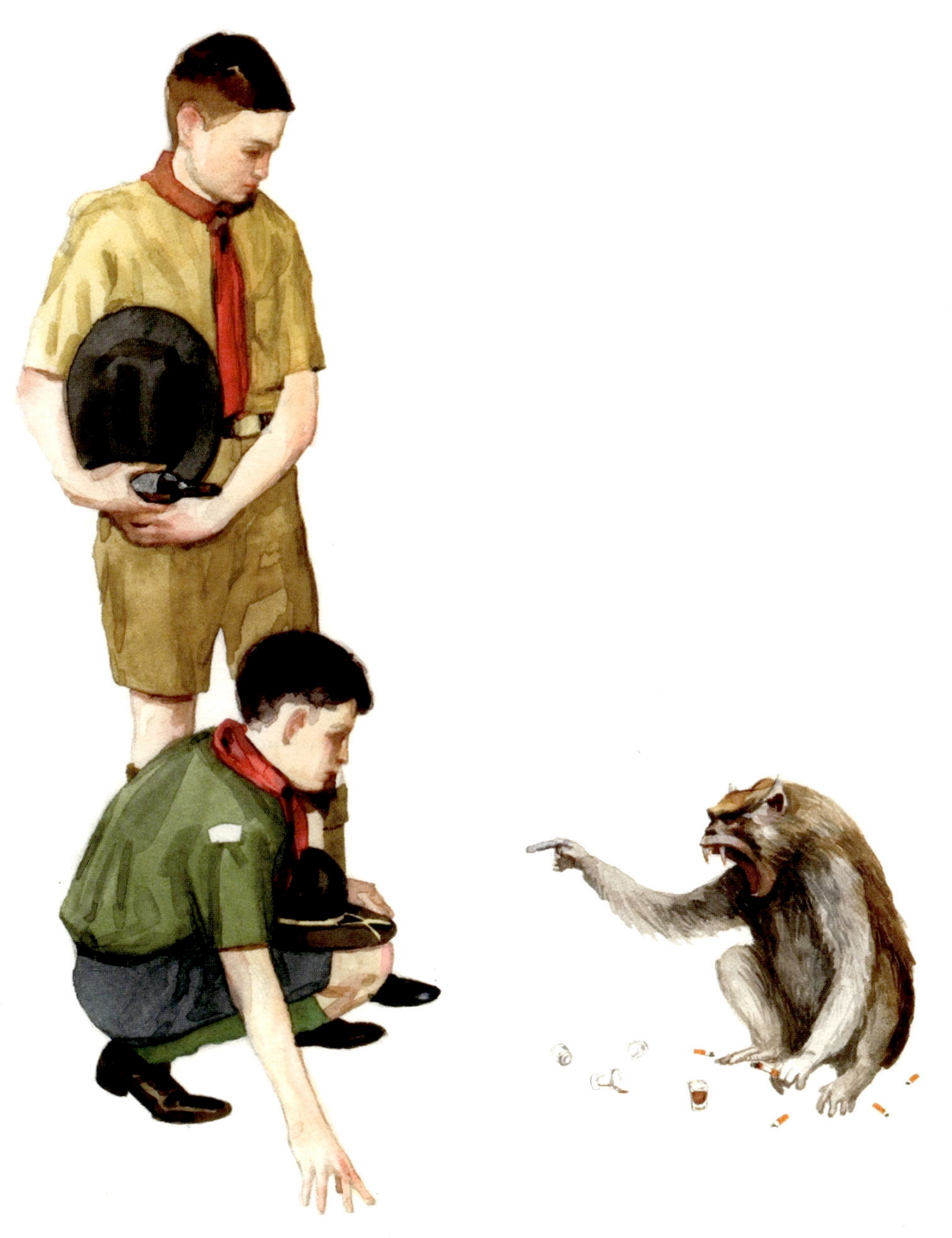

Intervention Merit Badge 2010

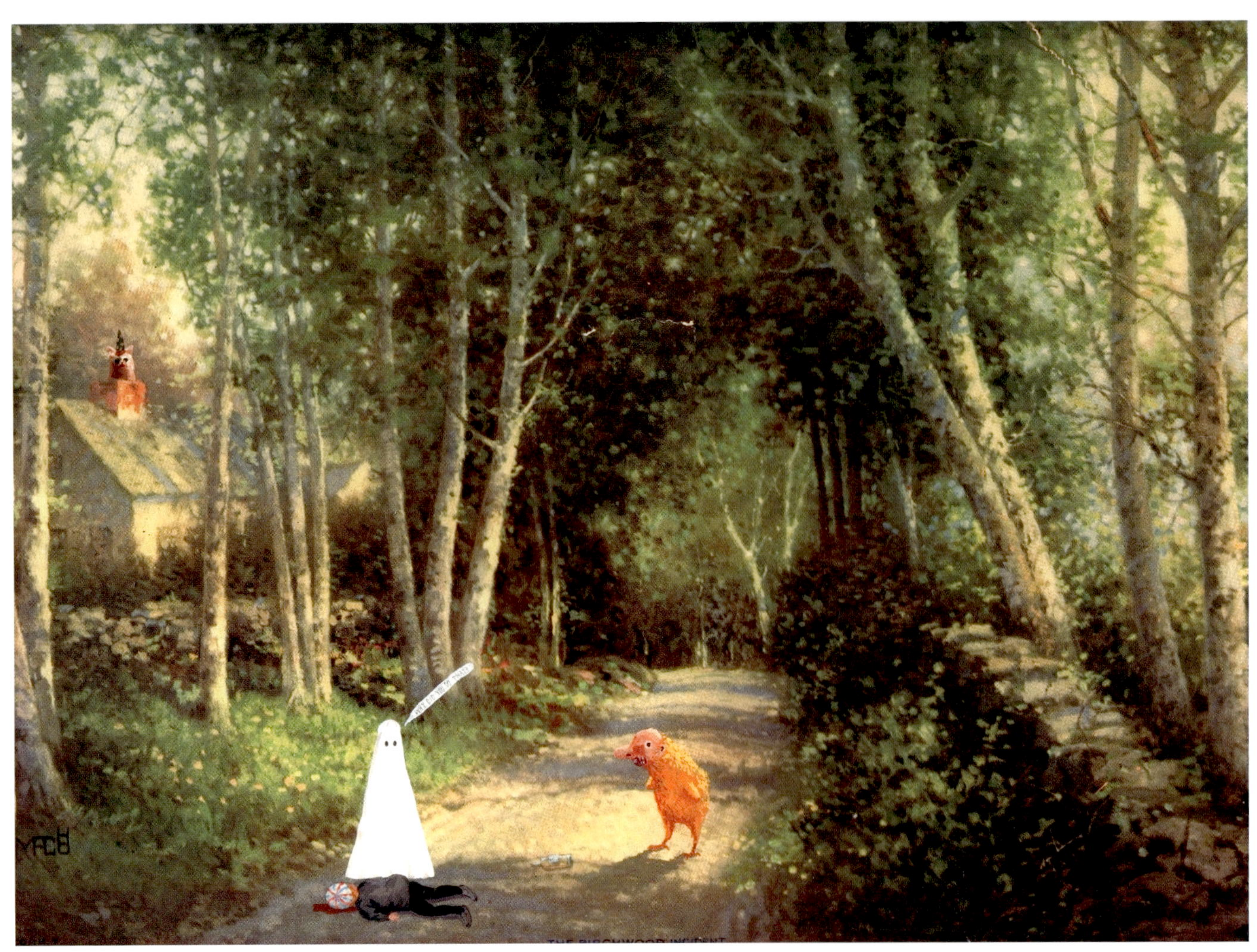

The Birchwood Incident   2008

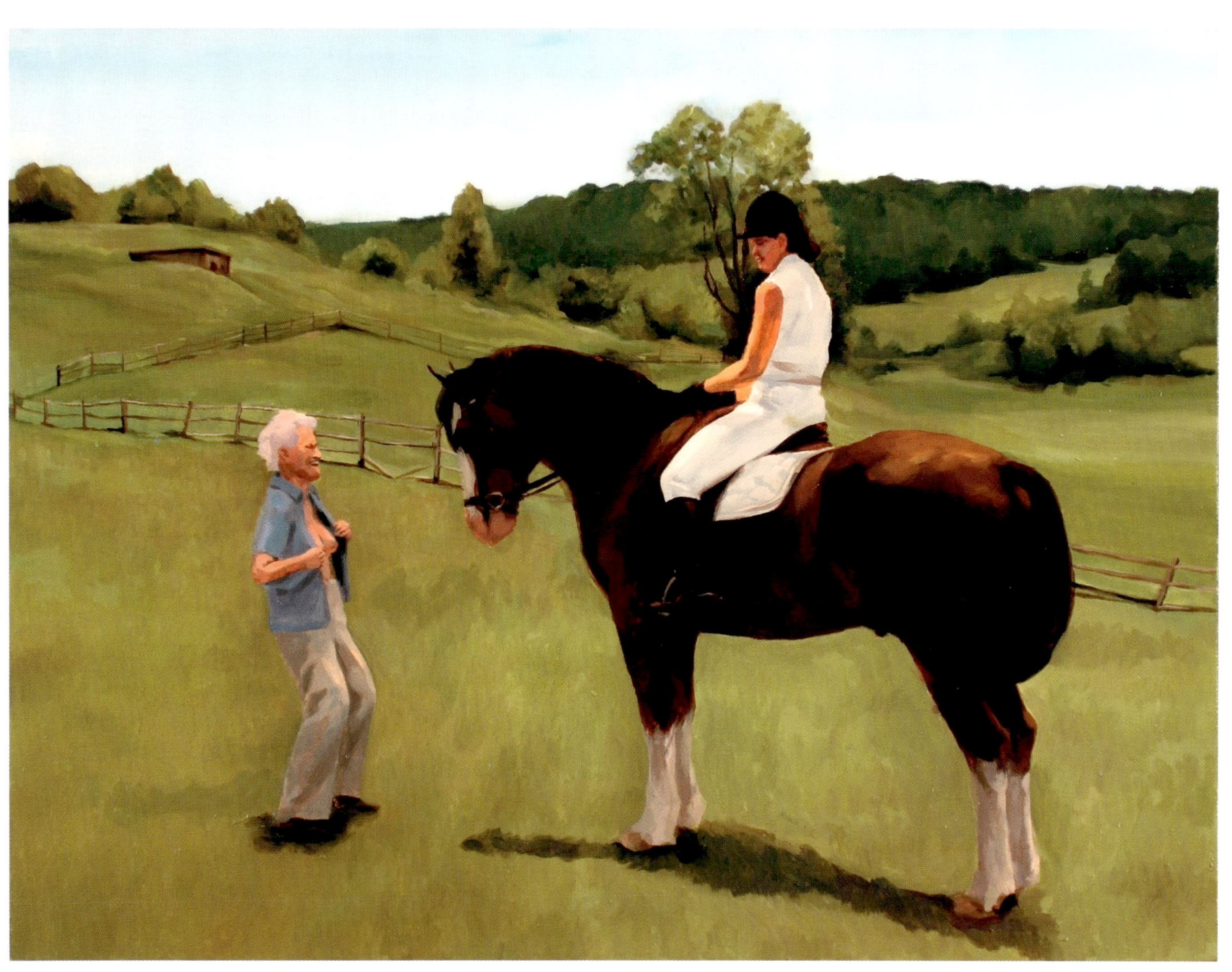

Swift Sally 2010

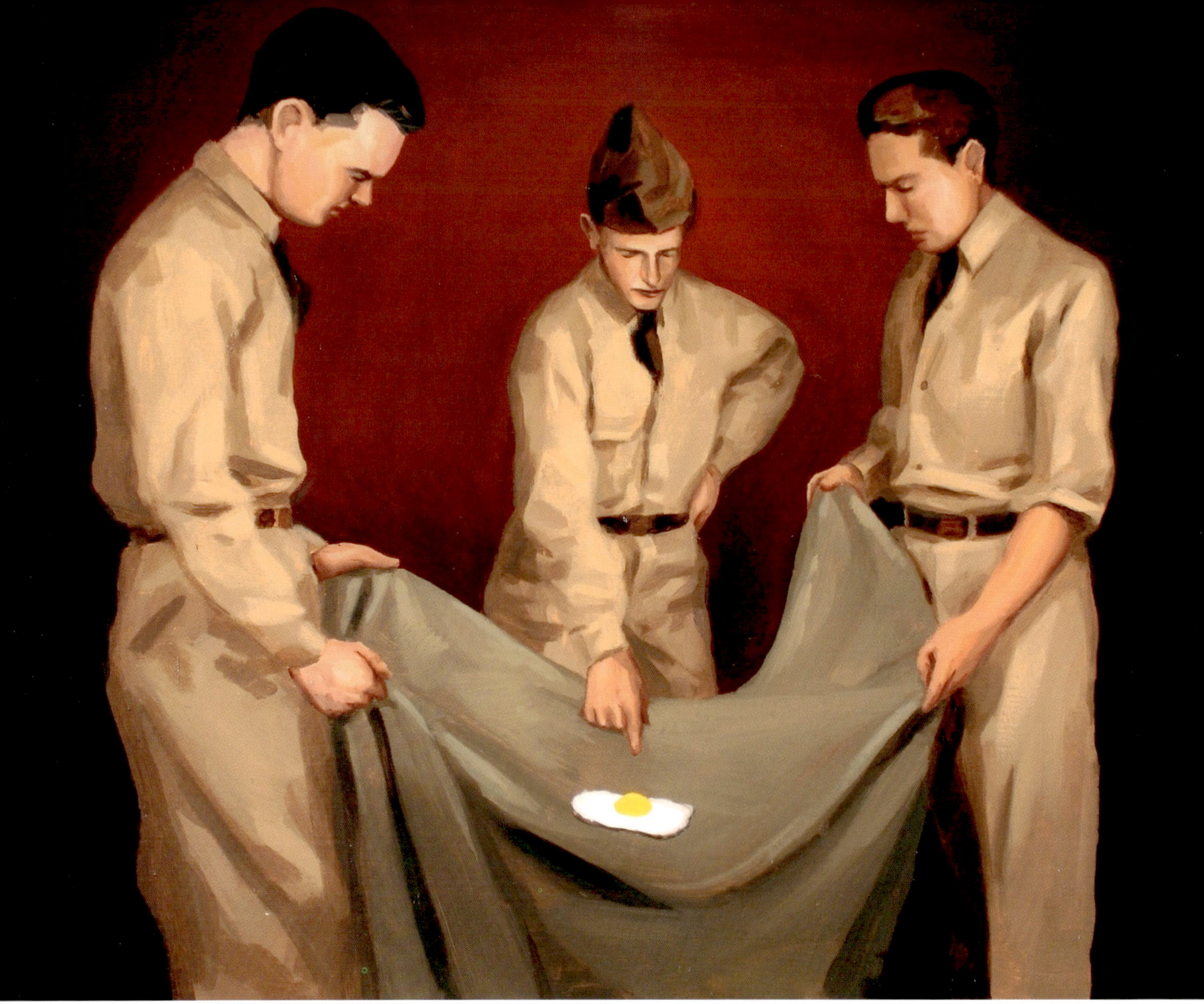

Gustatory Reprimand   2010

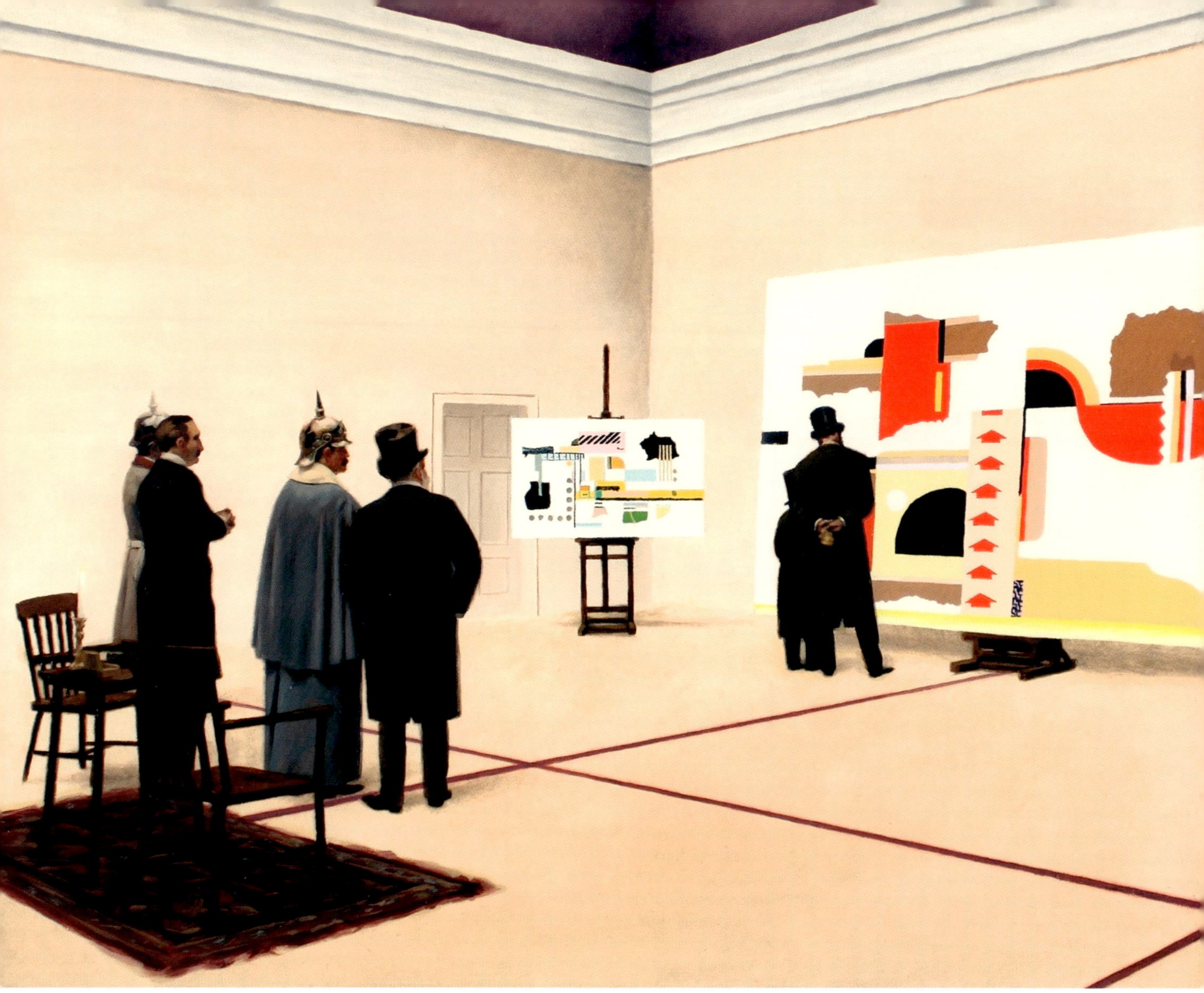

Little Master Whibley's First Exhibition   2010

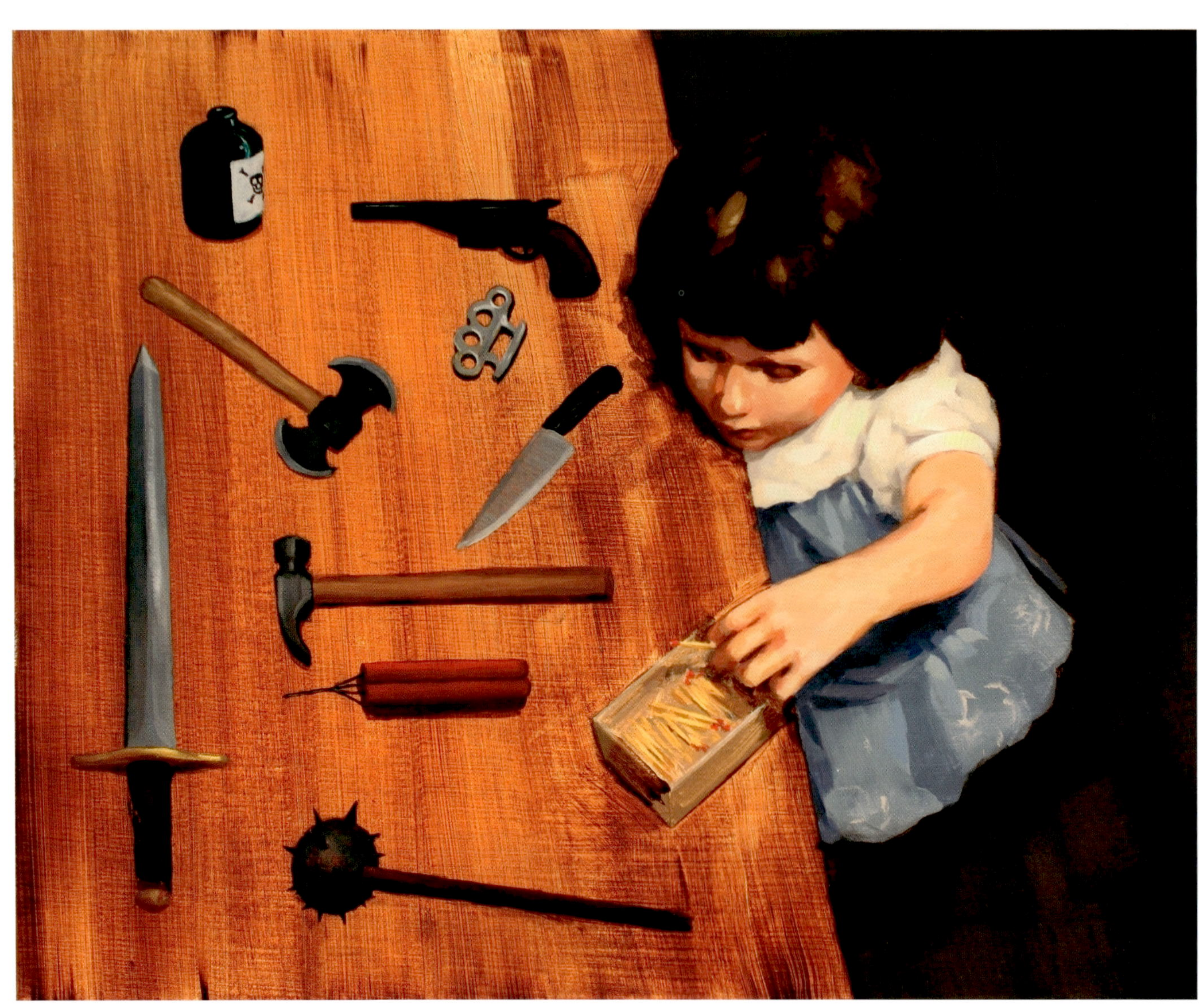

Choose Your Weapons Wisely   2010

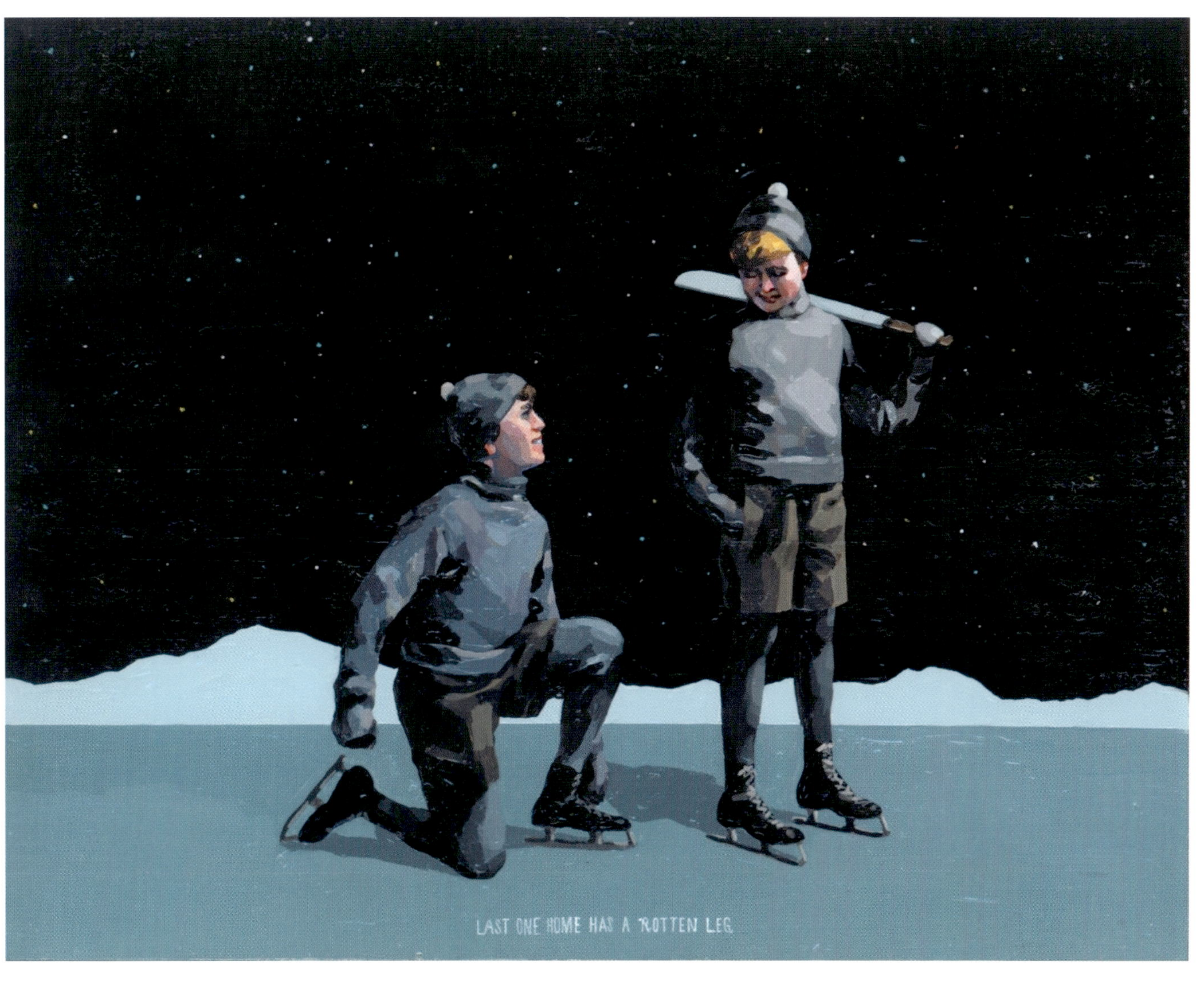

Last One Home Has A Rotten Leg 2008

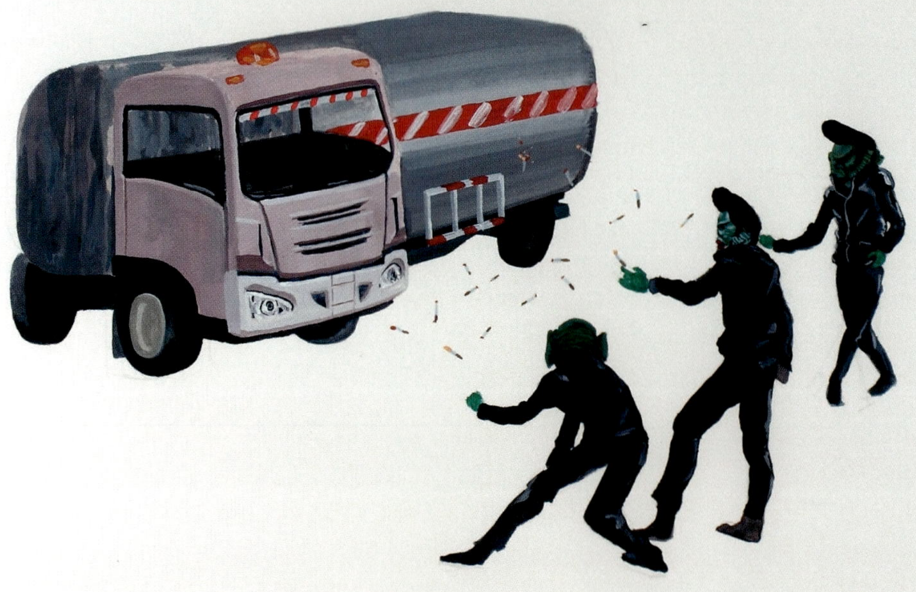

Rebels   2010
The Goode Shippe Munroe   2010

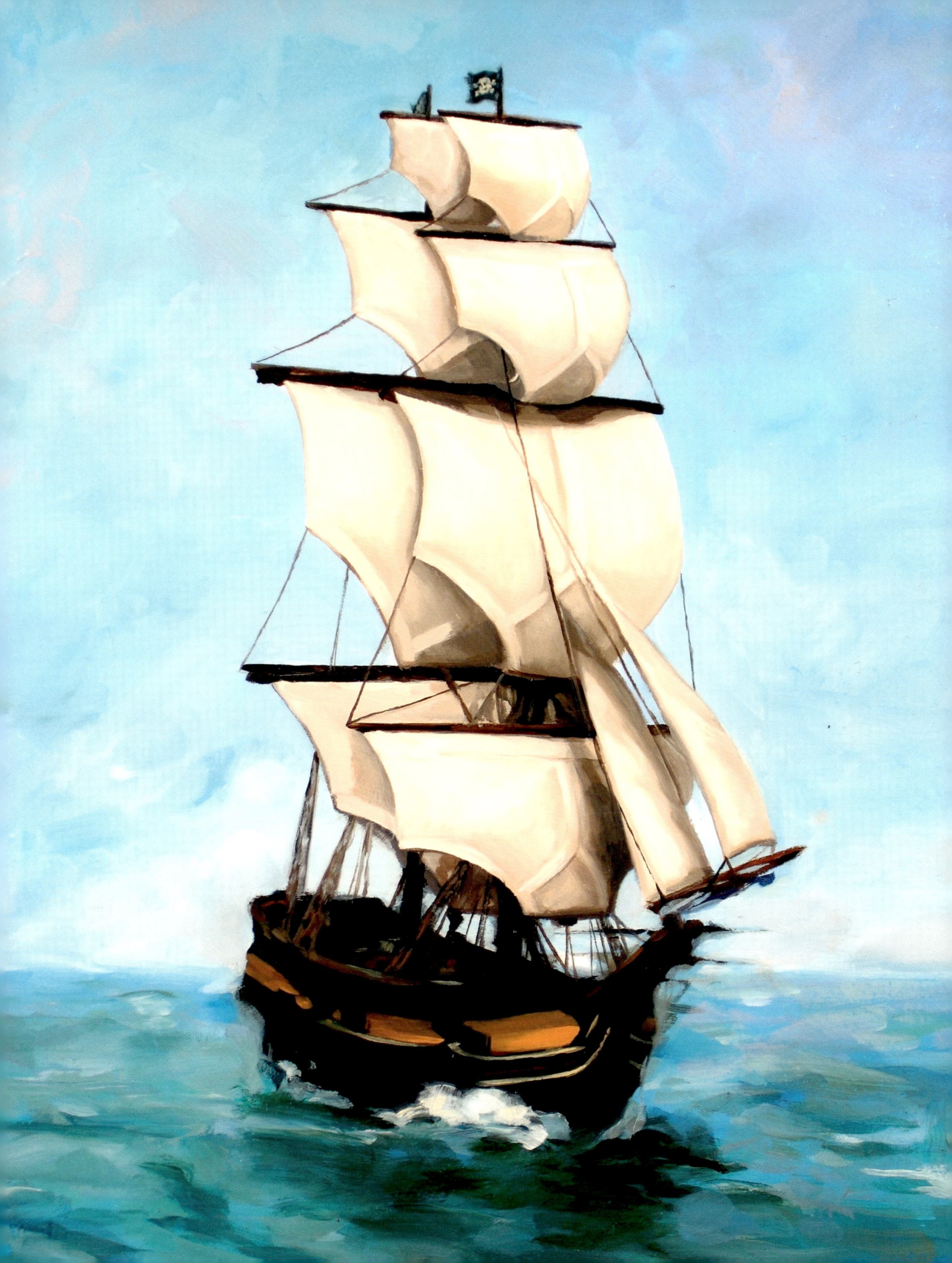

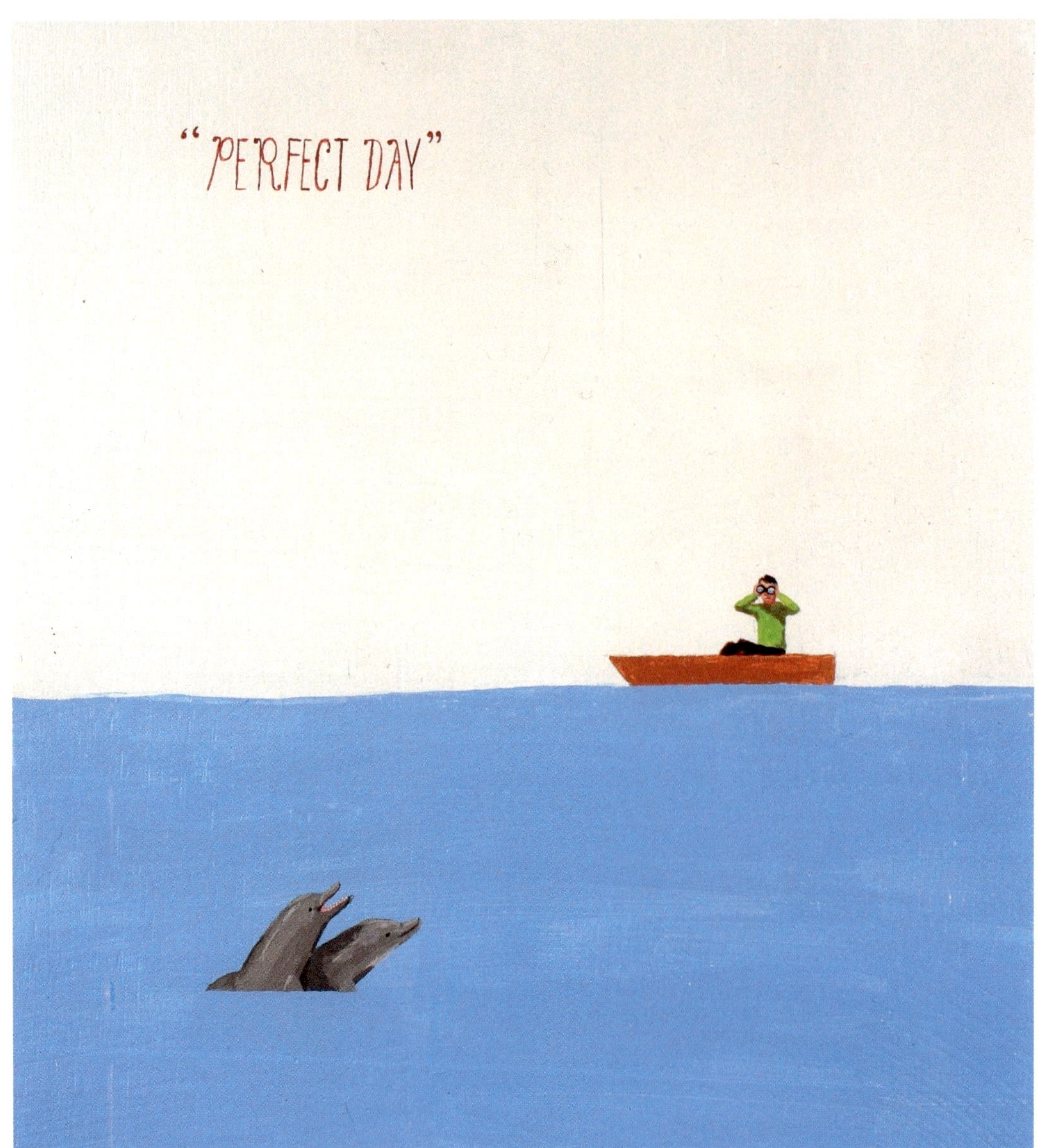

Perfect Day   2008

"WORST DAY"

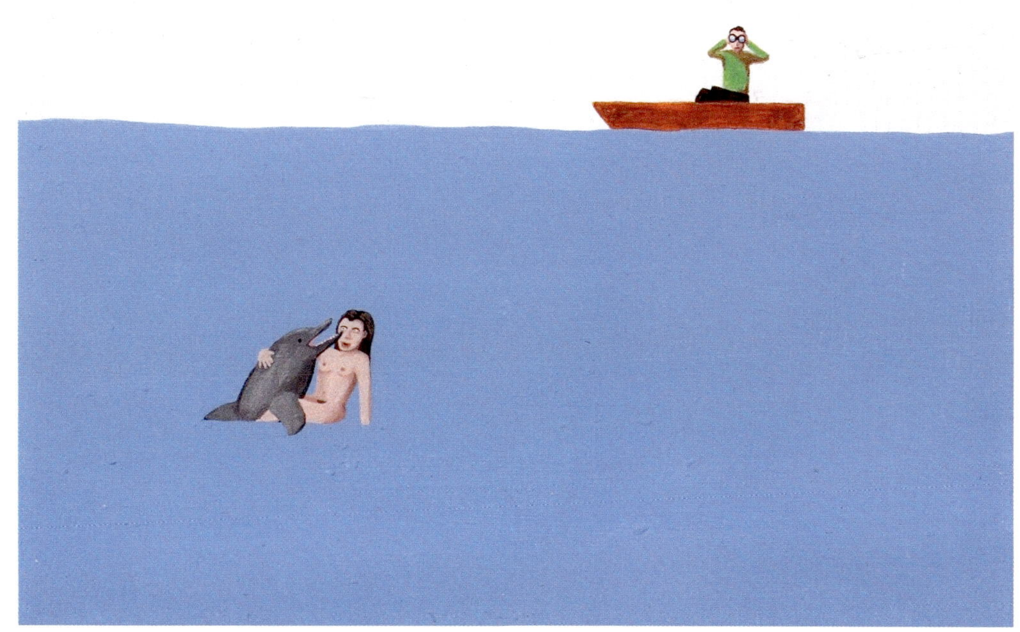

Worst Day   2008

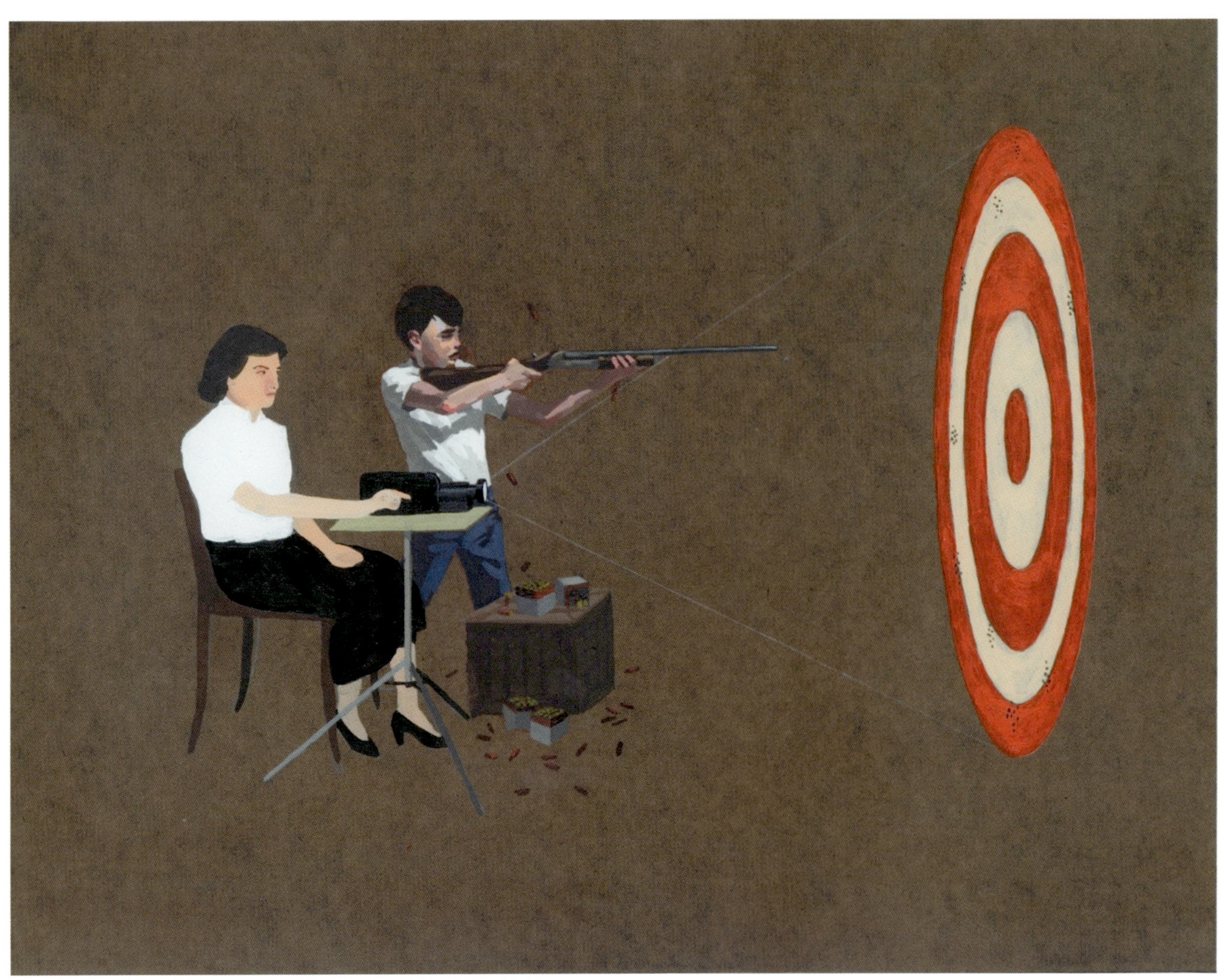

Target Practice   2008

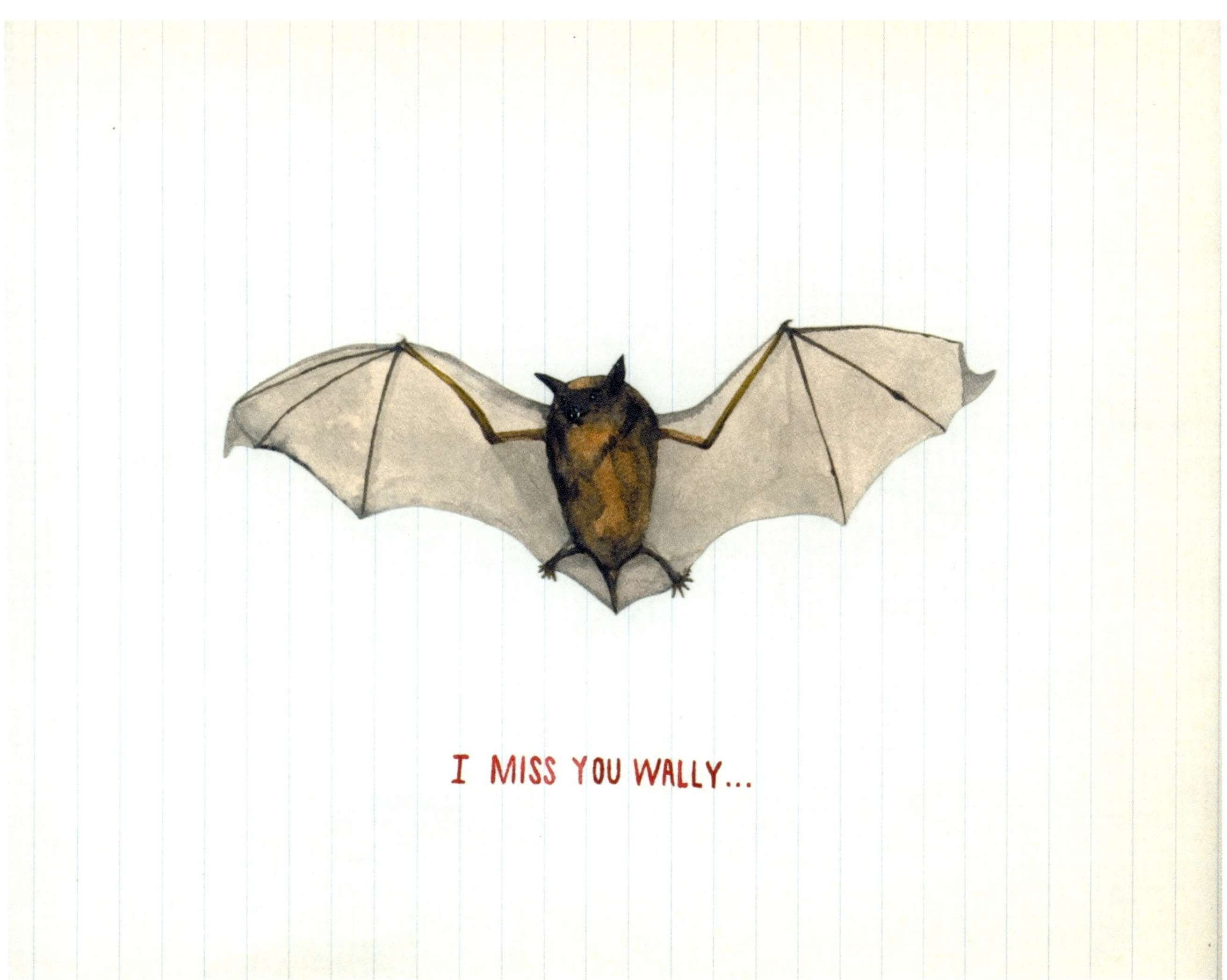

I Miss You Wally   2008

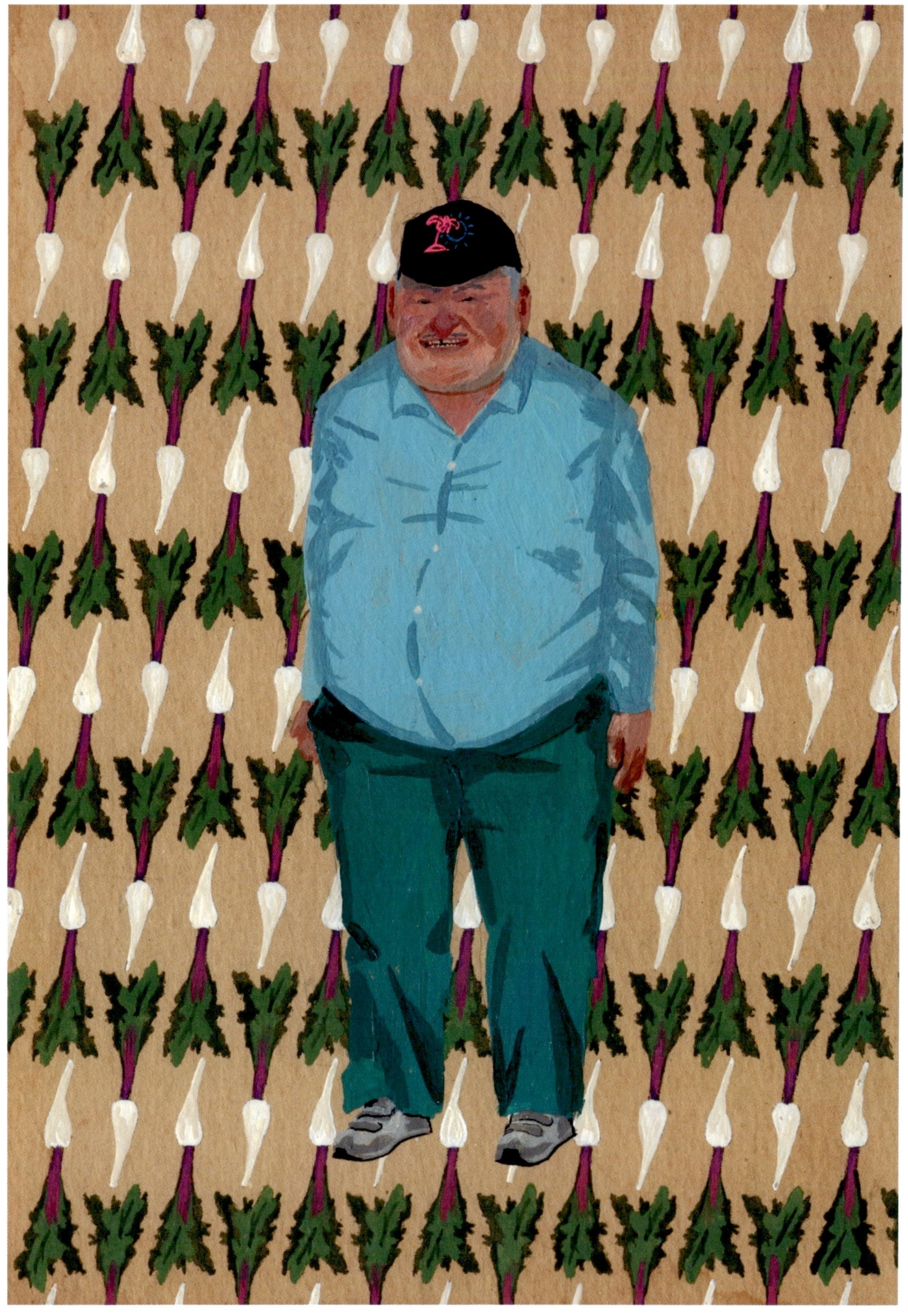

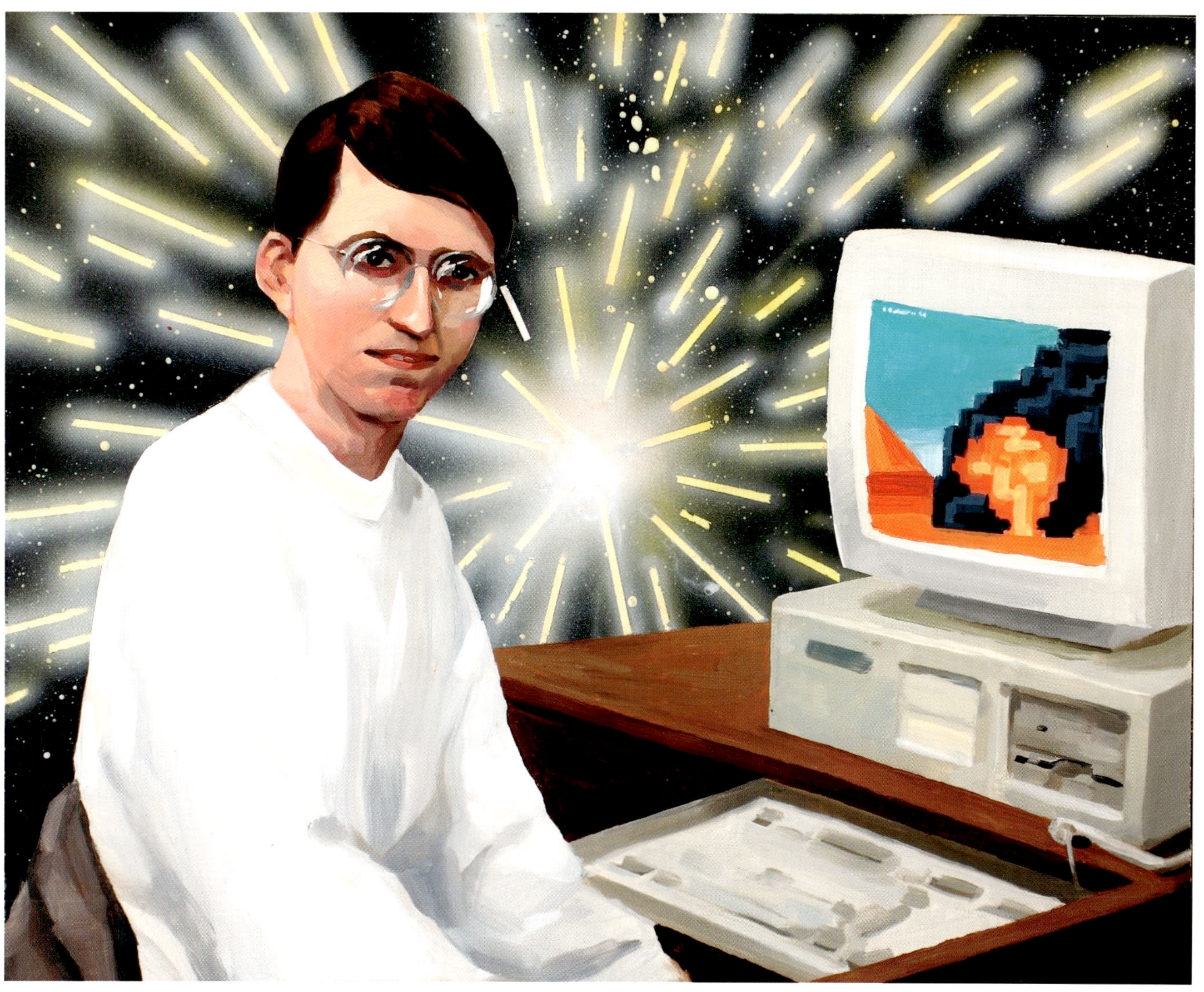

Goodbye Charlie Sweetbeet   2008
Game Over, Man   2008

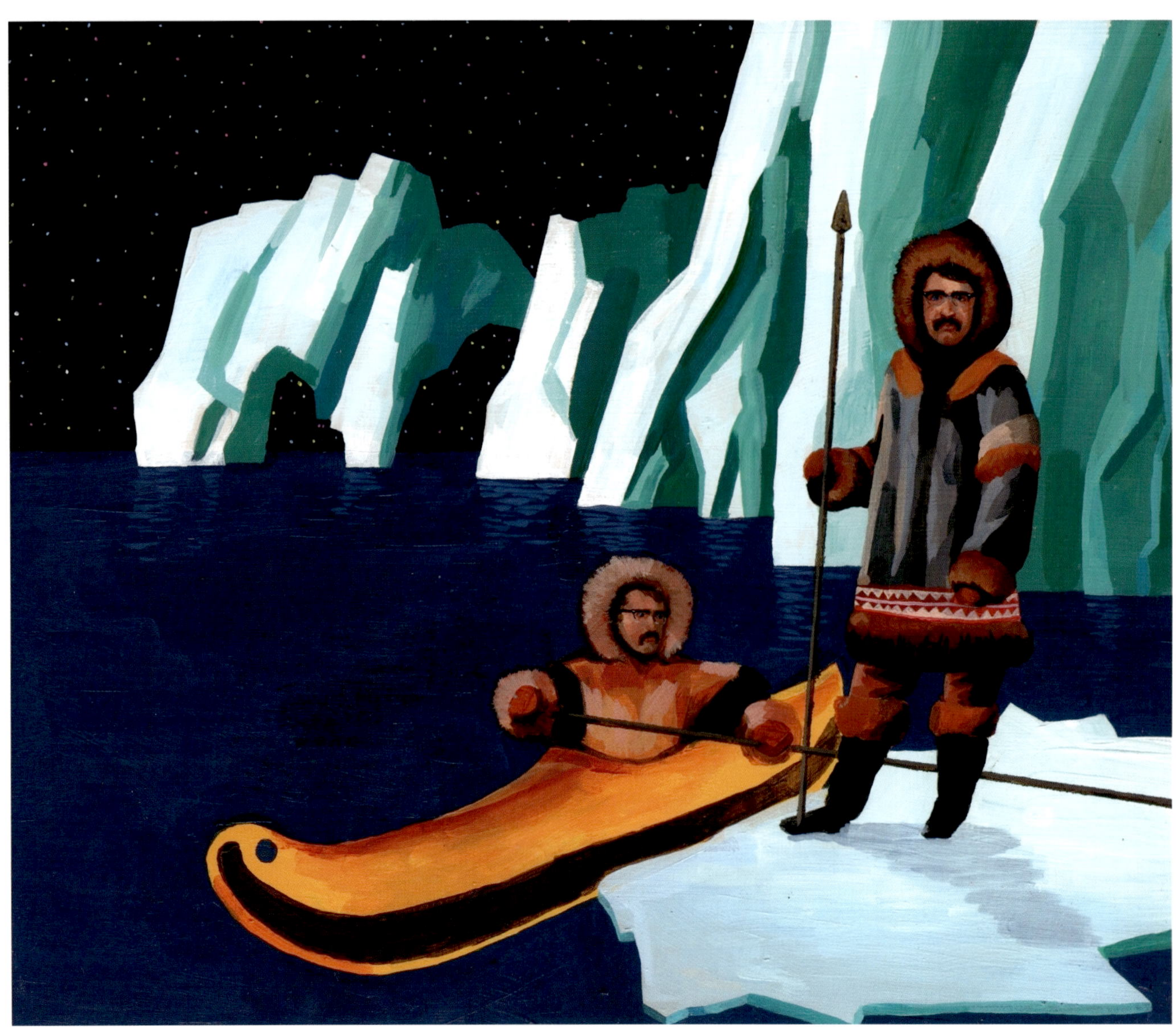

Self Portrait as Two Inuit   2008
One of Nature's Greatest Wonders   2008

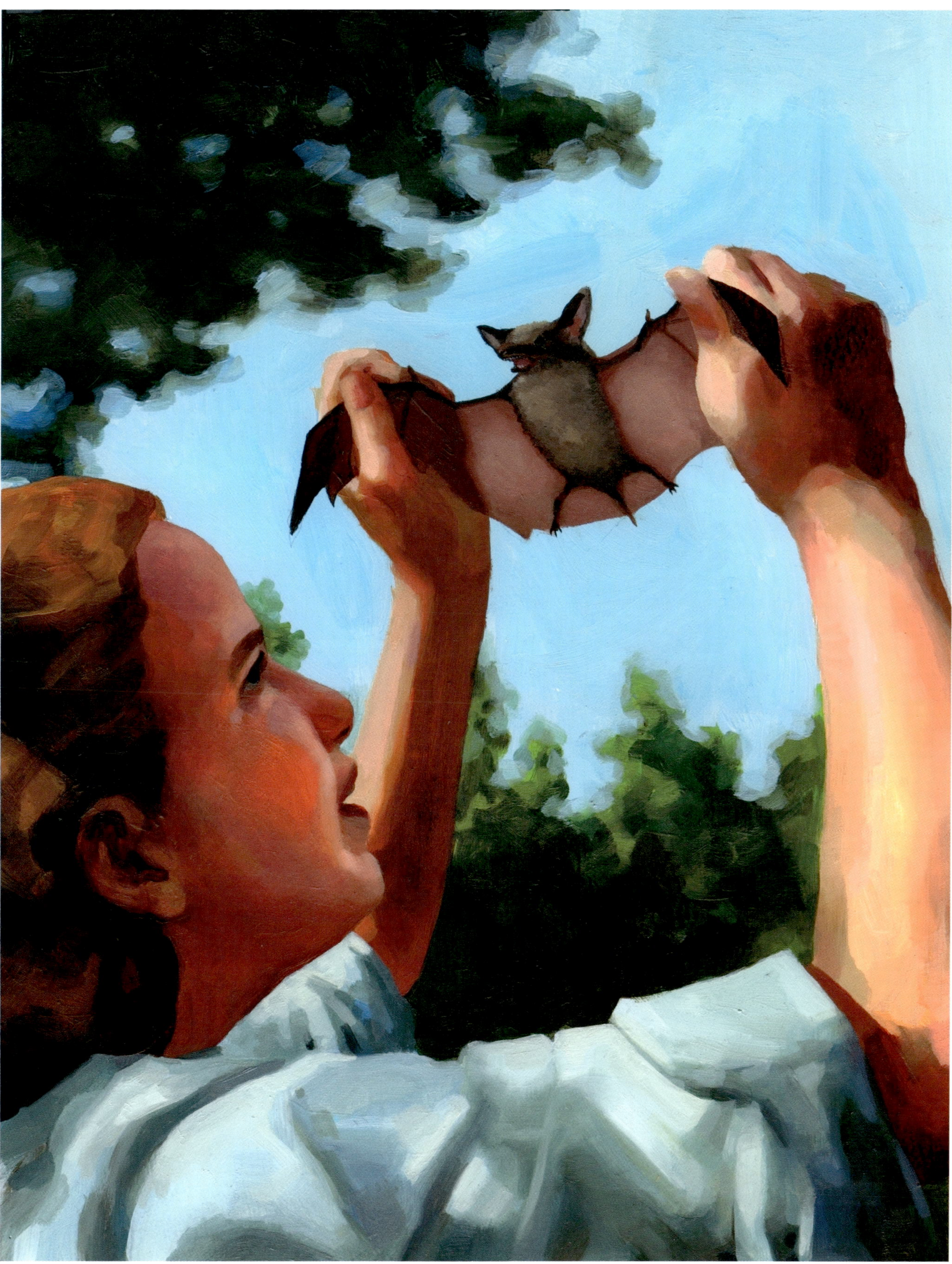

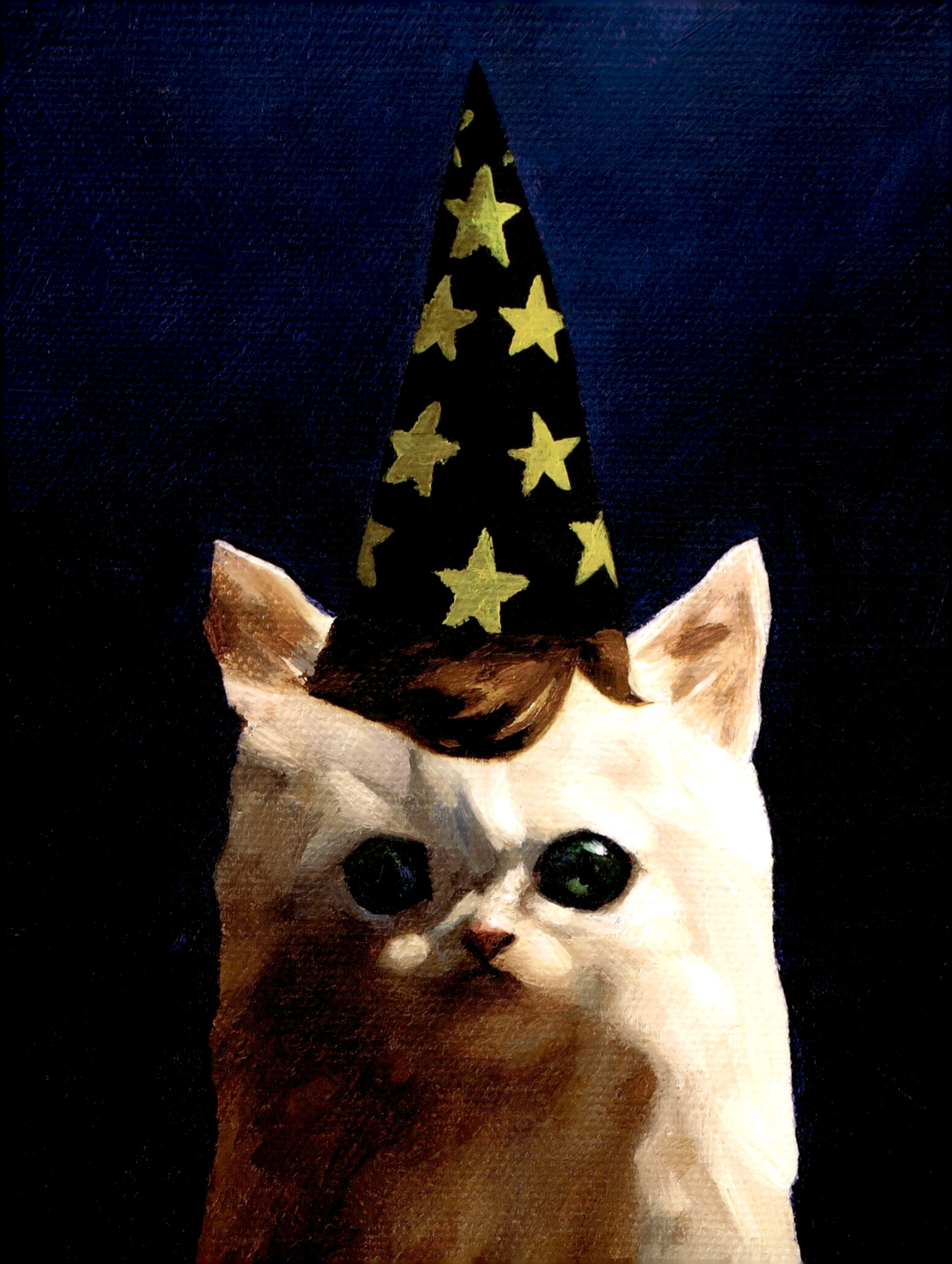

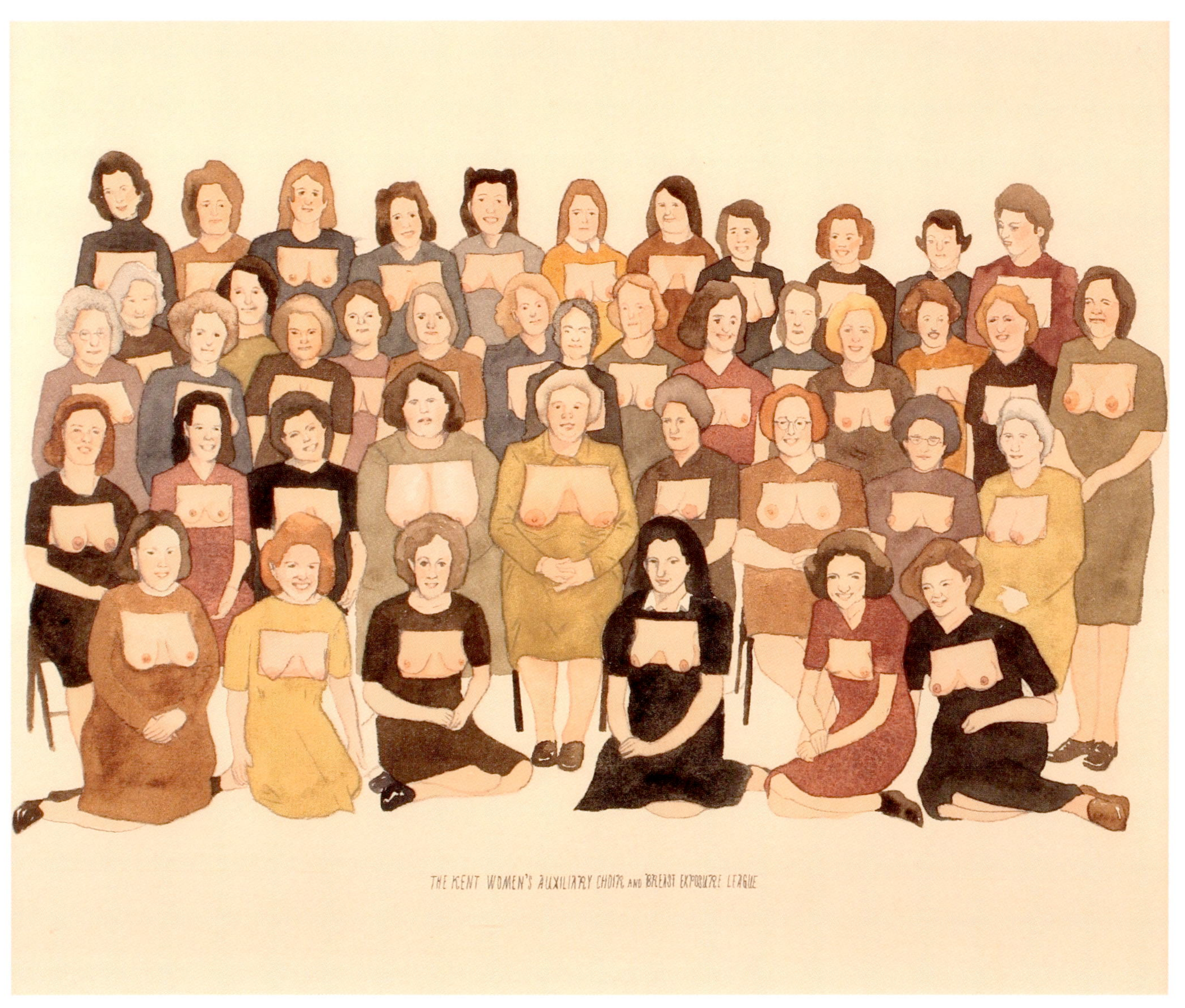

Fizzlekitten 2008
KWACABEL 2009

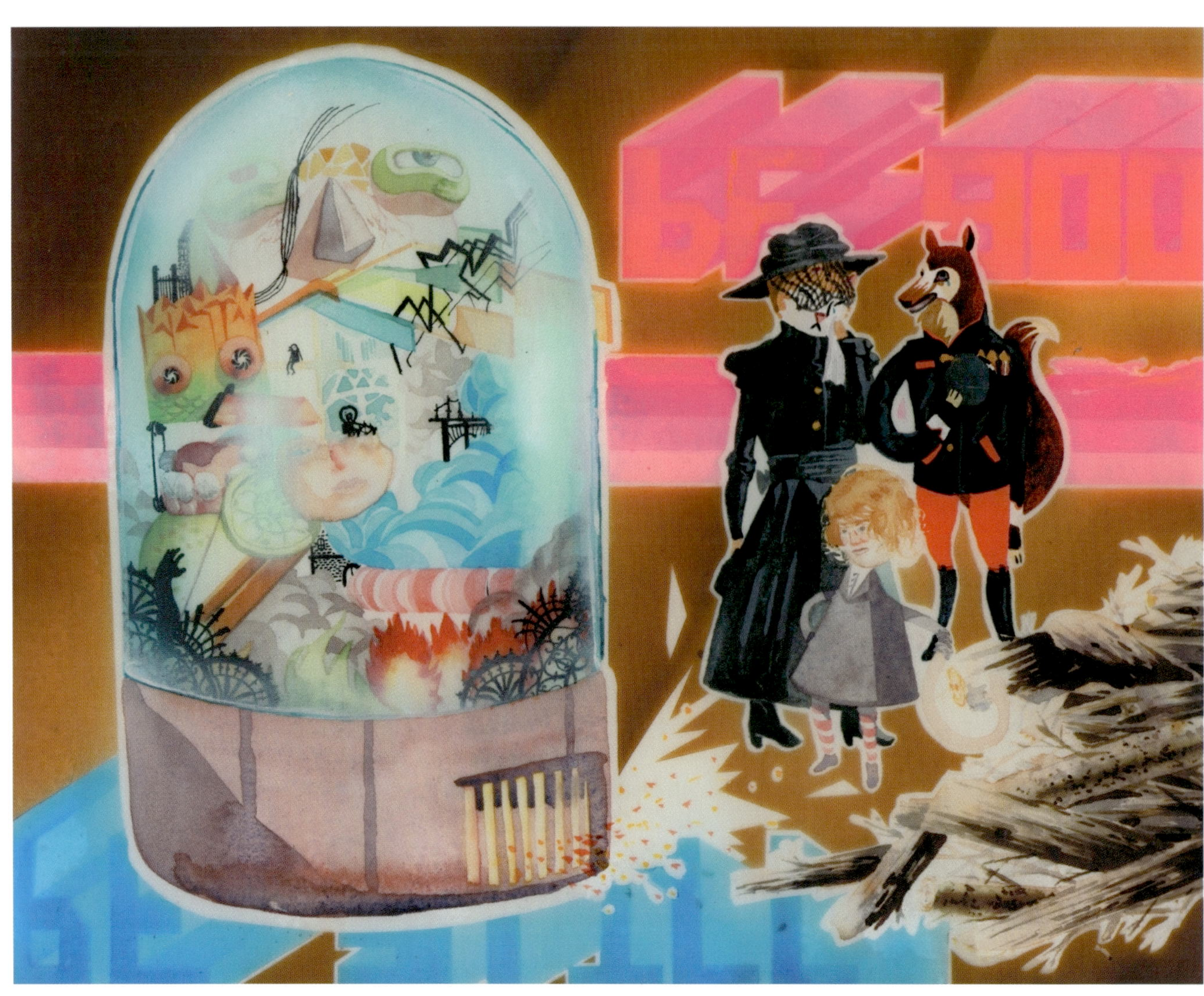

Be Good, Be Still   2008
We Salute Thee   2010

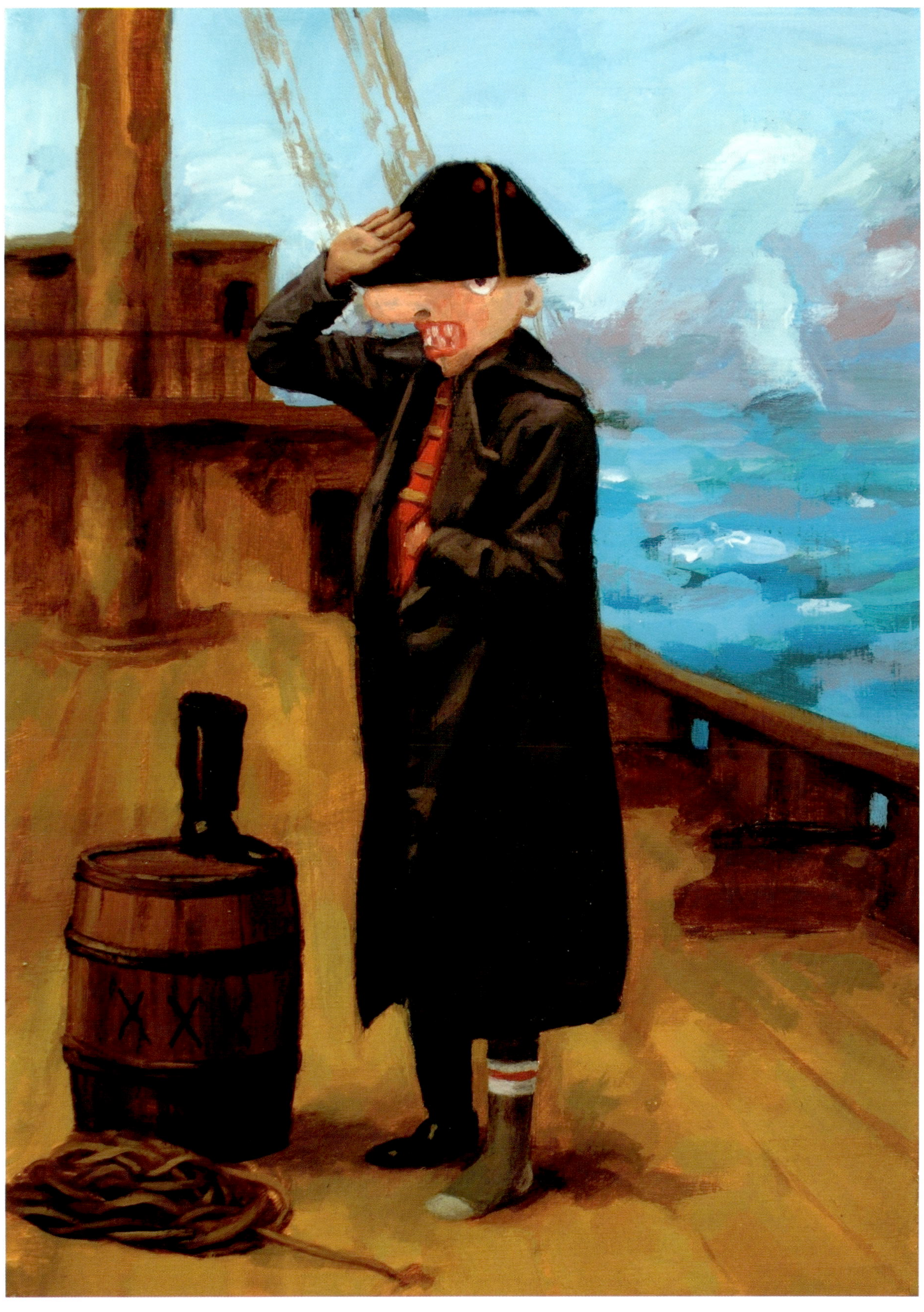

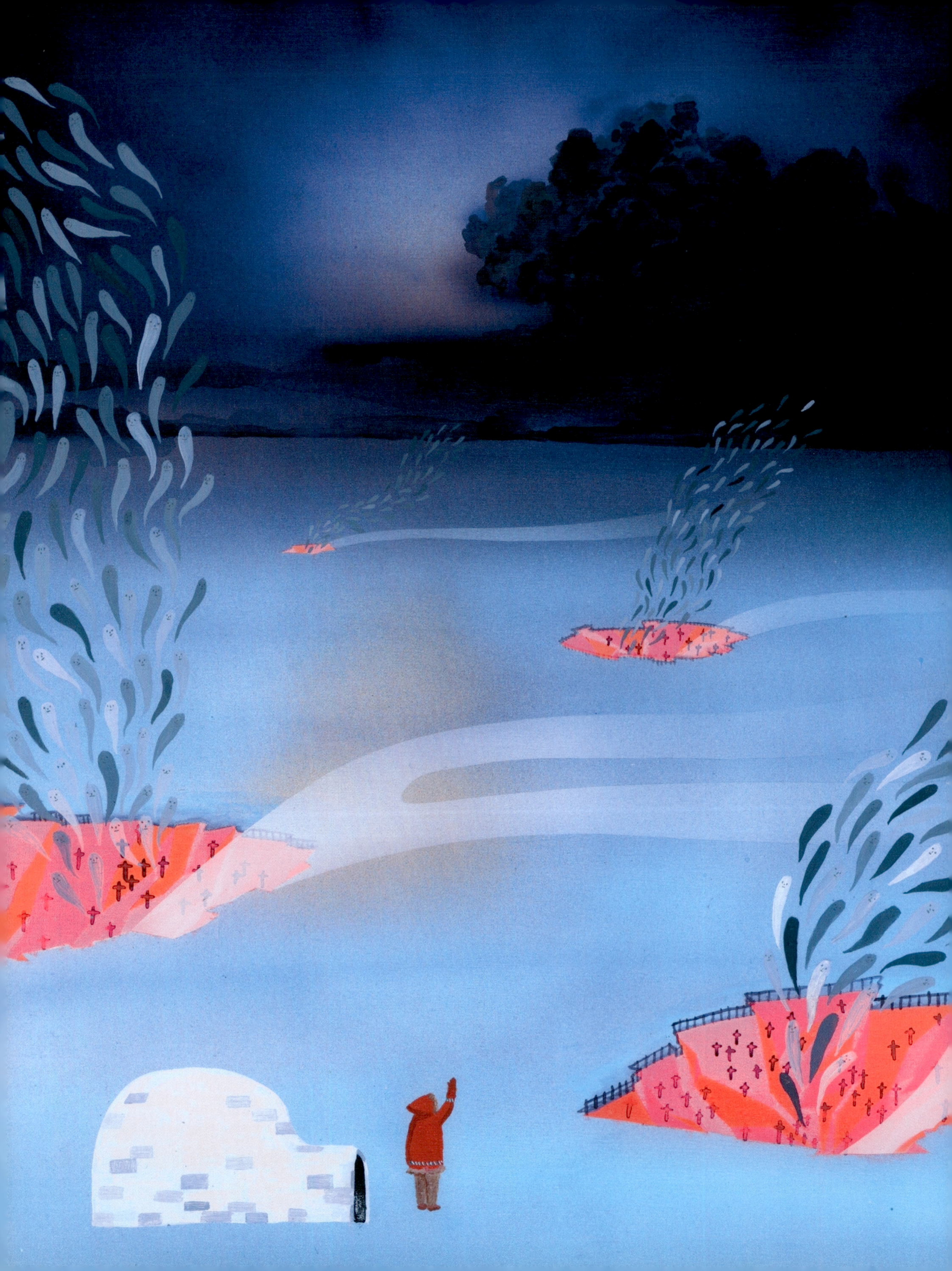

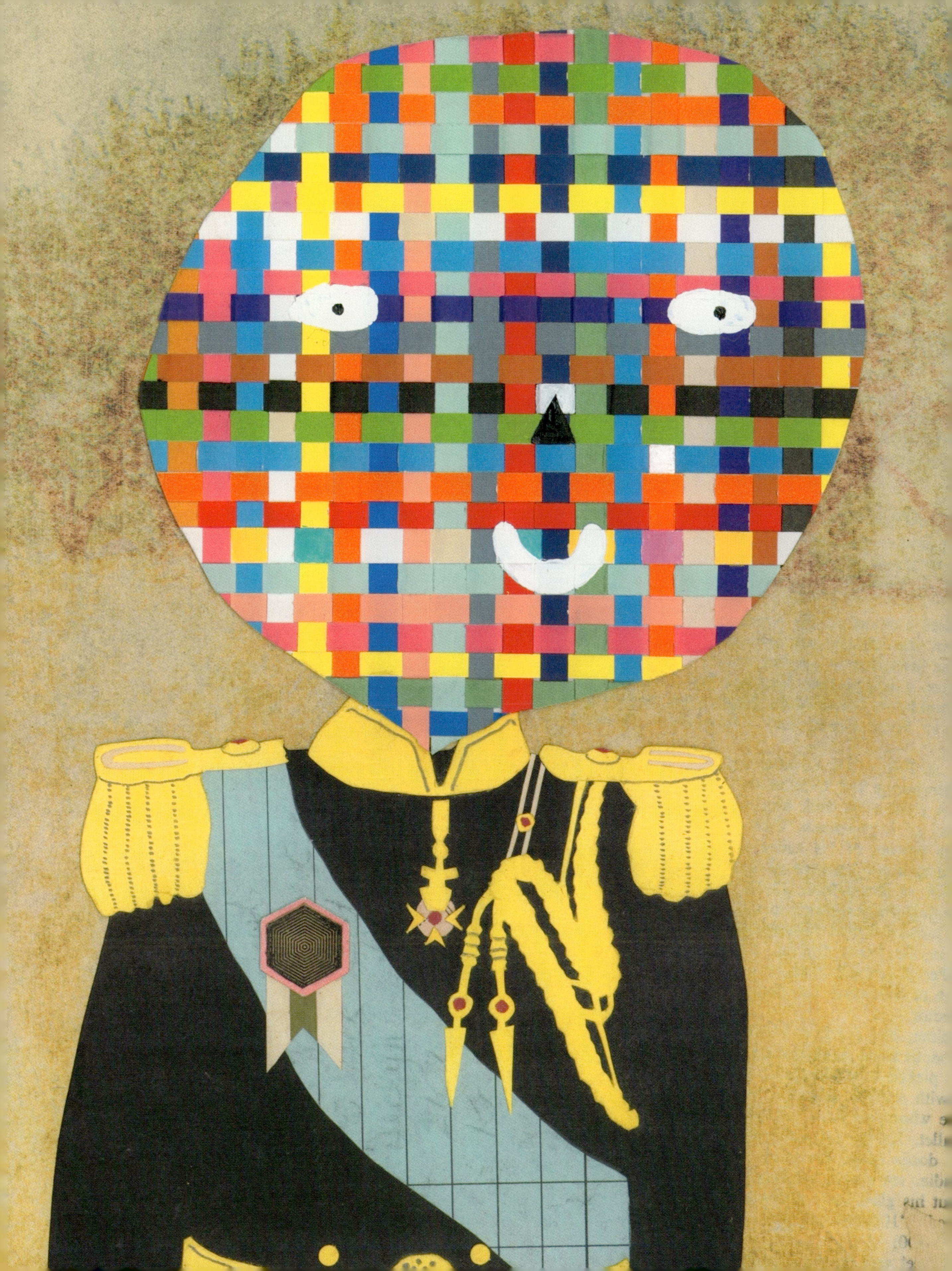

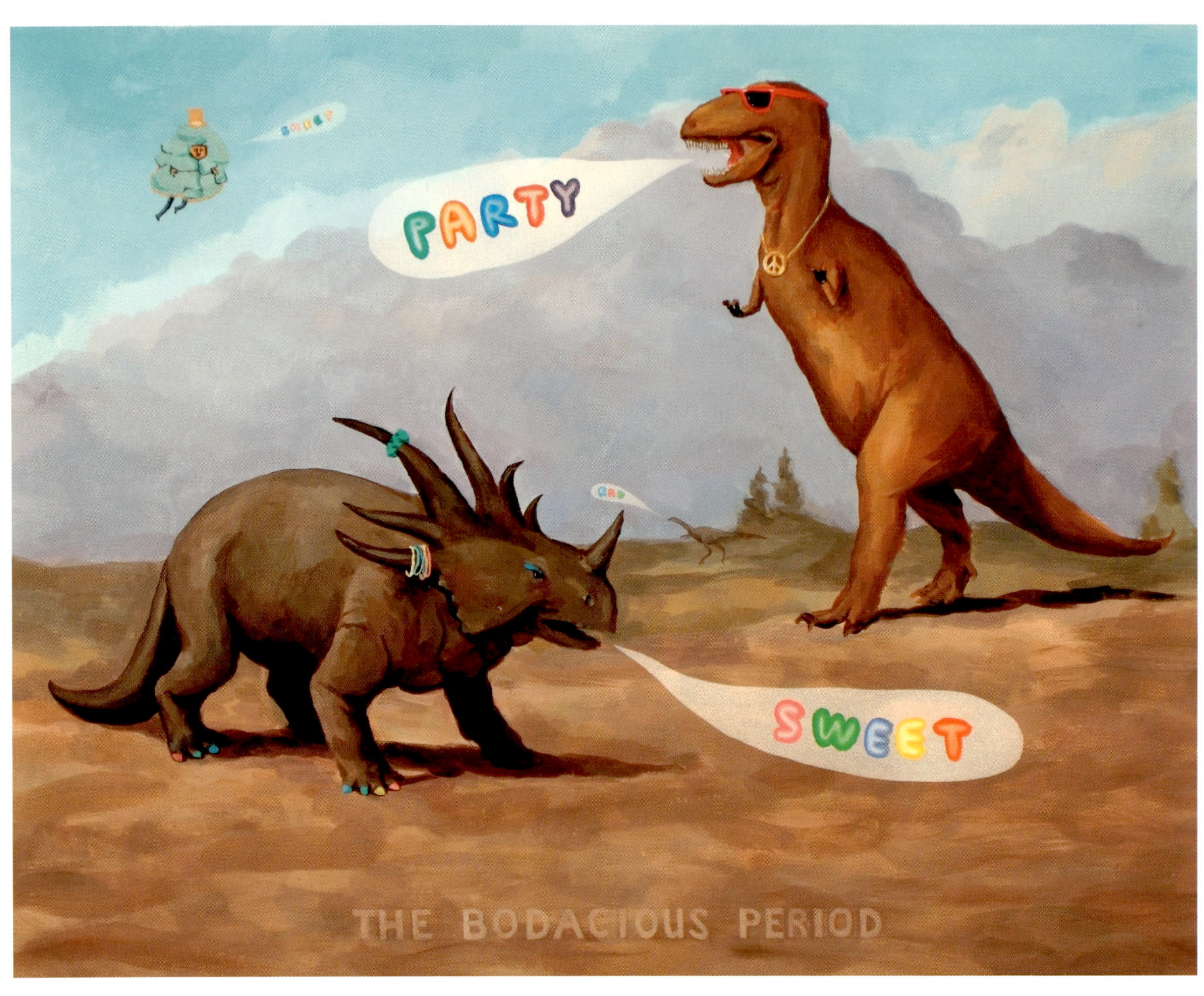

Bye Guys! 2008 (previous)
Sir Arthur Wellesley 2007 (previous)
The Bodacious Period 2010

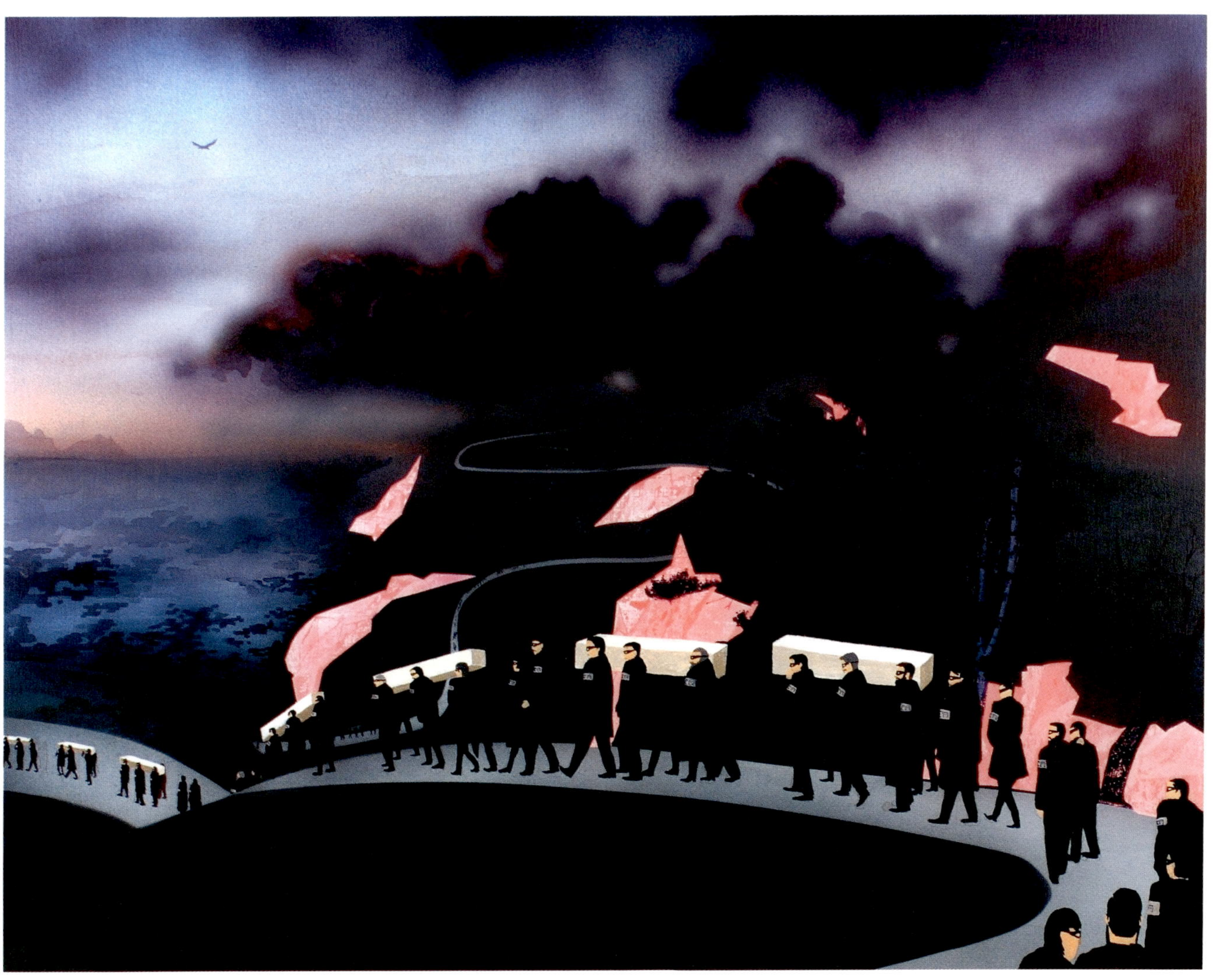

Raise Up You Glasses   2008

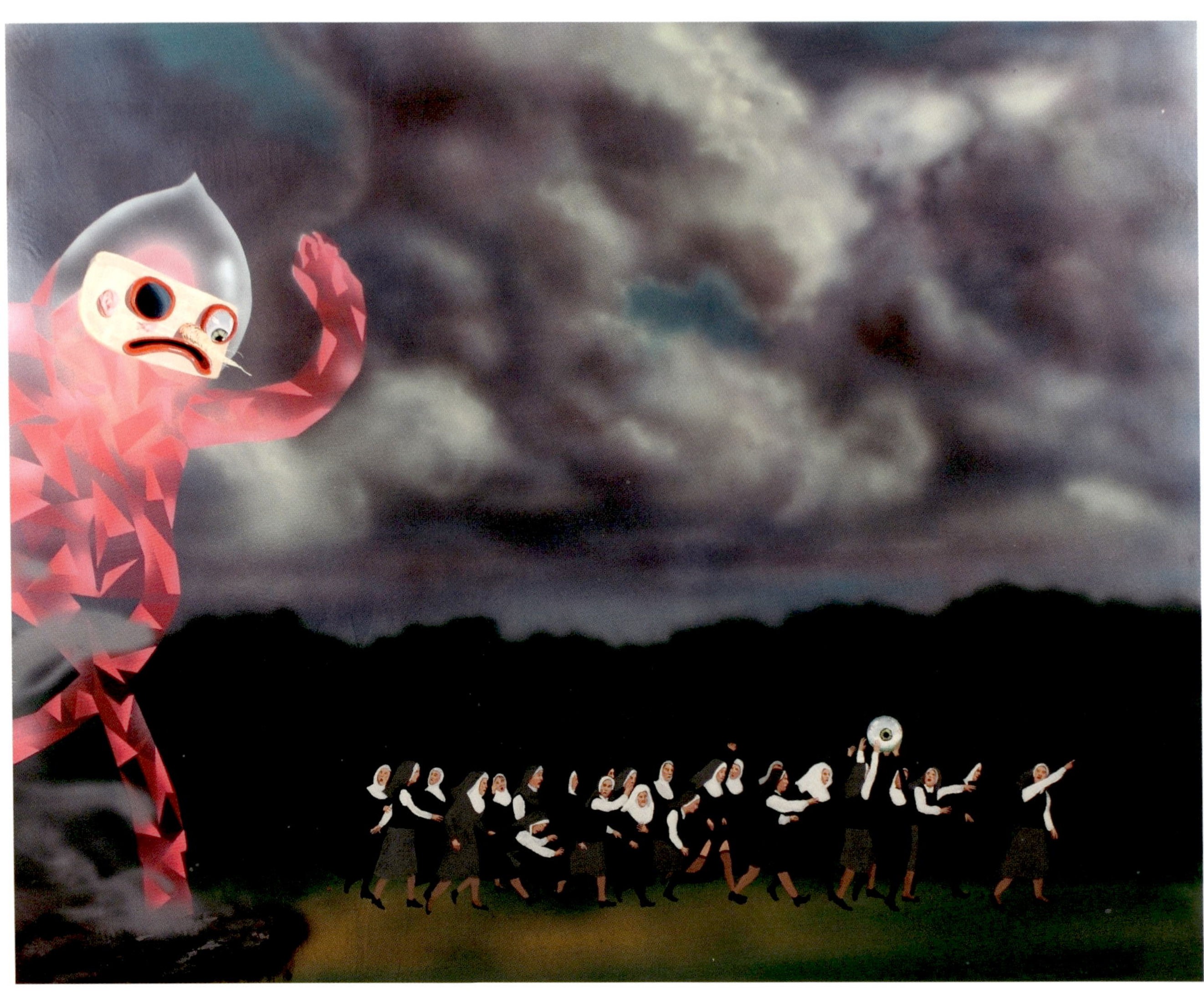

Ecclesiastical Initiation   2008
Ghost and Girl   2008

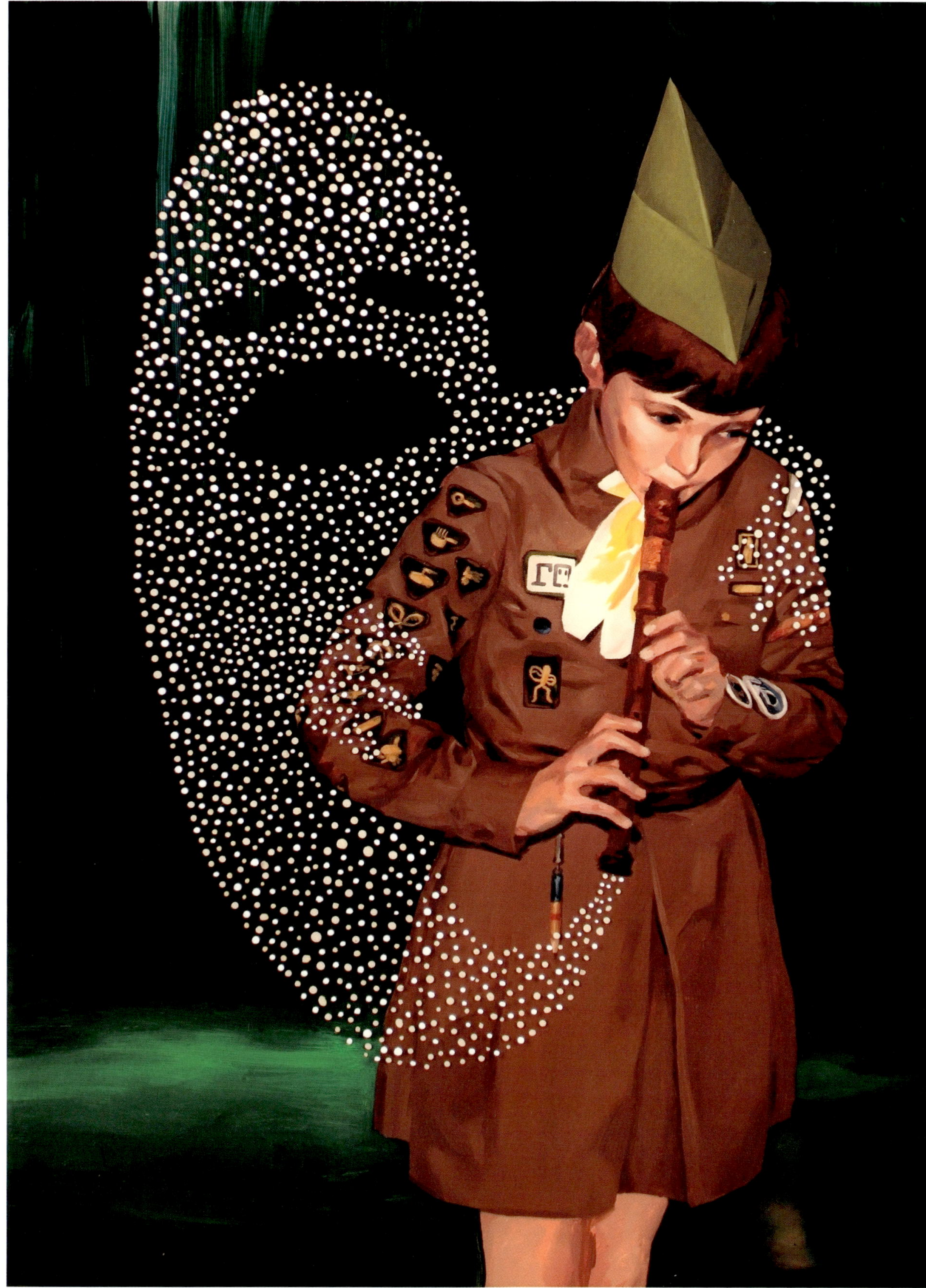

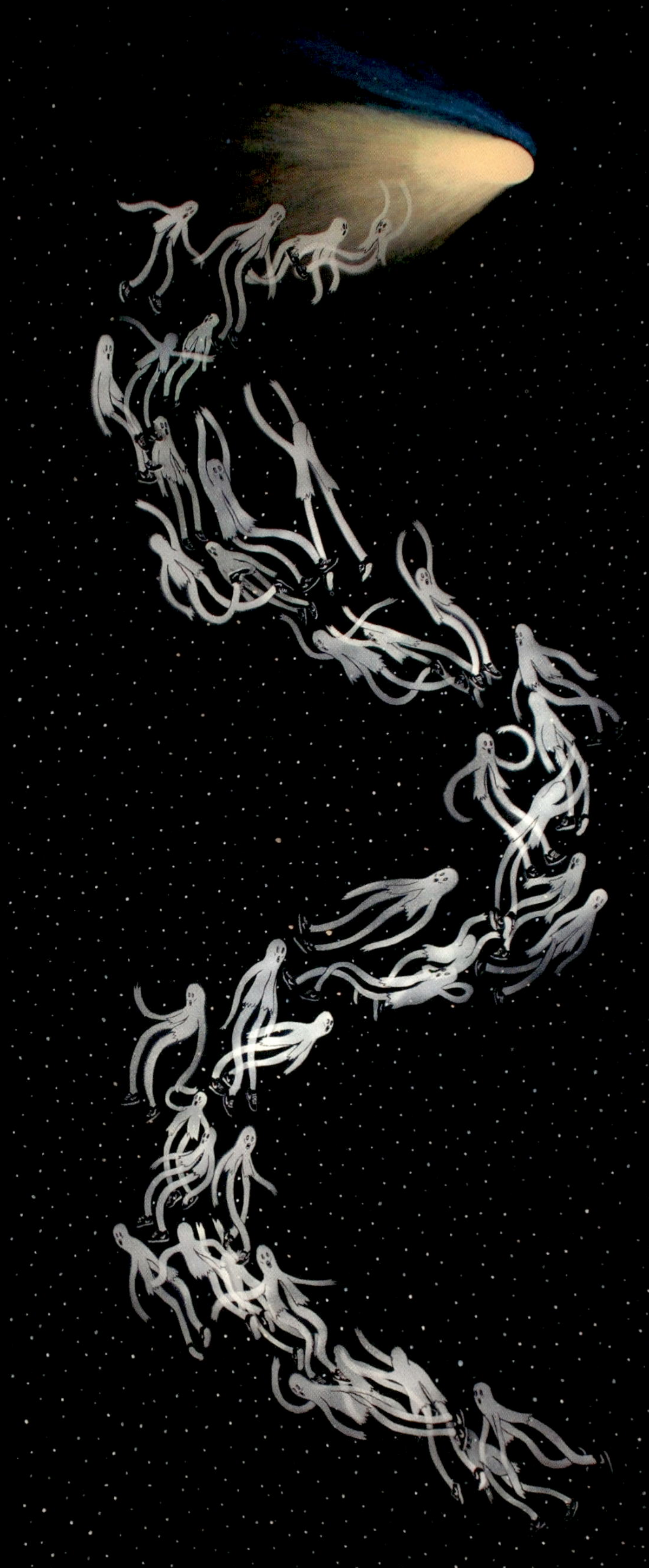

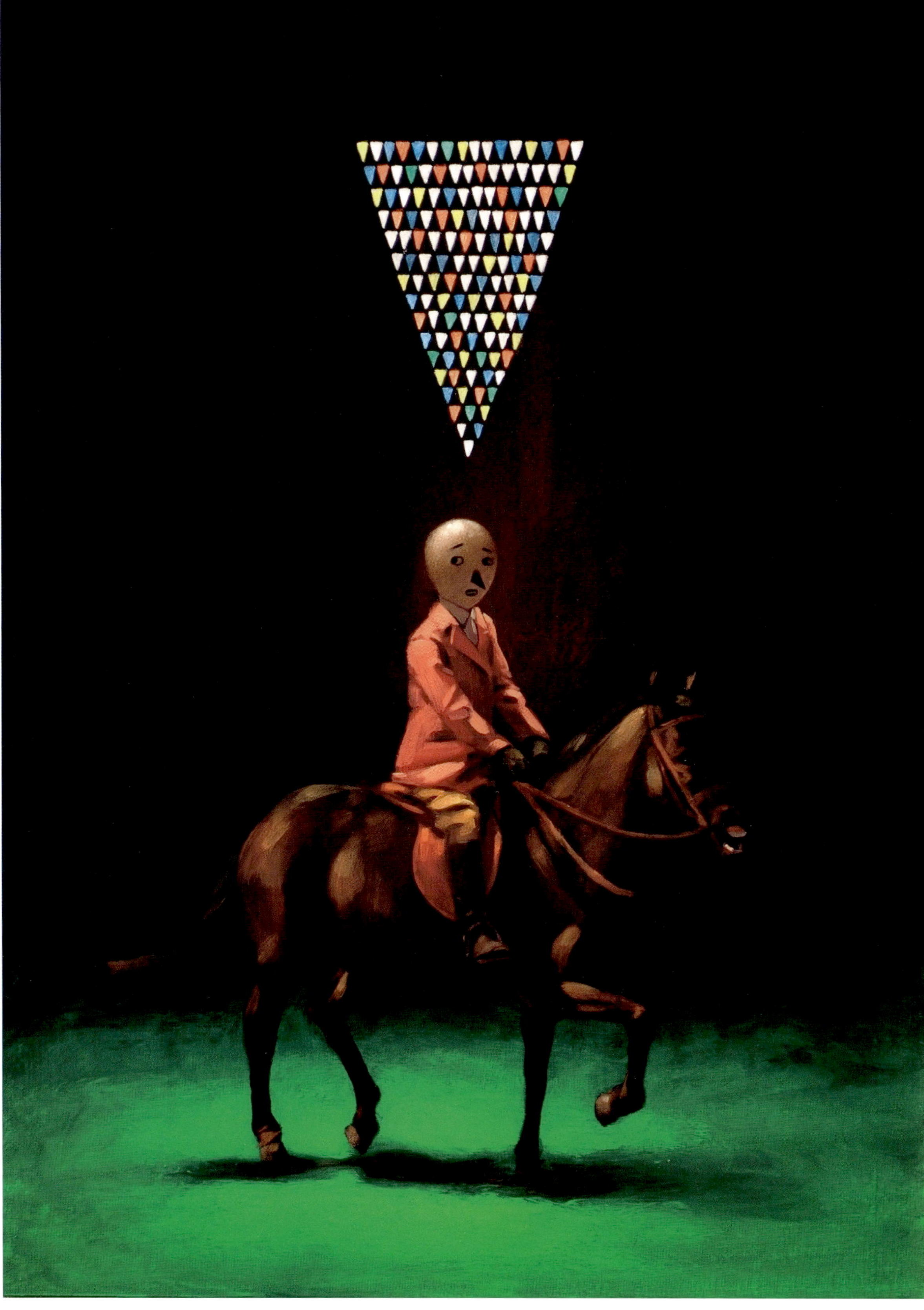

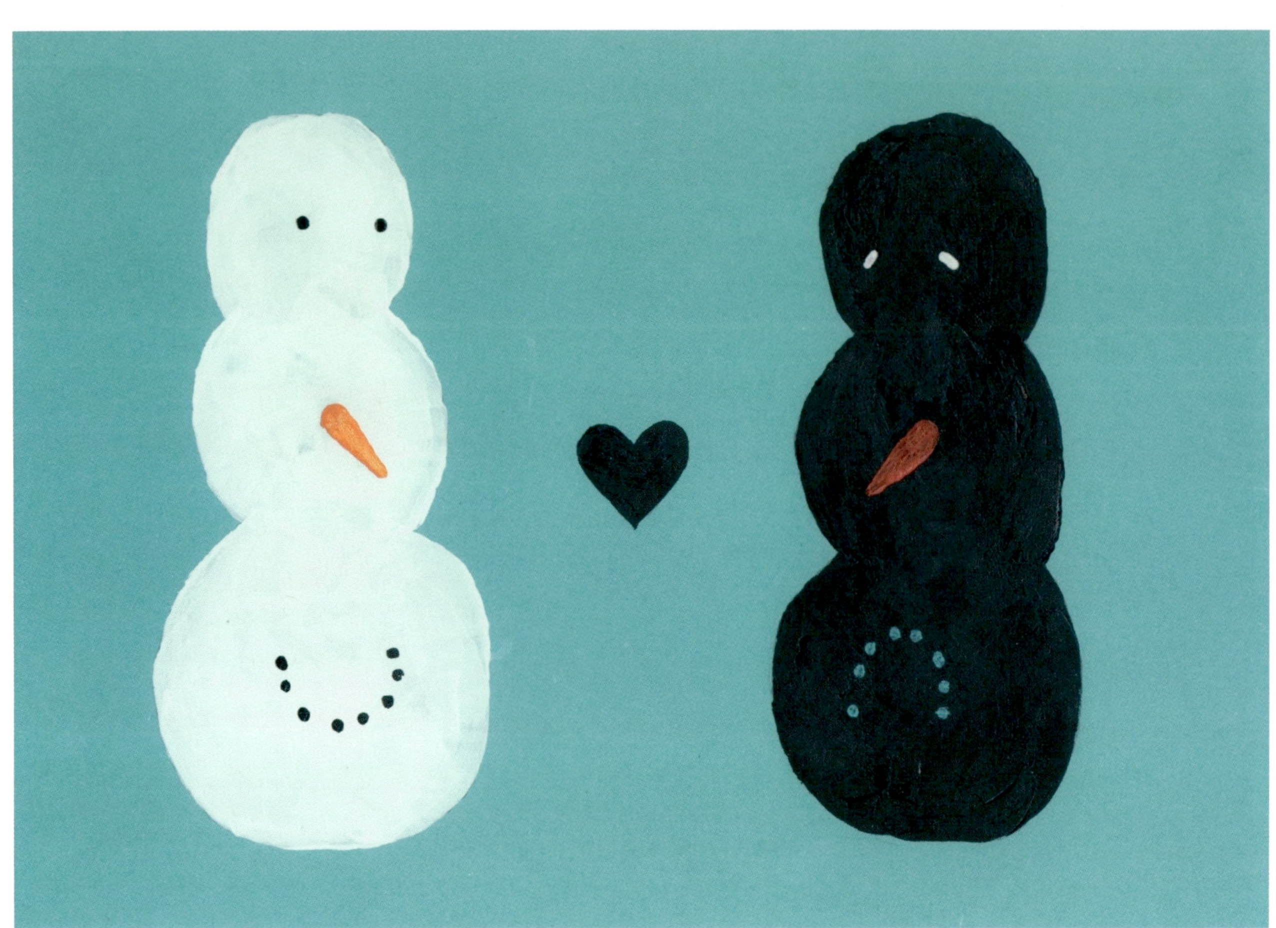

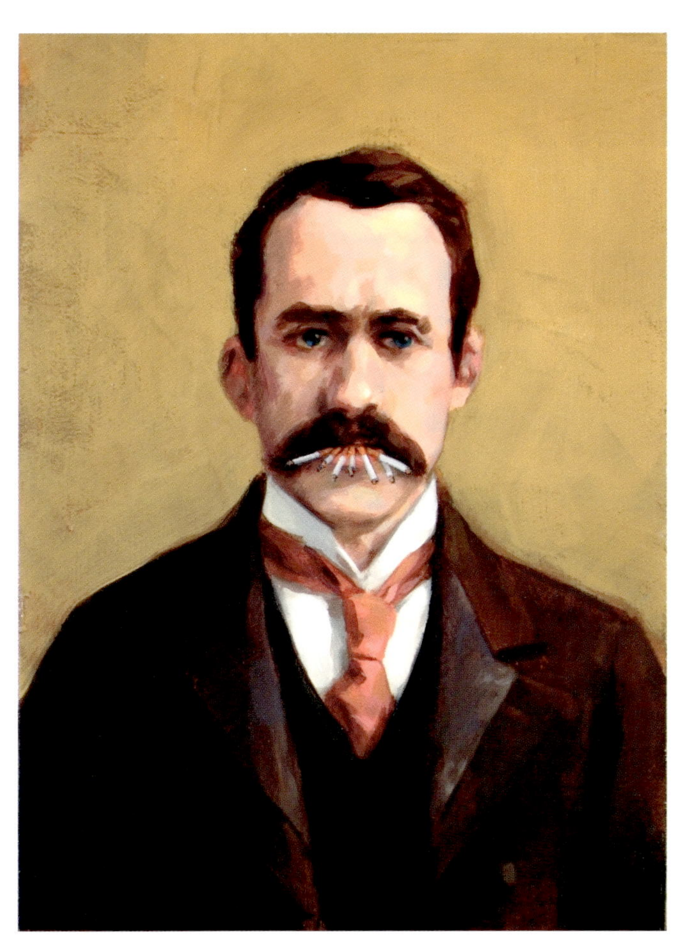
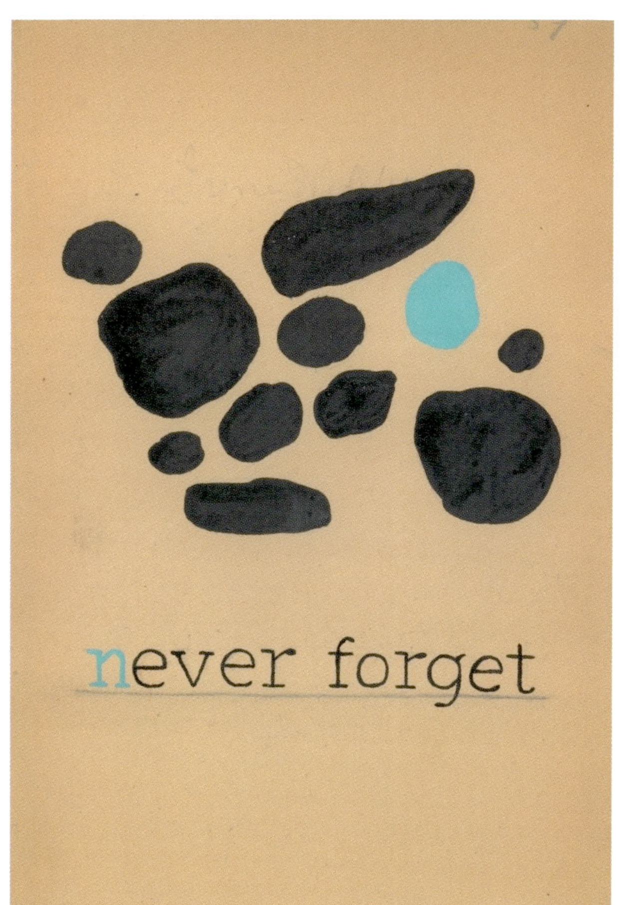
never forget

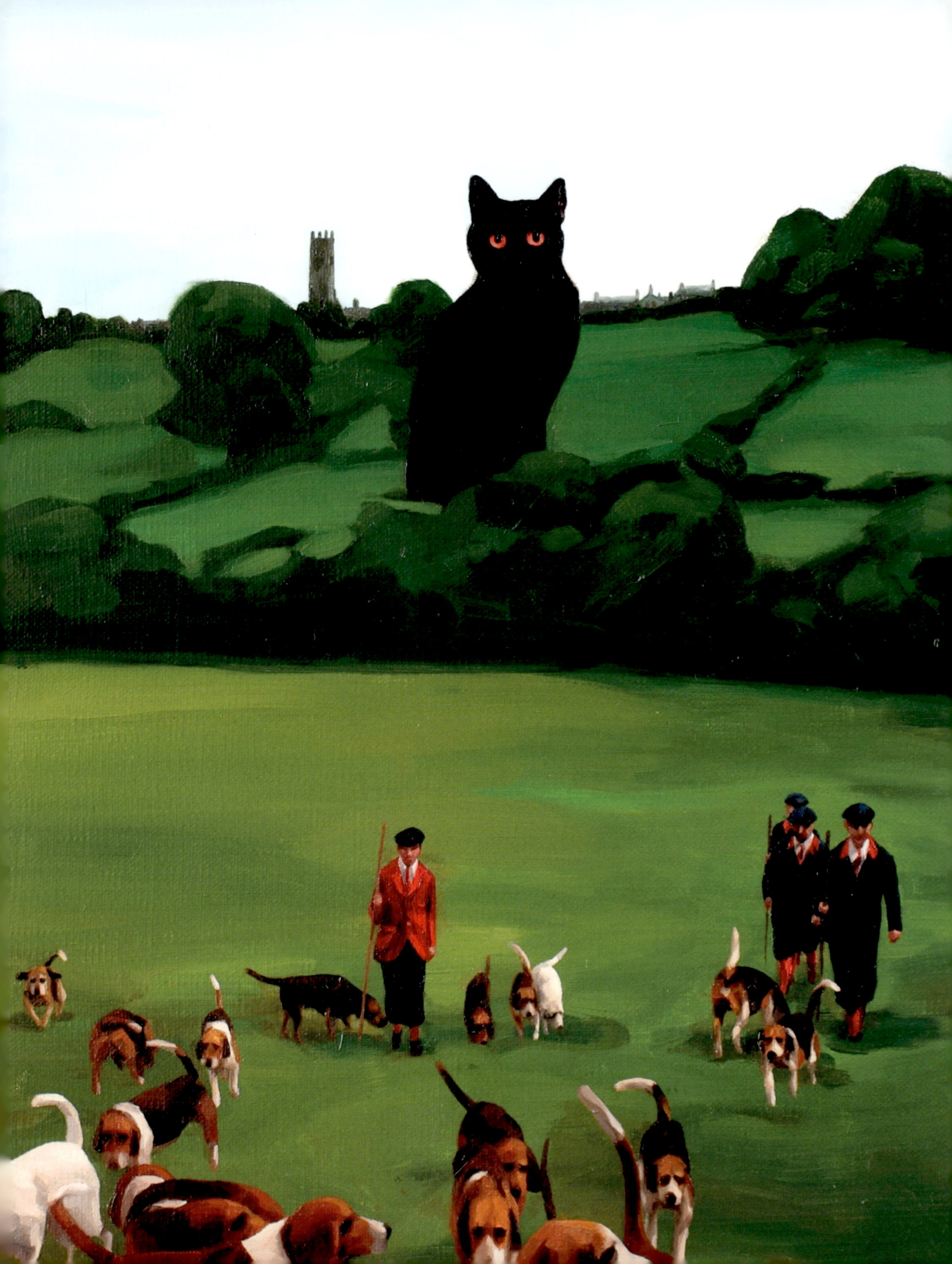

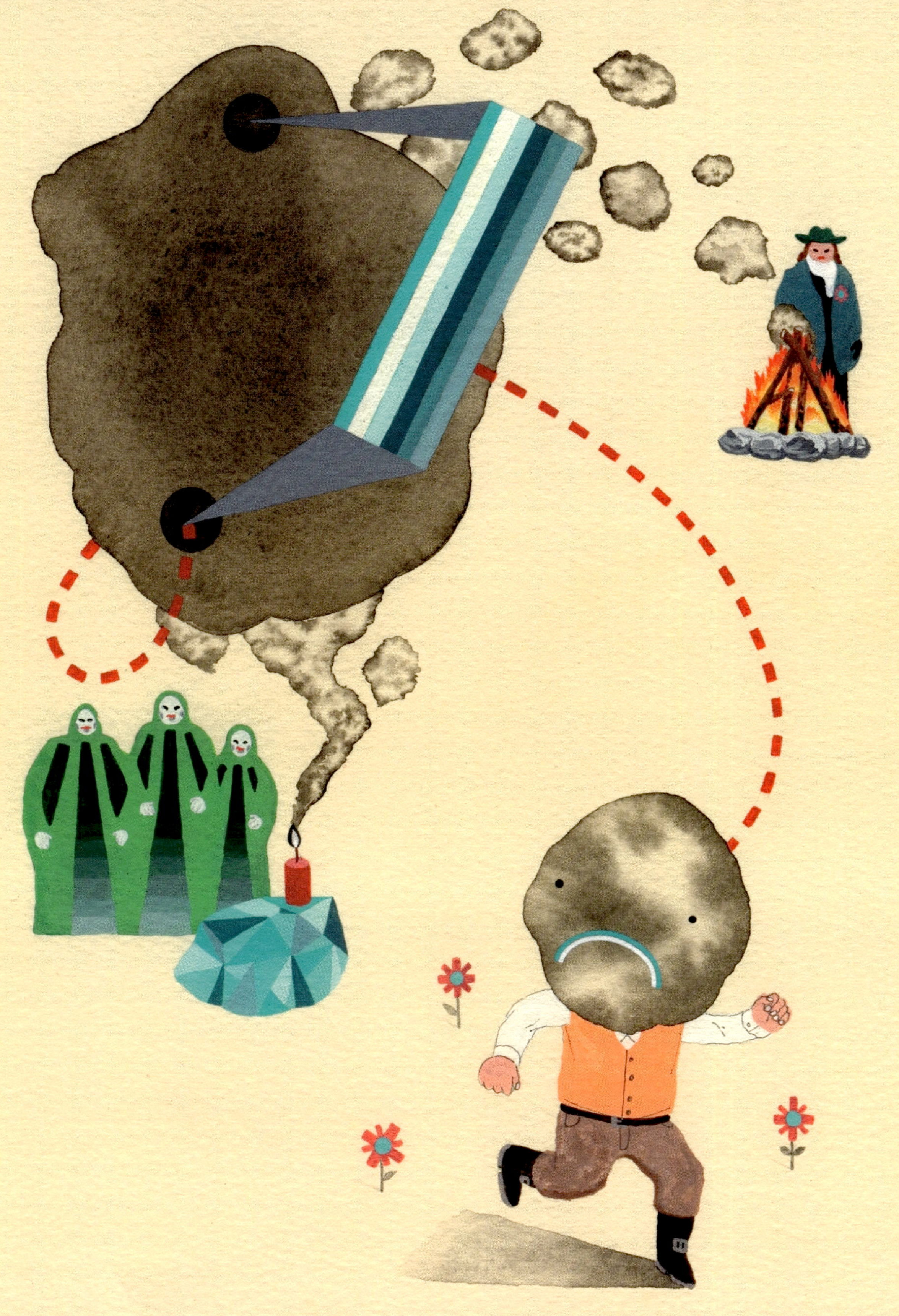

fig. 1

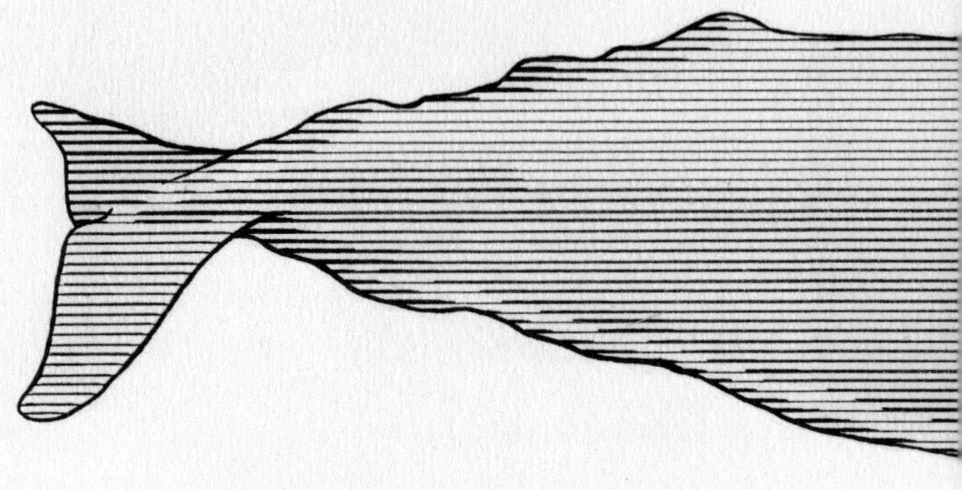

fig. 2

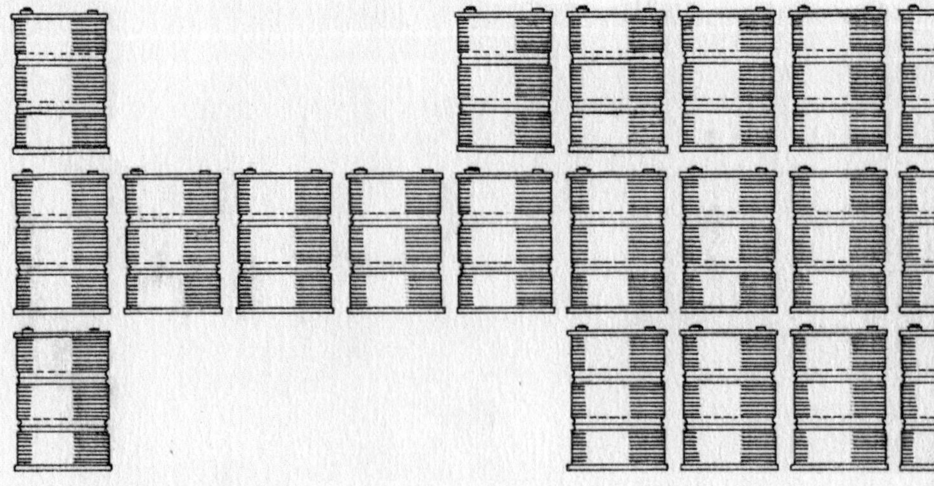

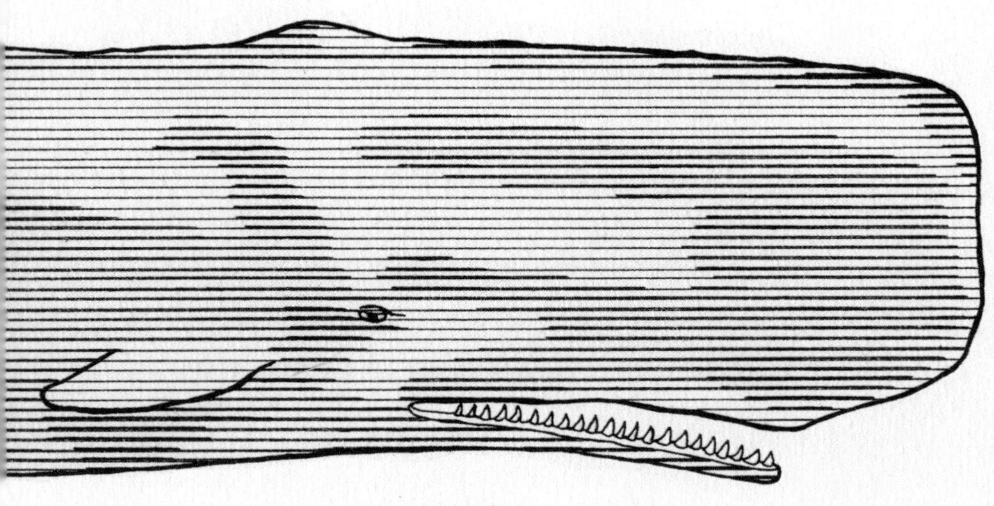

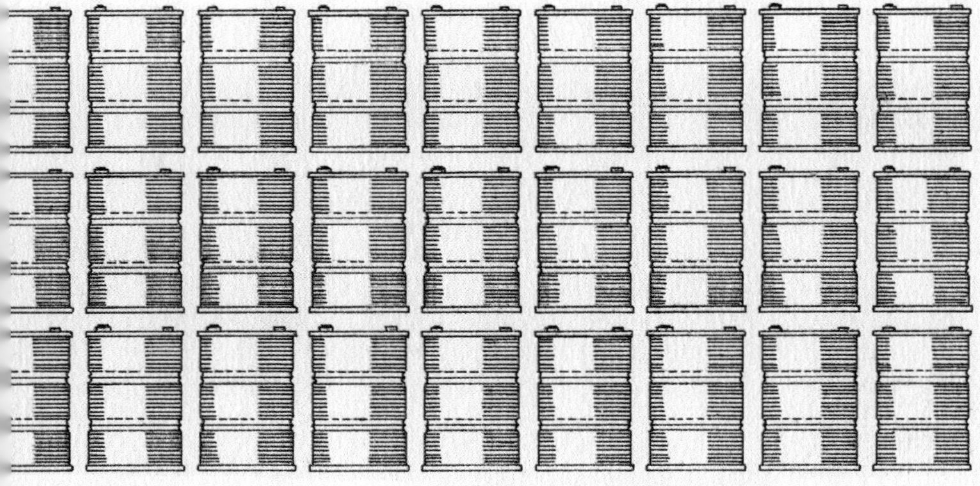

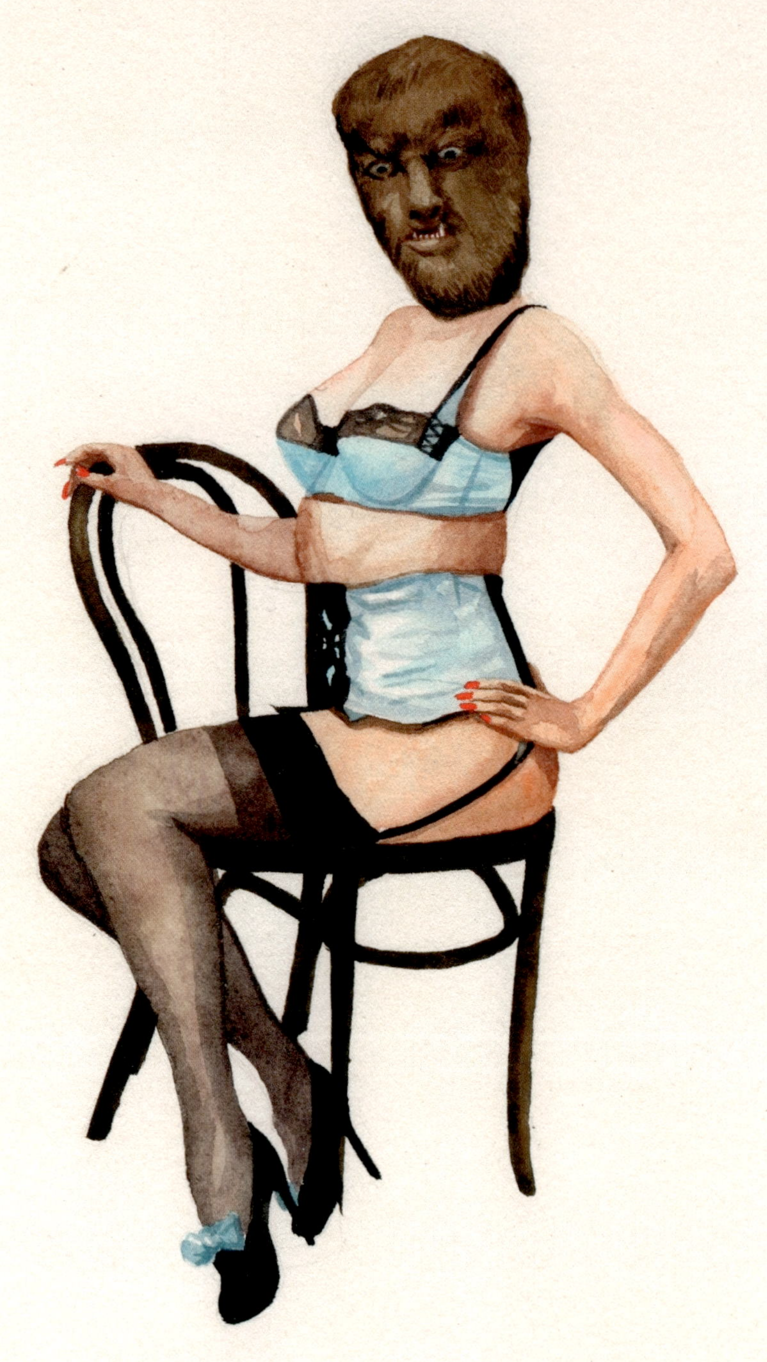

Whale Oil 2010 (previous)
Sex Wolf II 2010
A Fine Balance 2010

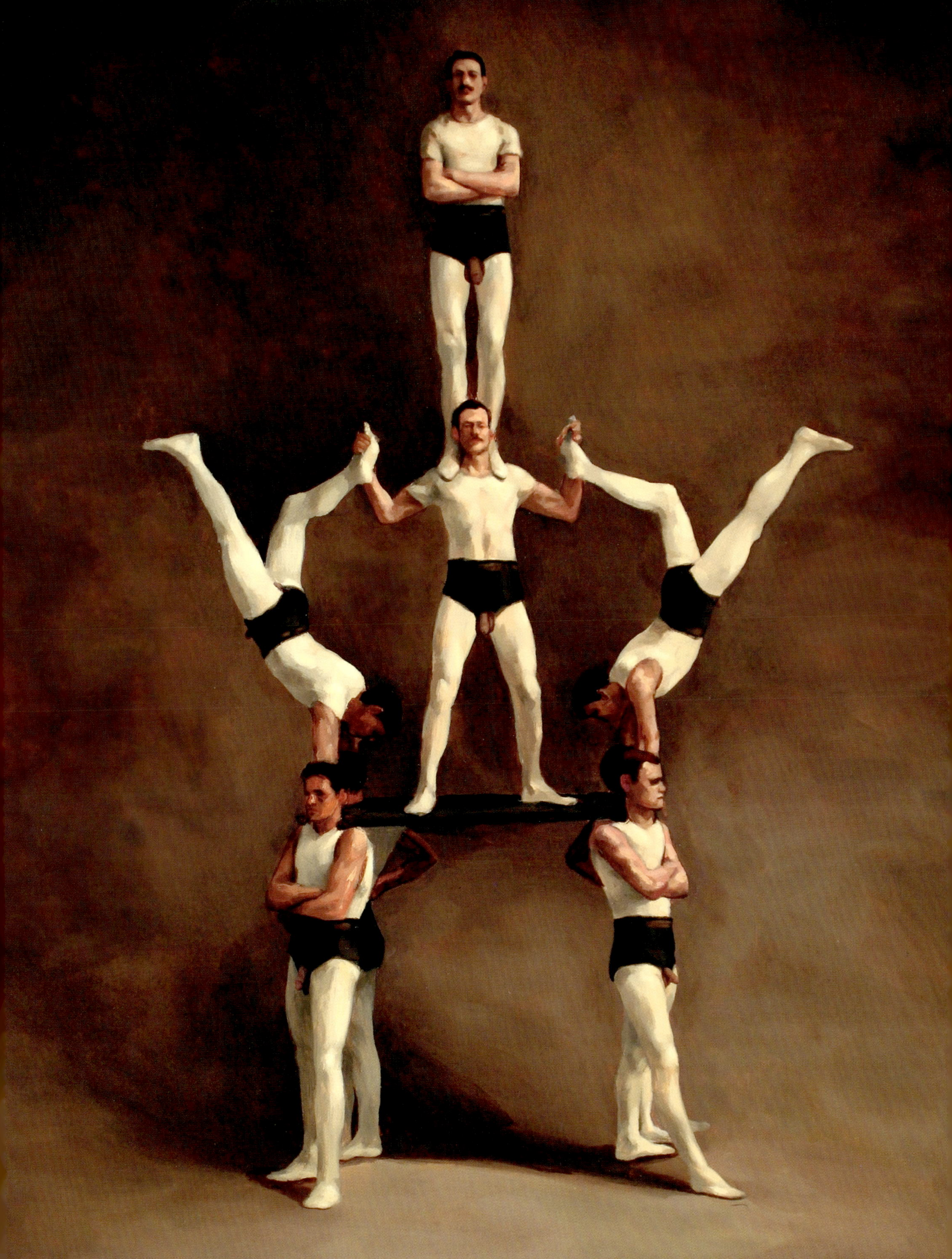

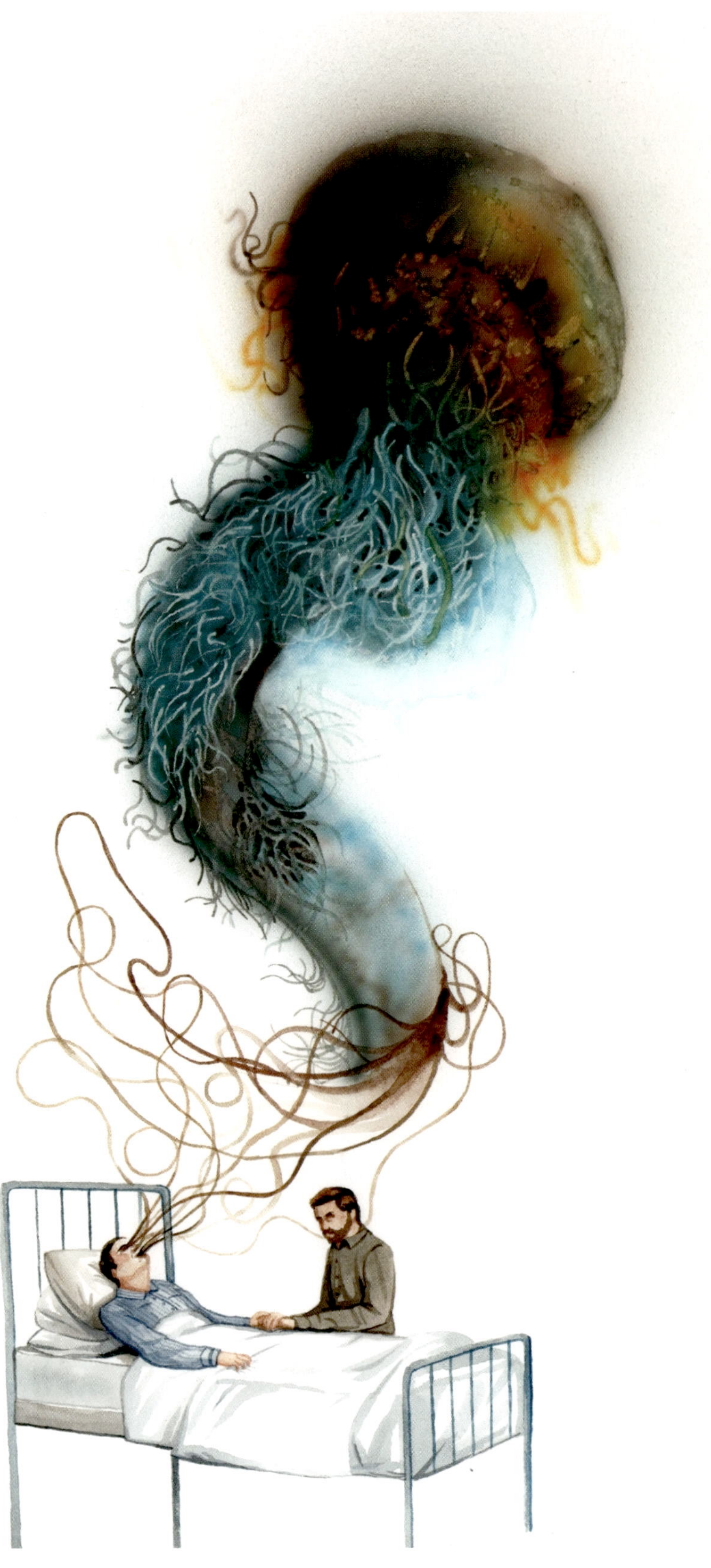

Merry Maladies 2010

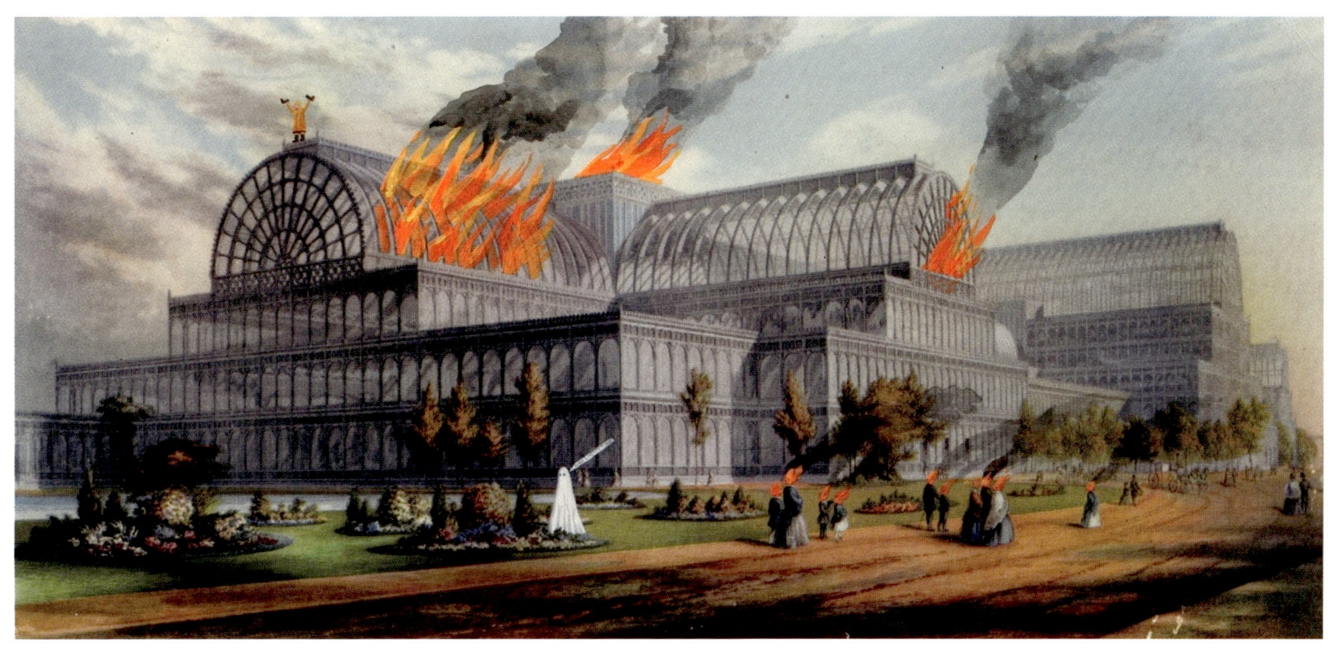

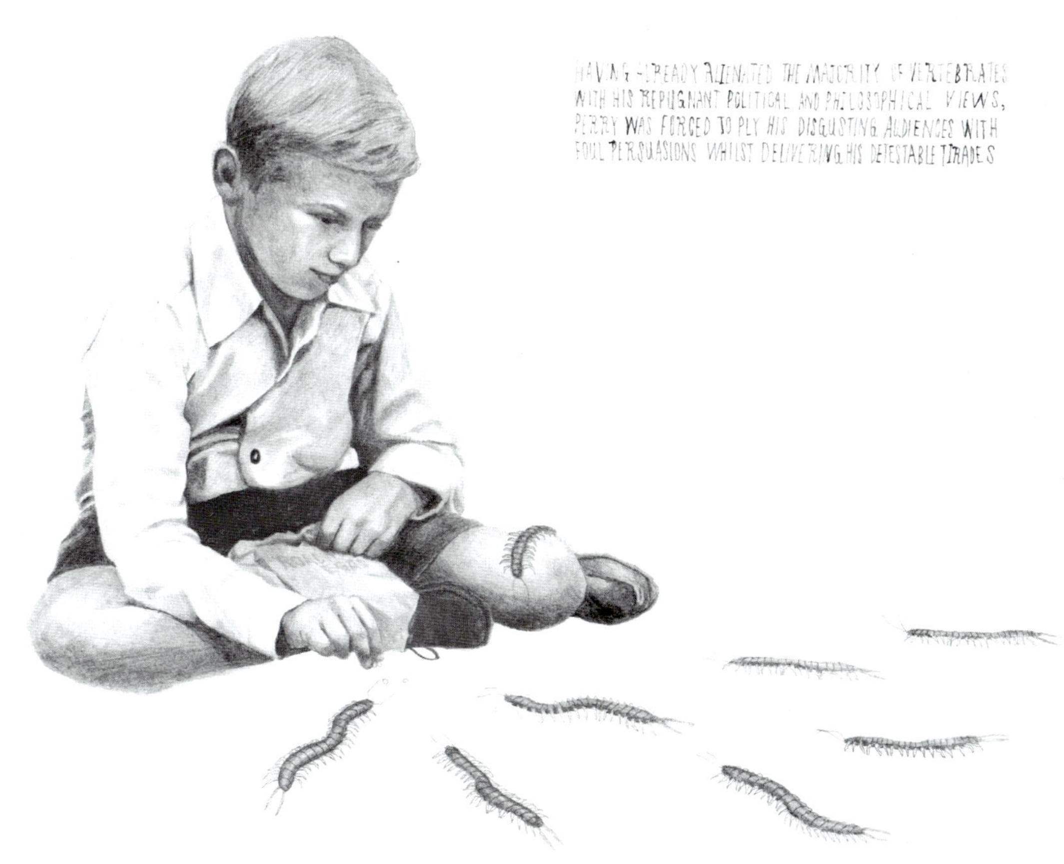

November 30, 1936 2008
Deplorable Little Shit 2010

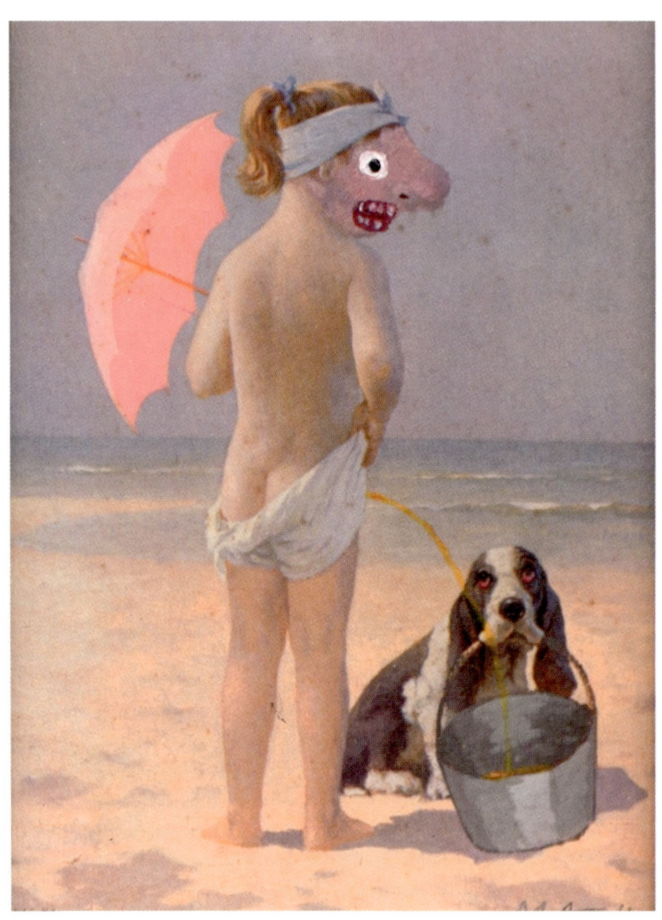

The Unbearable Tightness of Peeing 2008

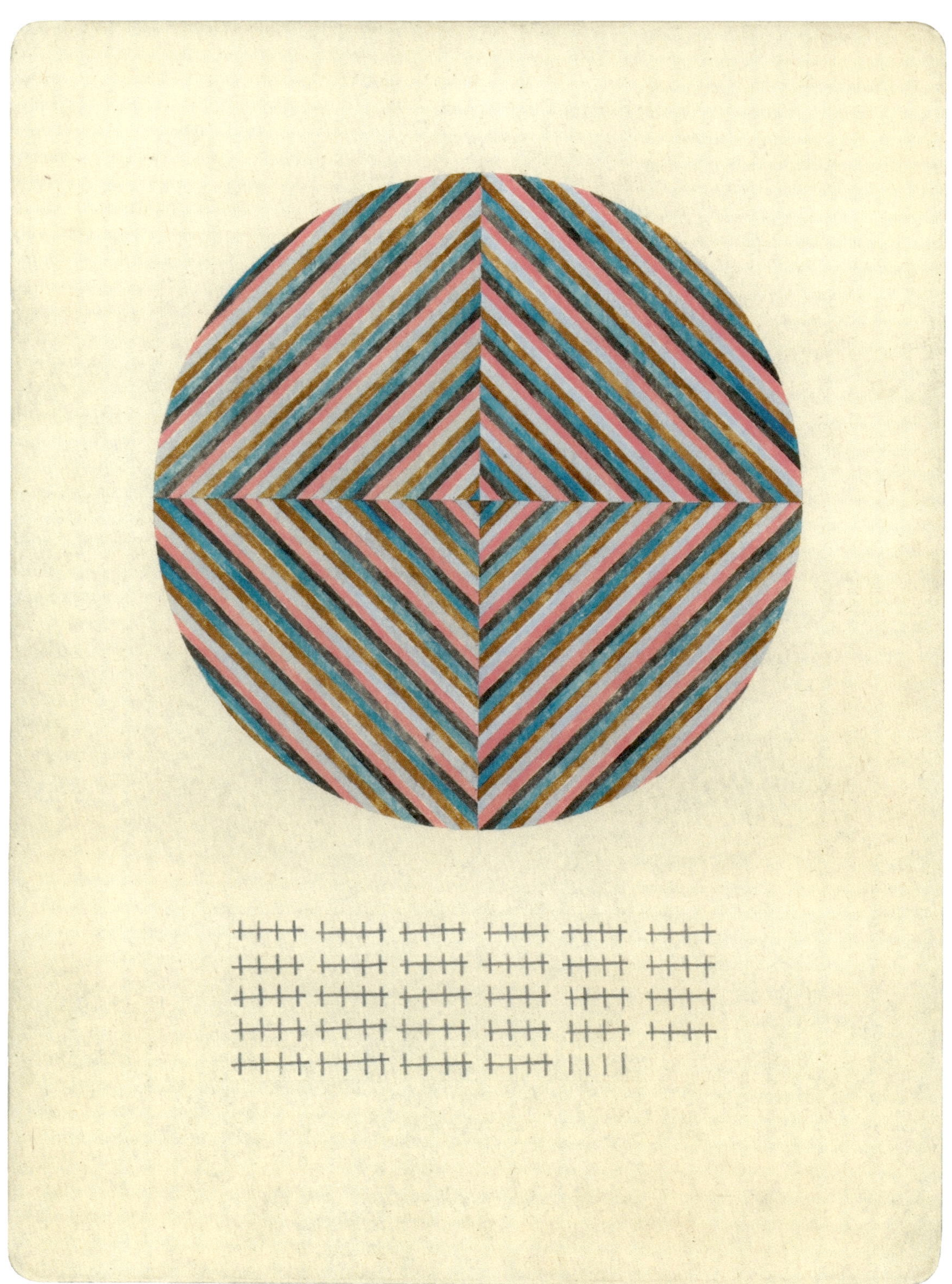

Bundle Spectrum   2008

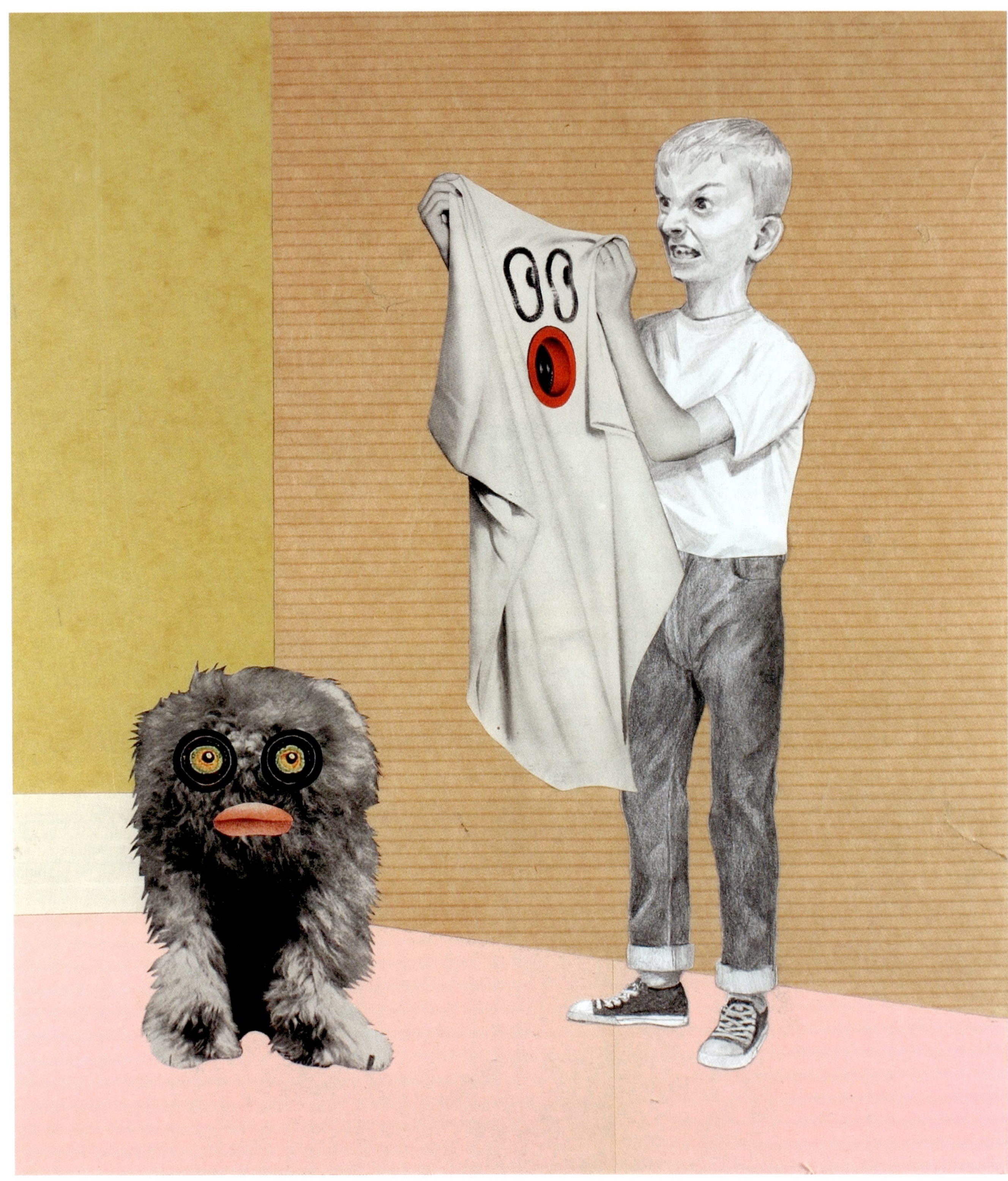

Reverse Poltergeist 2010
Quantum Percolator 2010

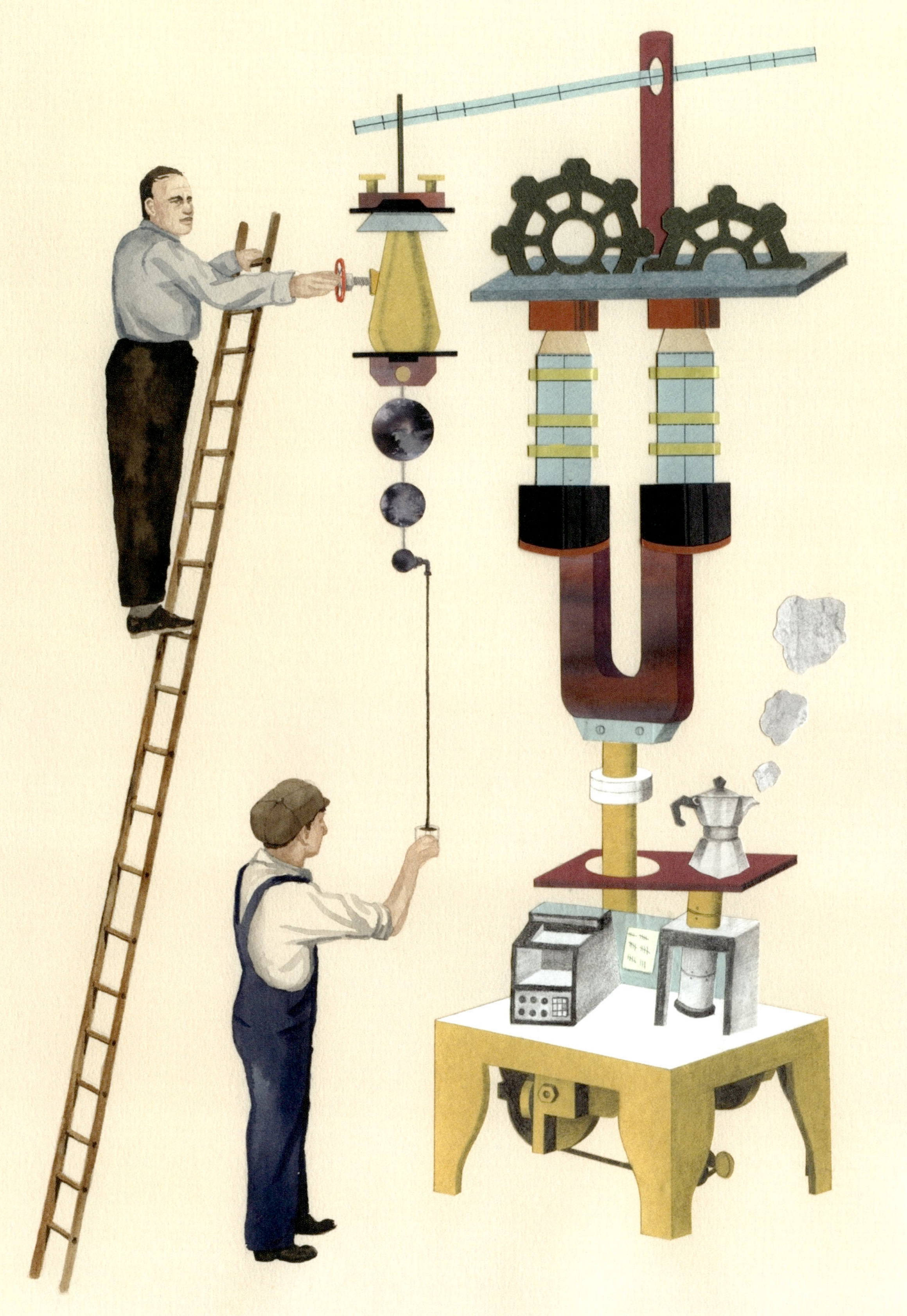

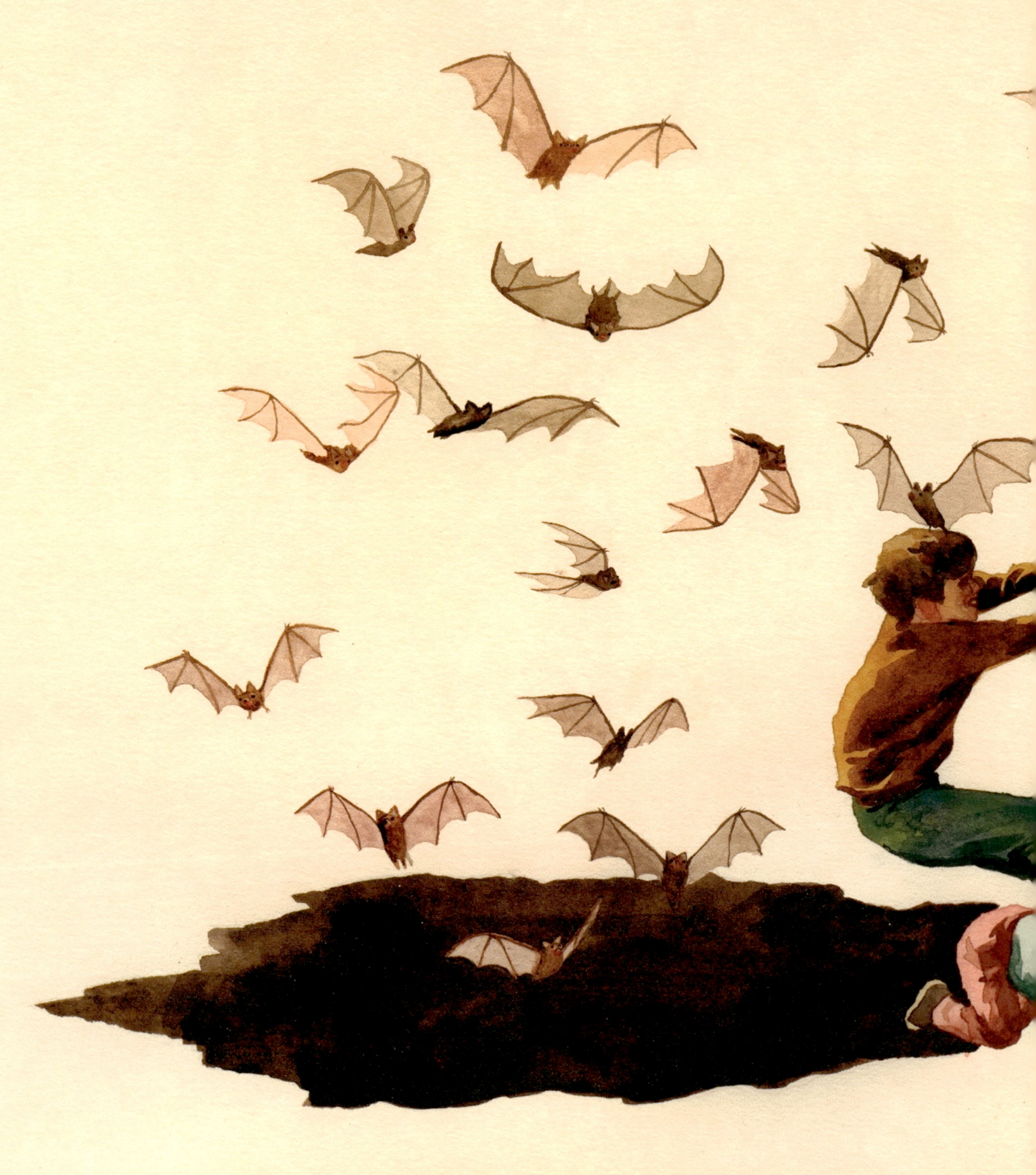

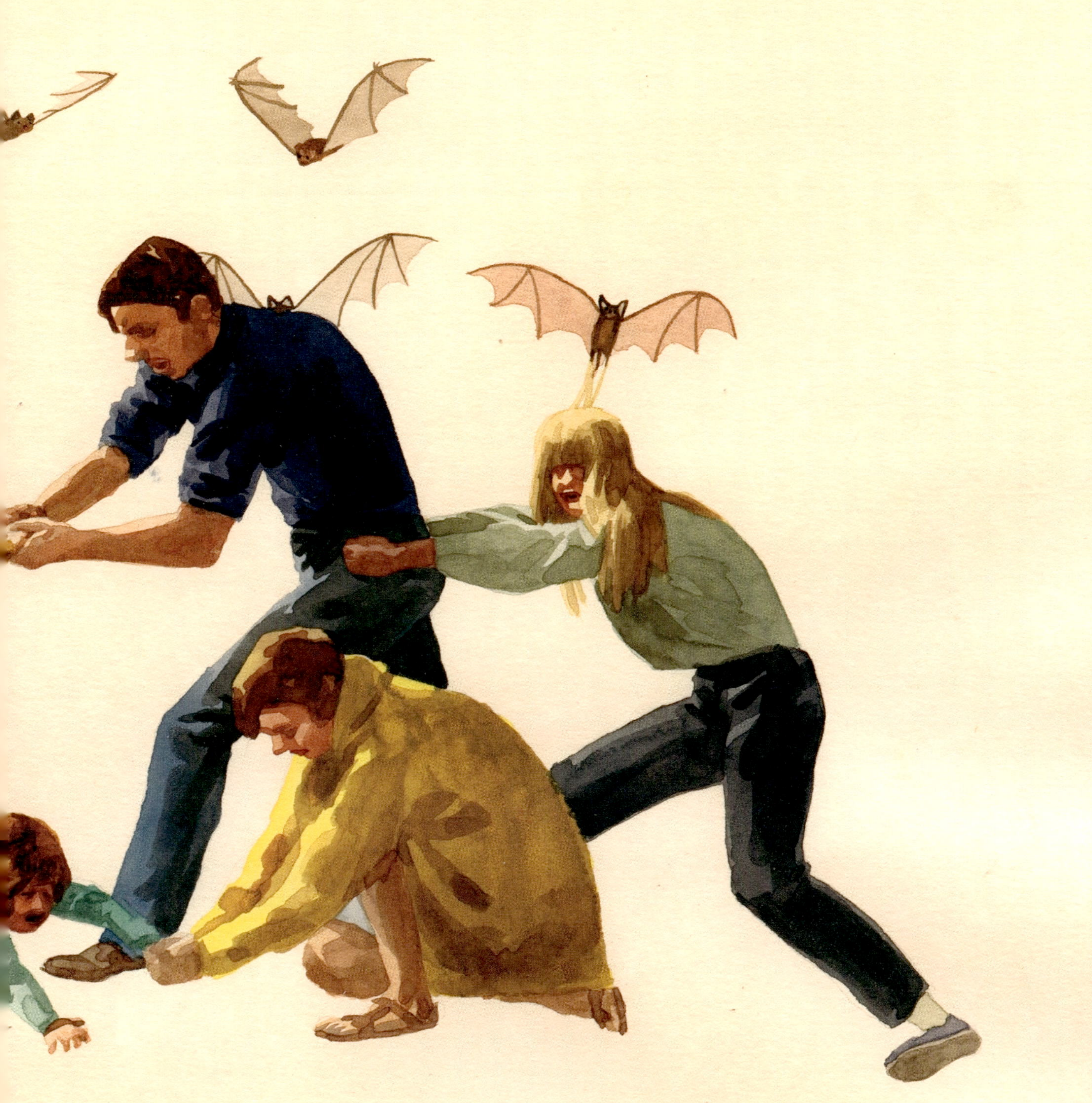

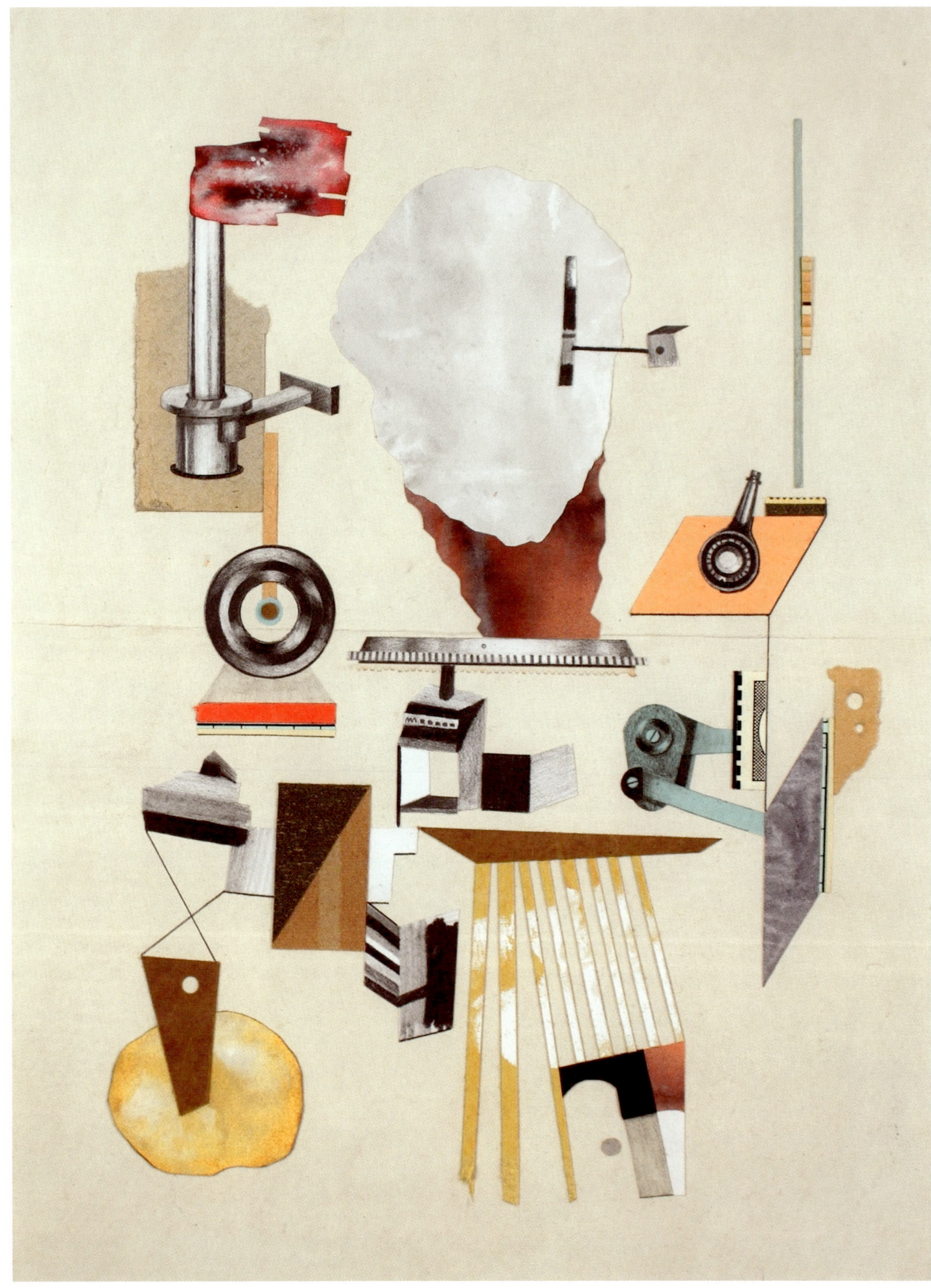

Caution: BATS!! 2010 (previous)
It Never Worked 2010
Oh Creeping Hell 2010

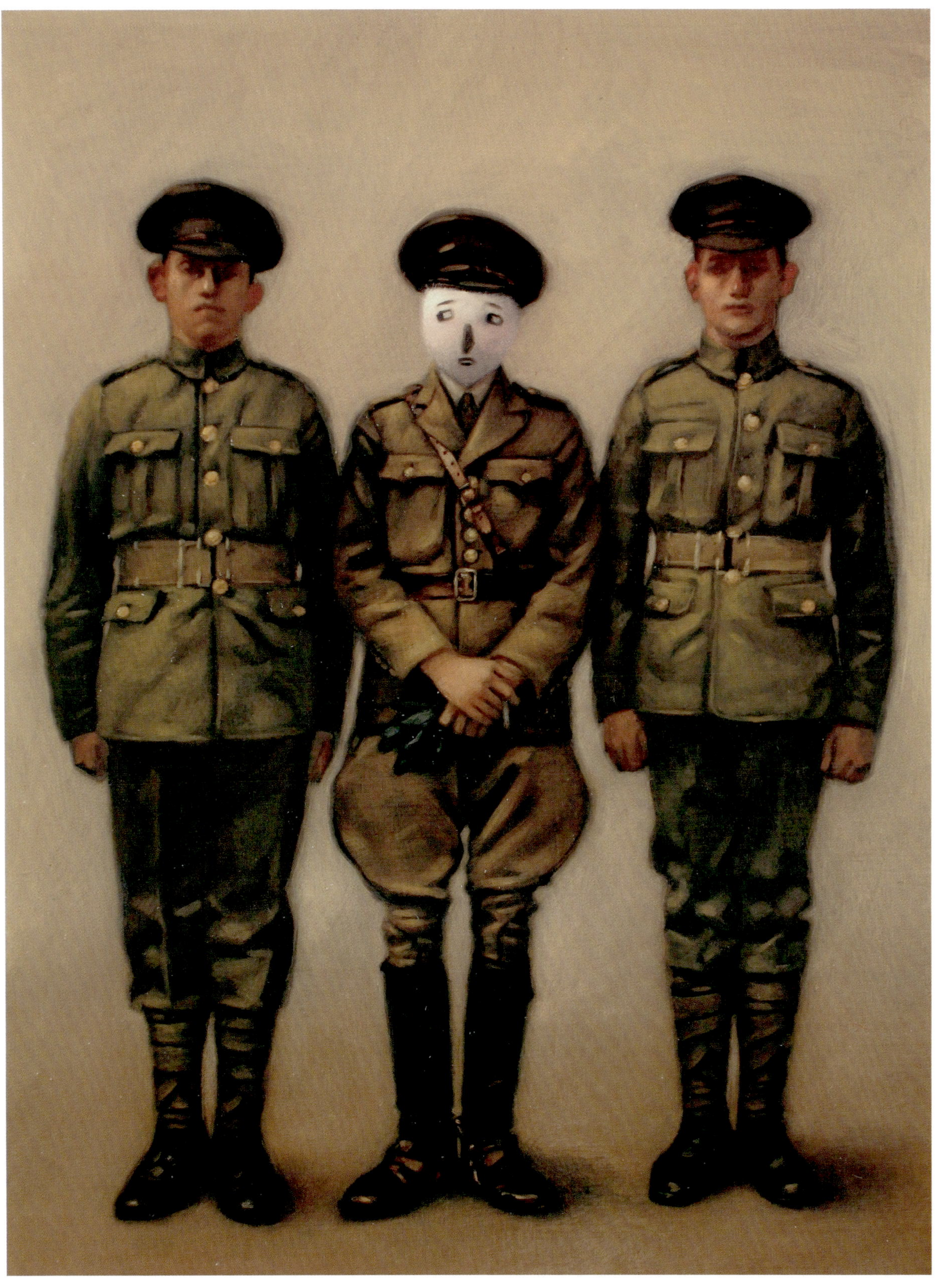

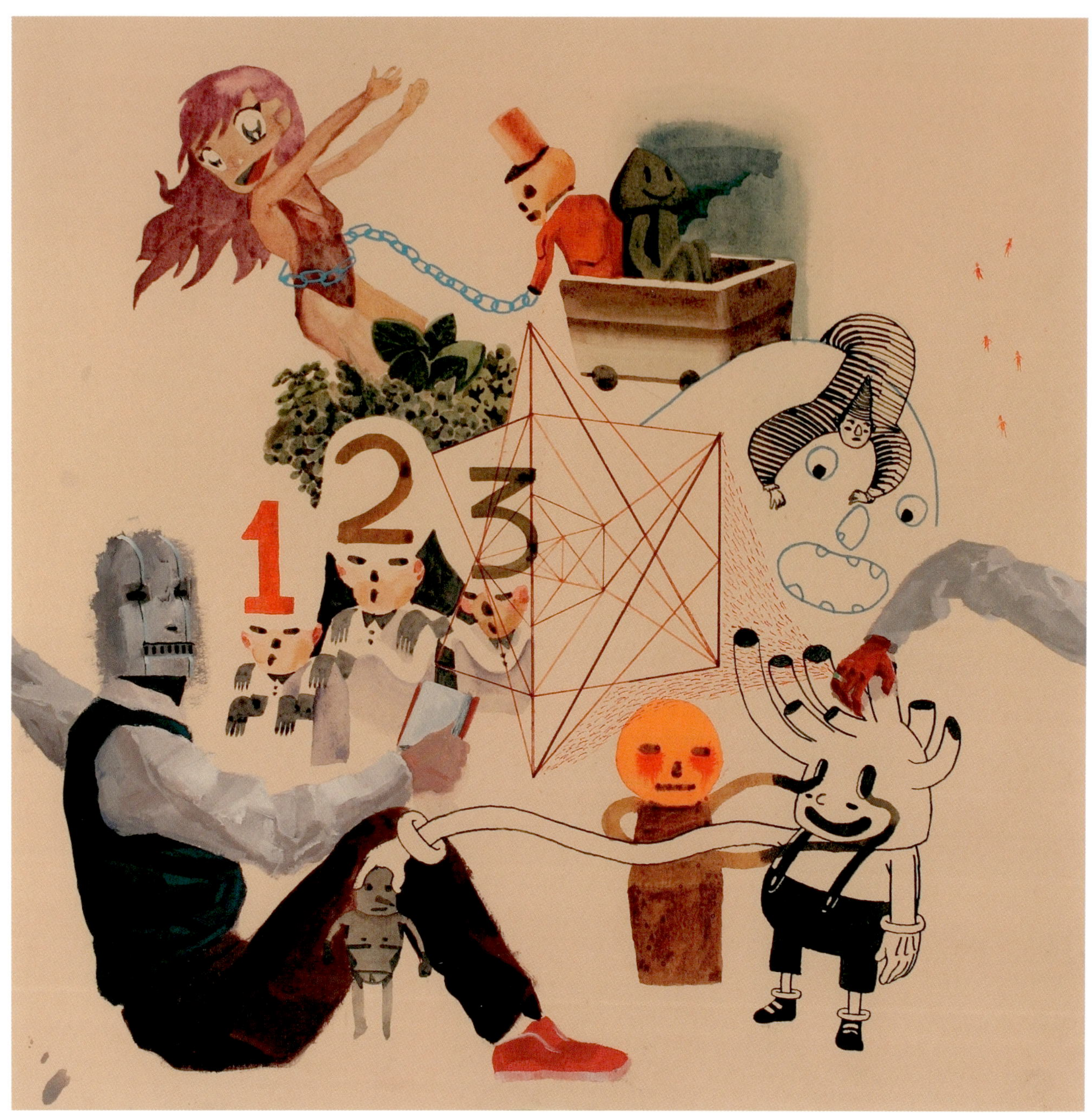

ABC 2010

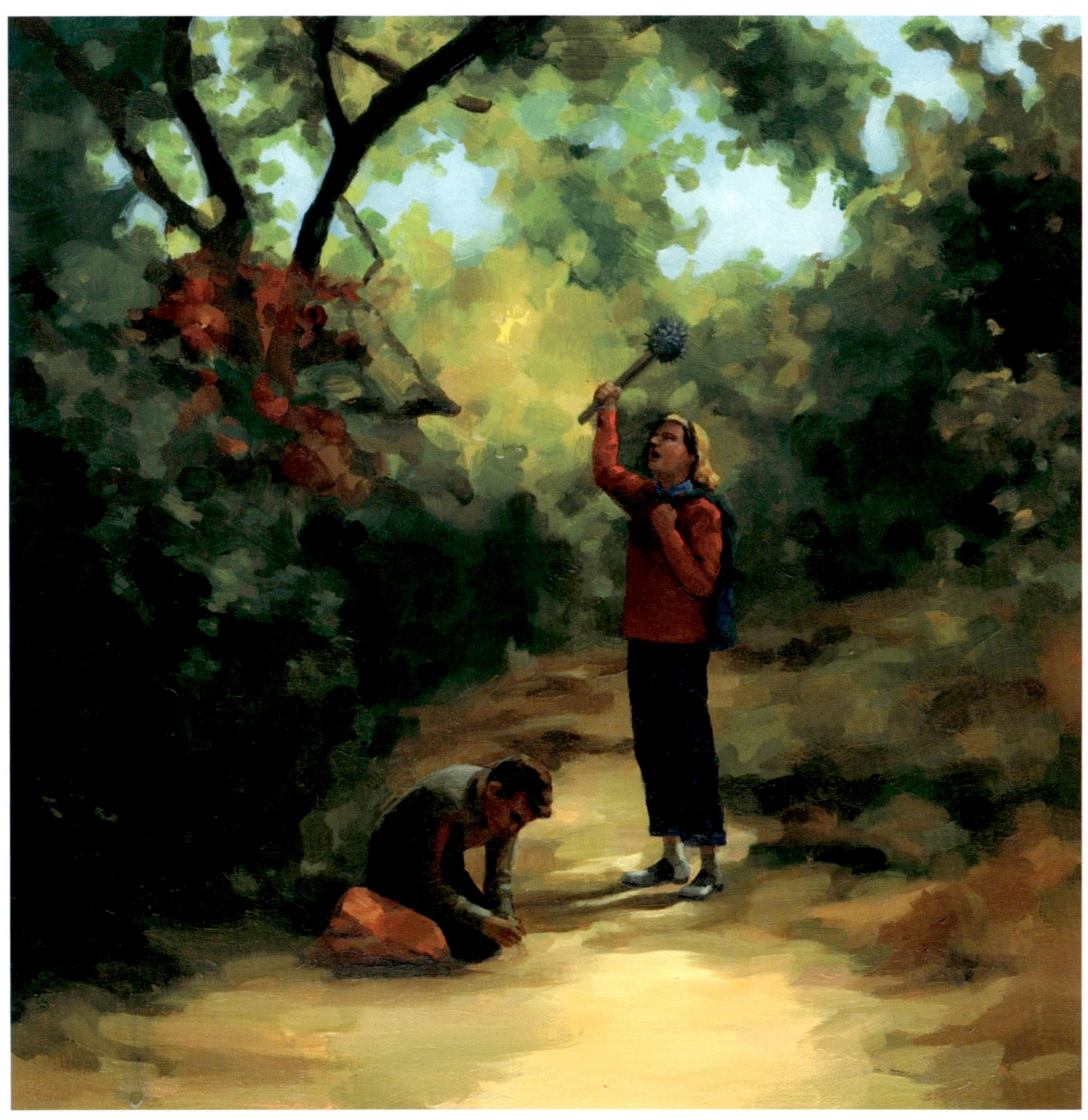

Let's Go Nutting   2009
Anne of Green Gables   2008 (over)
My Teeth Are Leaving   2008 (over)

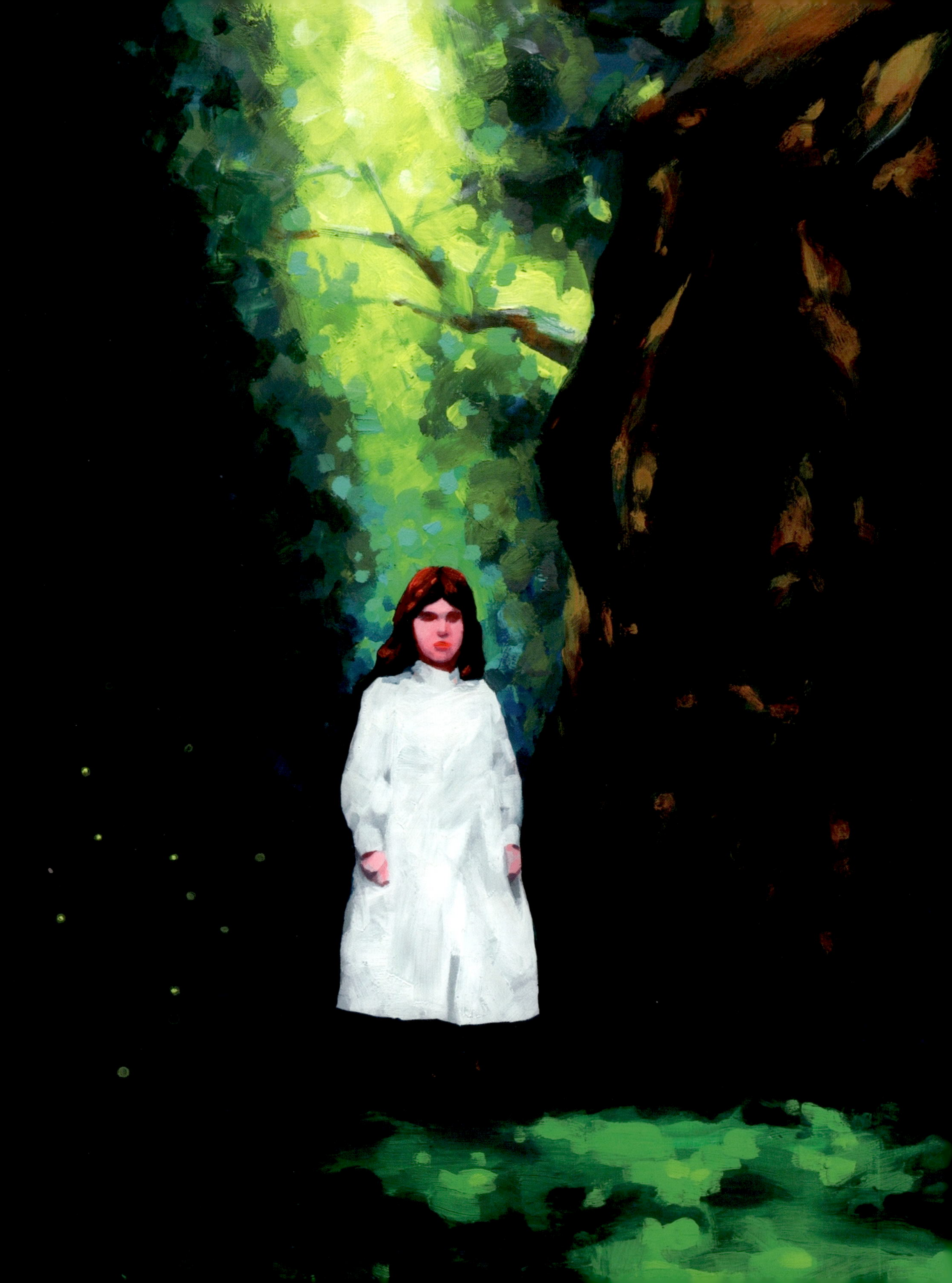

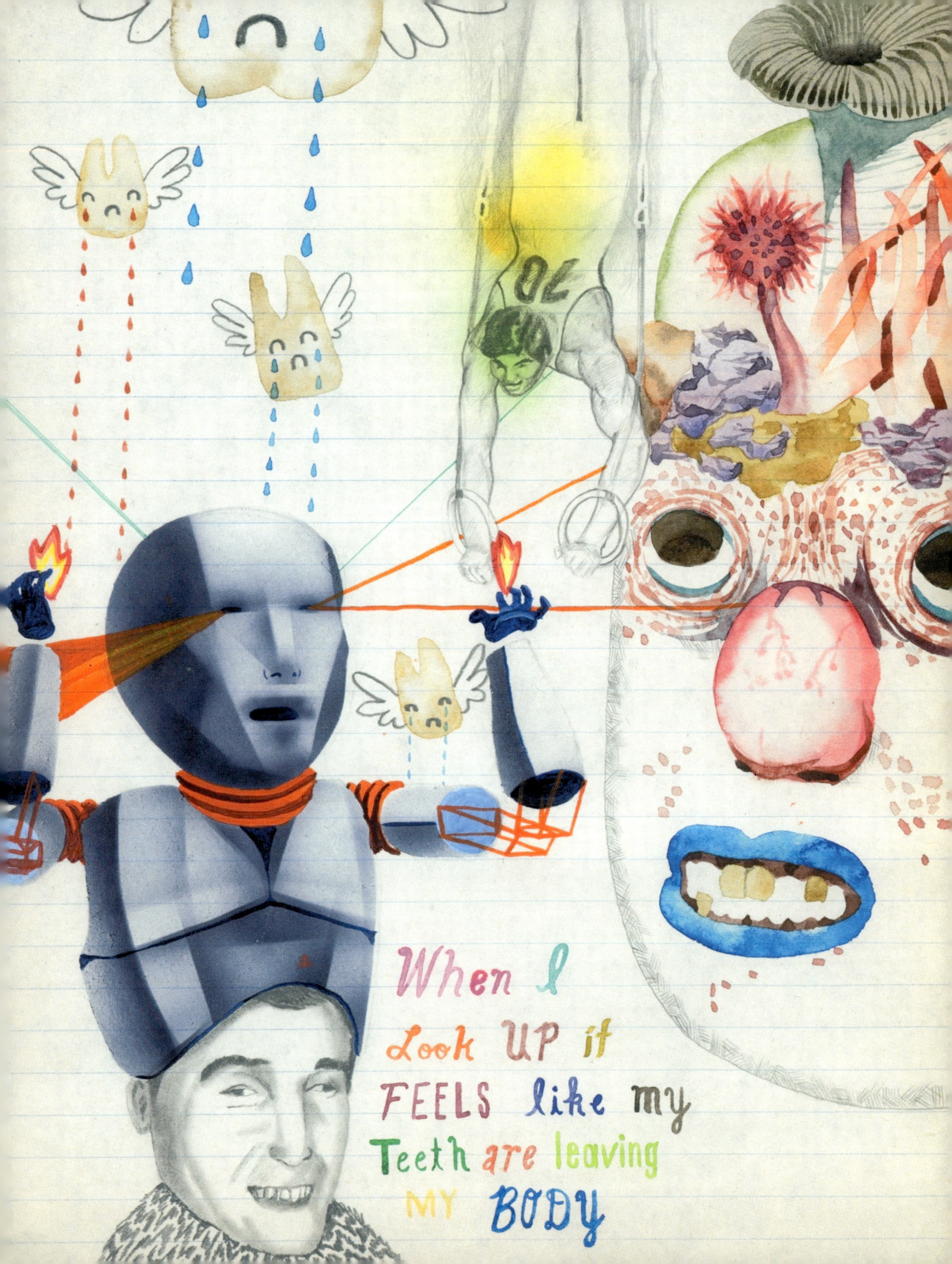

When I
Look UP it
FEELS like my
Teeth are leaving
MY BODY

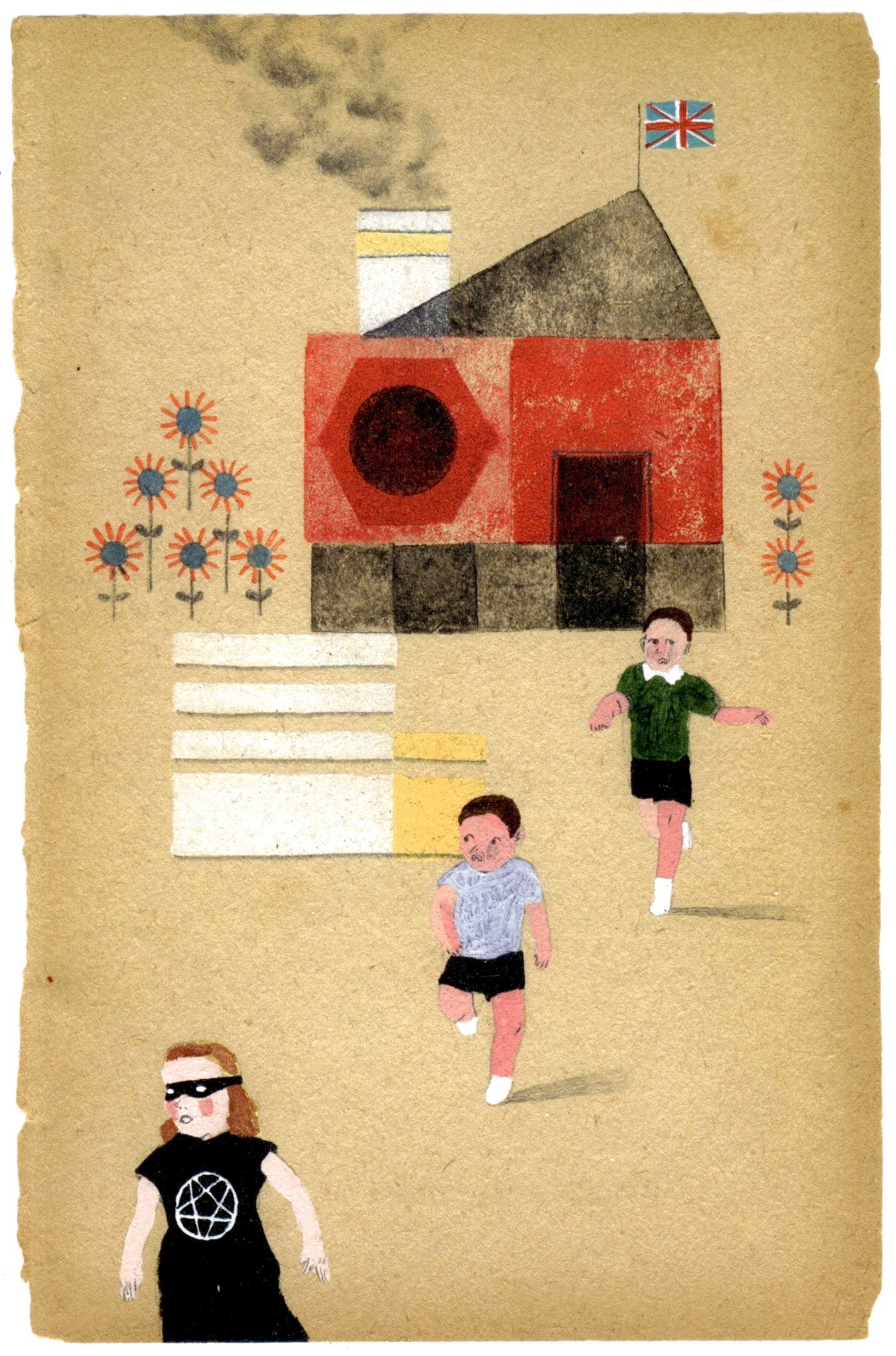

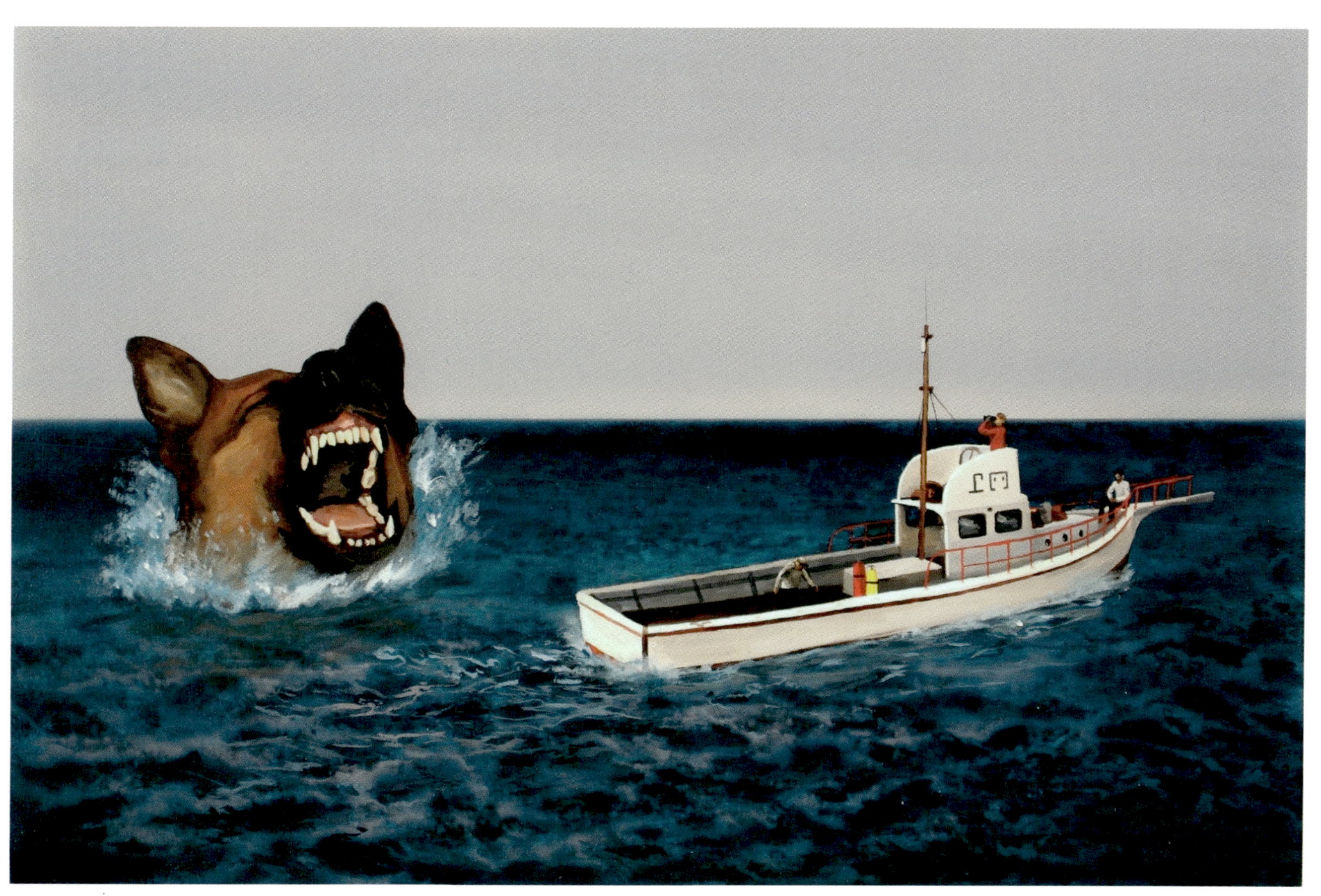

Go Back To Canada   2009
We're Gonna Need a Bigger Bone   2010

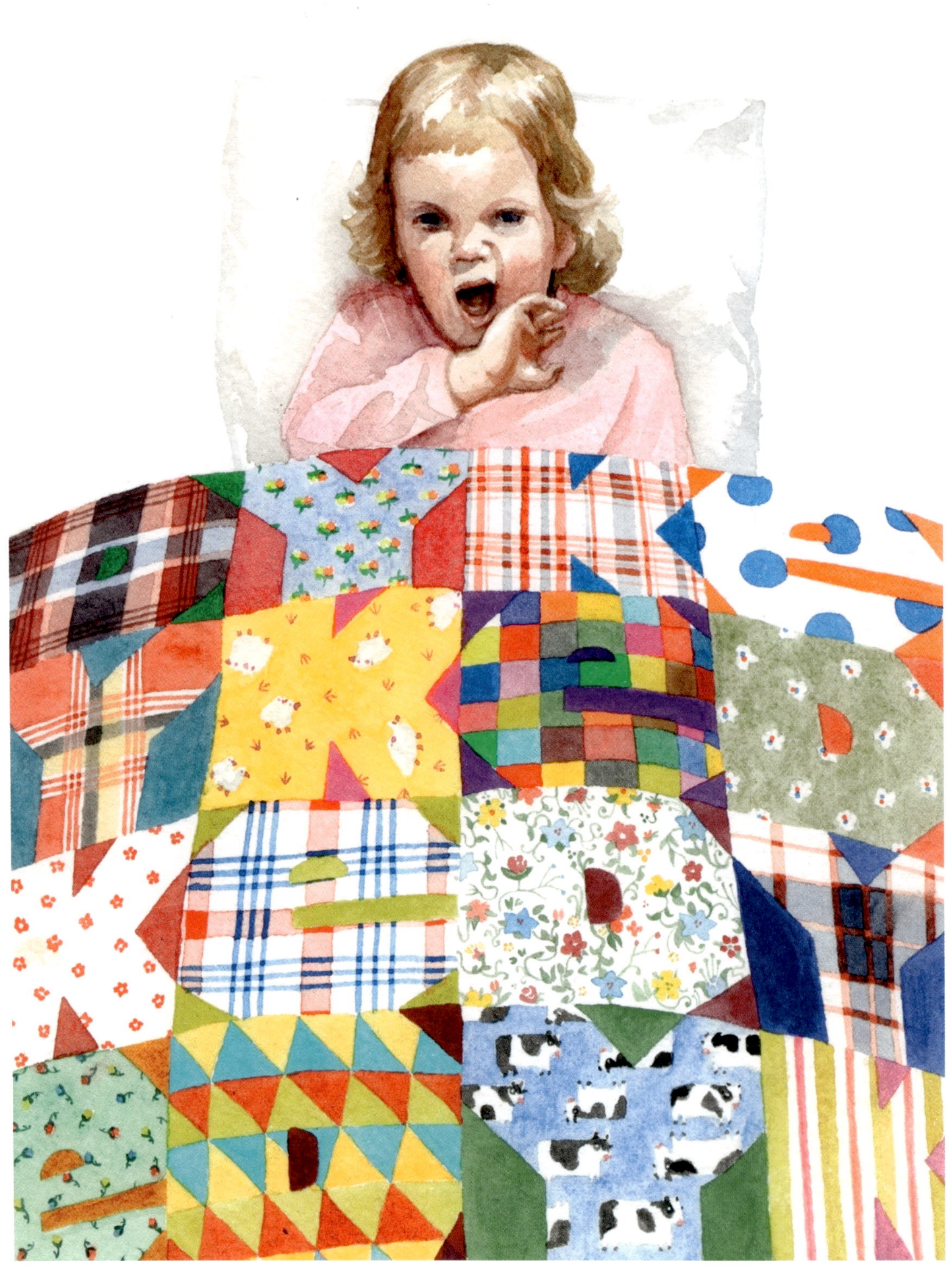

And She Grows   2010
Running Free   2008

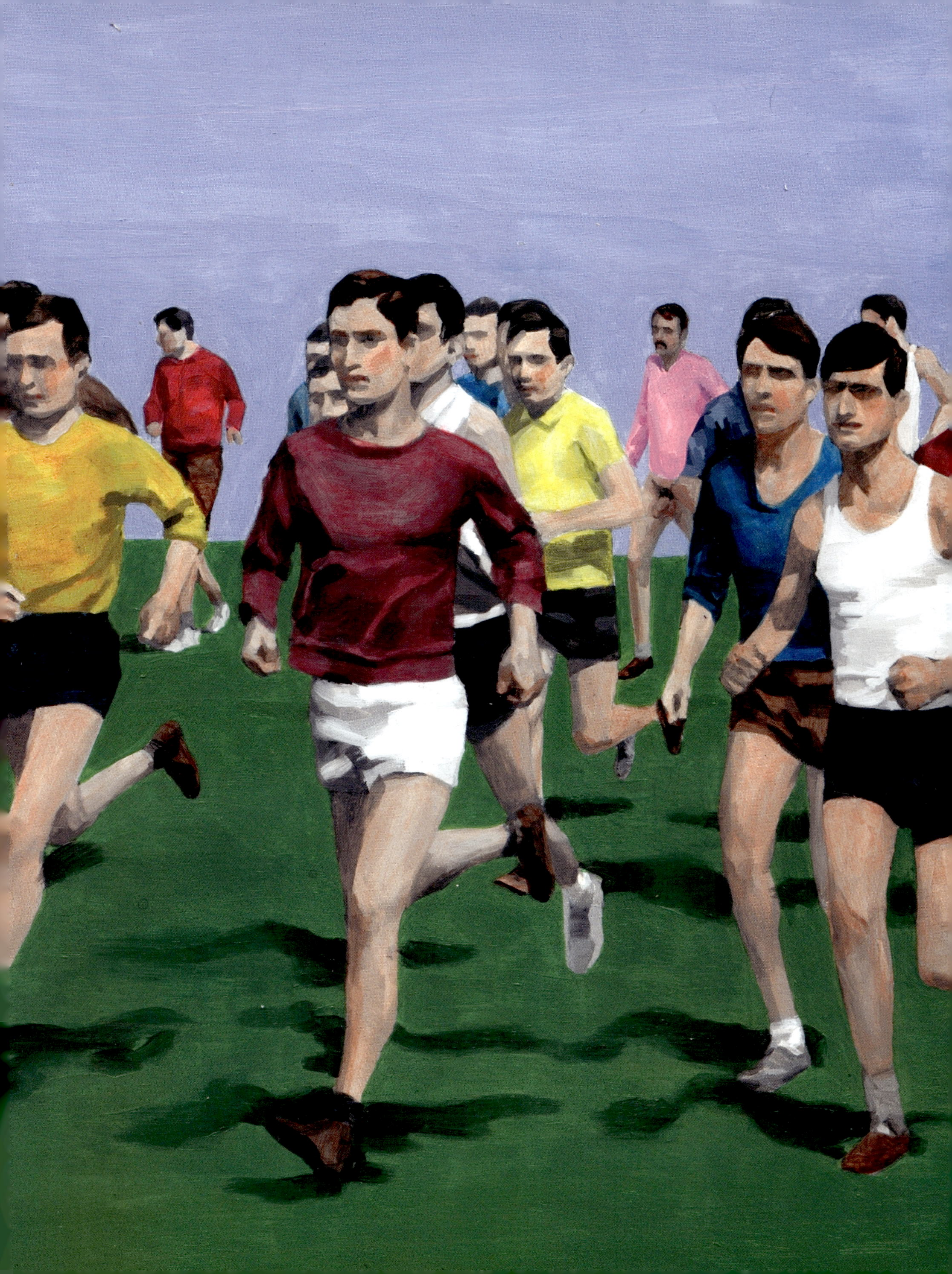

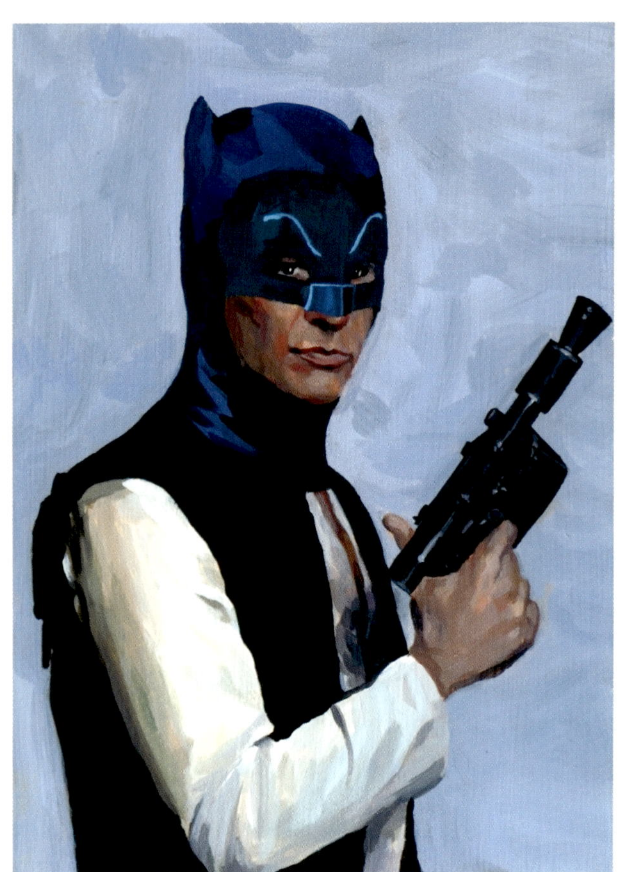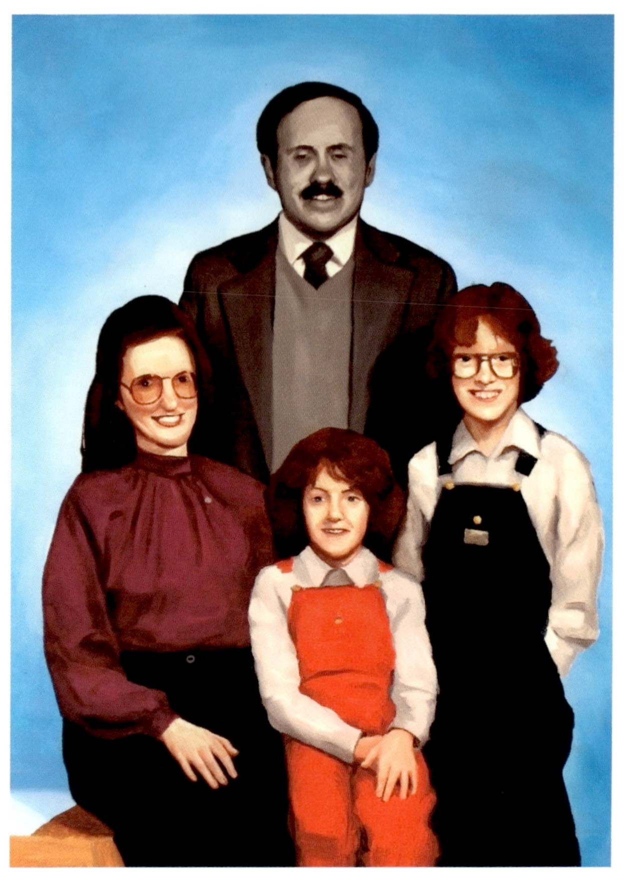

Spock 2010
World's Grayest Dad 2010

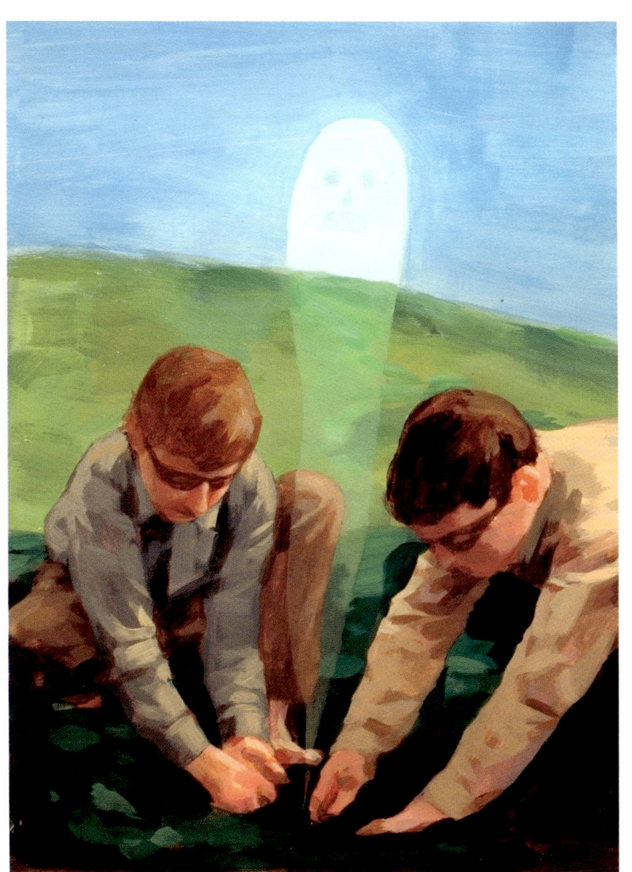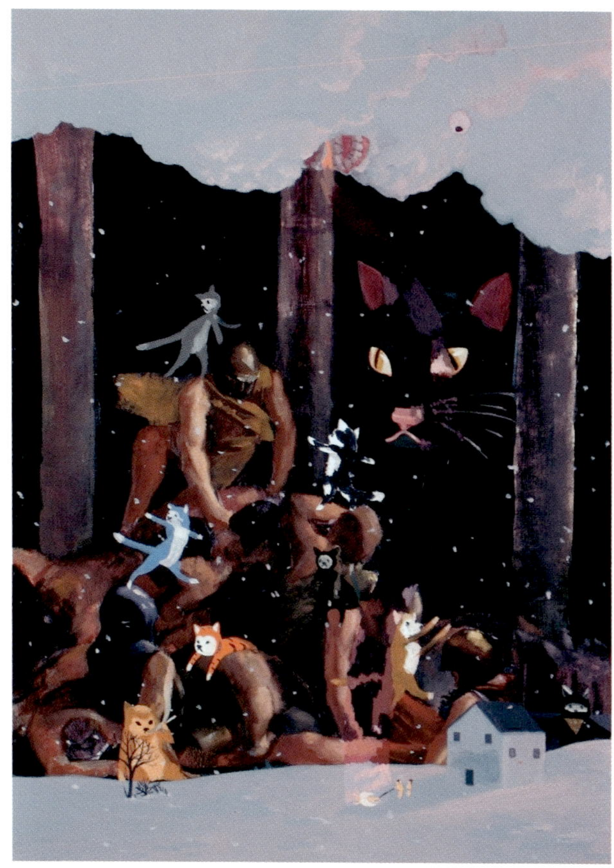

Bringing The Past To Life   2010
Expulsion of Lucifer   2010

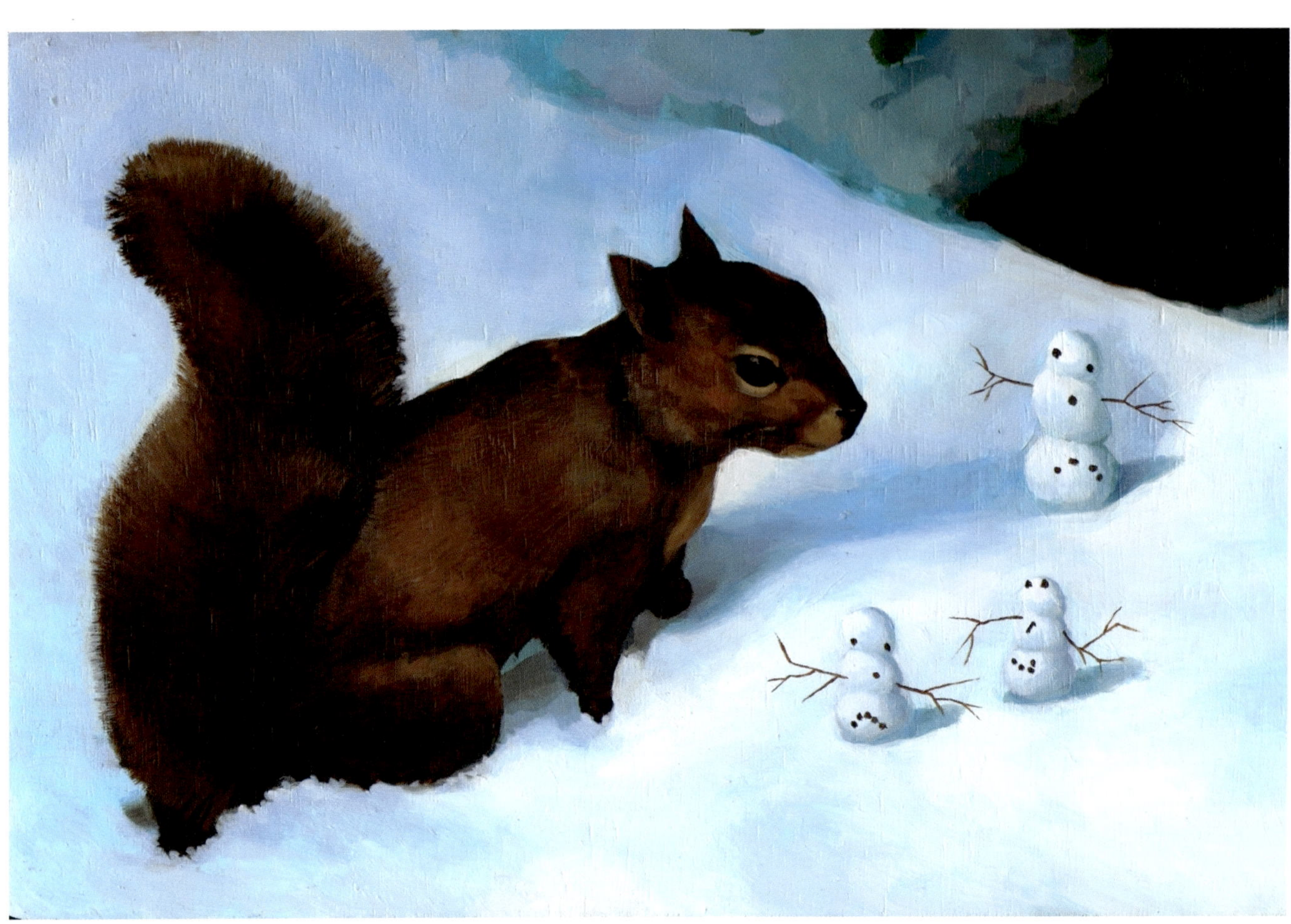

To Outwit Unwanted Guests 2009

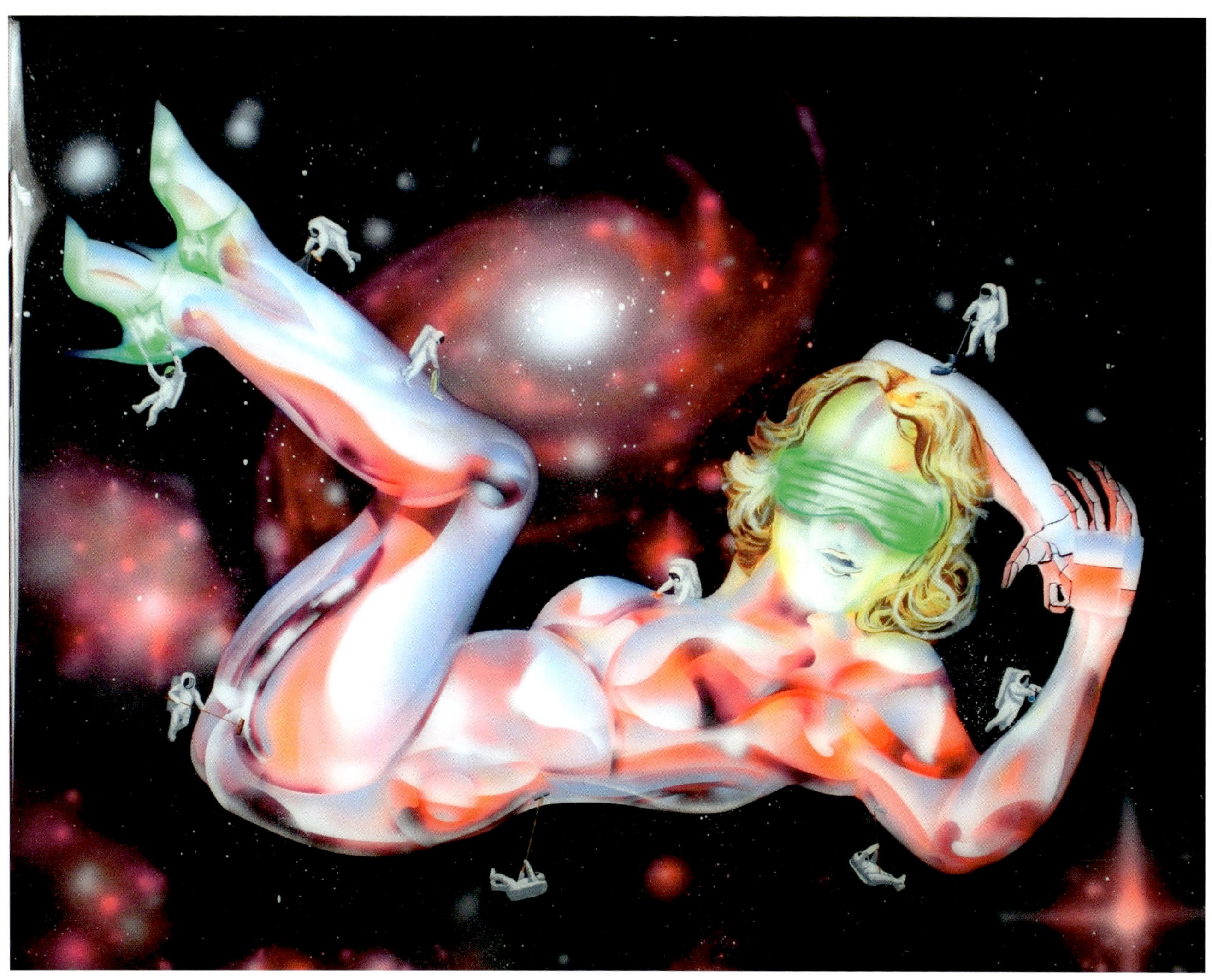

Space Lady 2008

THE MERLIN YEARS

AXIS MUNDI

Interactive Installation

Art Gallery of Ontario

2012

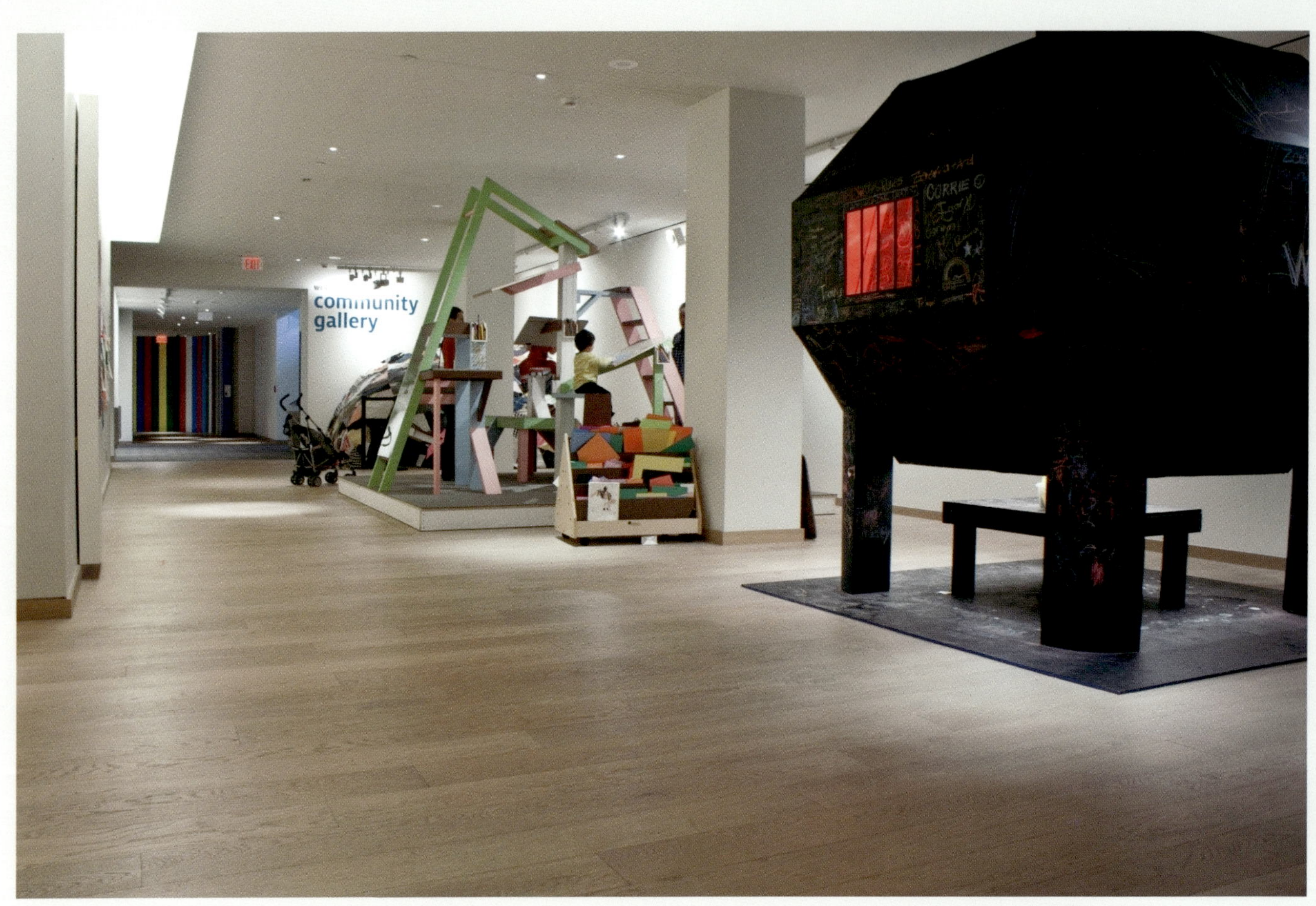
community
gallery

AXIS MUNDI
A DIY Guide

By Ann Marie Peña

It began as a series of rather basic questions about space.

How can a space in an art museum be used to engage the public, intimately and directly,
with the artistic process?

How can this engagement with the public be used in a real and significant way to highlight
and support that very artistic process - and by extension to support art communities themselves?

Finally, what happens when you ask an artist, or in this case an artist collective, what they would do
if they were given a platform within a museum to consider, highlight and toy with the real issues they
think most affect practitioners living in these fluctuating socio-economic times?

In the case of Team Macho, what arose from posing the questions were conversations surrounding the problems of access to space for art practitioners, and how they have developed their own collective survival mechanisms to push their practice forward. Team Macho is a group of four men – strong-minded, able, opinionated, romantic, and importantly who like to make pictures.   Born from similar interests as illustration students in college together, they had their first venture out as a collective identity in 2005 with their exhibition Friends for Life in Toronto. With these roots in illustration, what radiates from Team Macho artworks is a particular kind of visual story-telling, one akin to the experience of secretly looking through boxes of found photographs and objects hidden away in an attic somewhere. You encounter what appears to be a series of collected memories, gathered ephemera and experiences, and just when you think you can draw some kind of lineage through them, a new image pops up to disturb the narrative you have established.   The subjects of their drawings and paintings range from boy scouts and monkeys, to foxes, lawnmowers, cats (many, many cats) and icons like Freddy Mercury. In the earlier days of working together, a drawing might have been started by one of the four artists and then set aside, only to be picked up at random and completed by another member of the Team. There was no preciousness involved, only

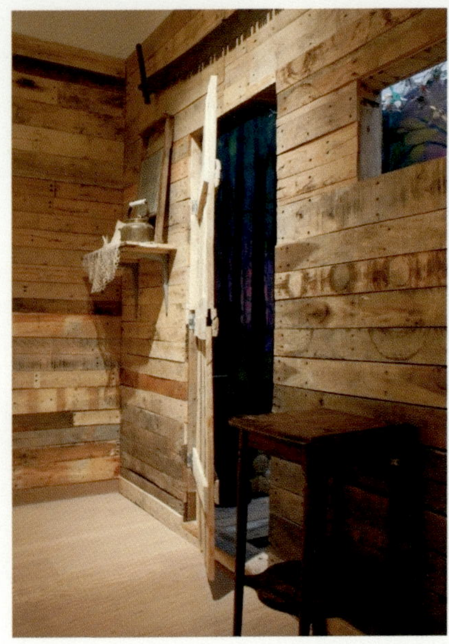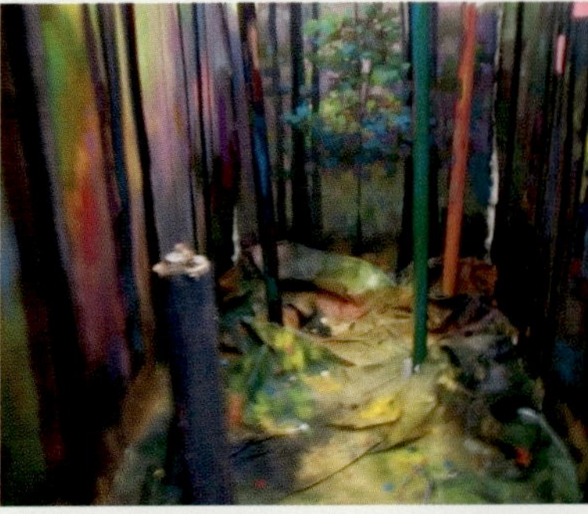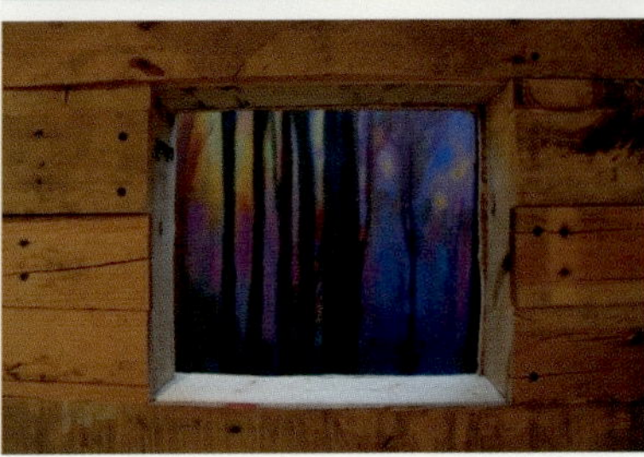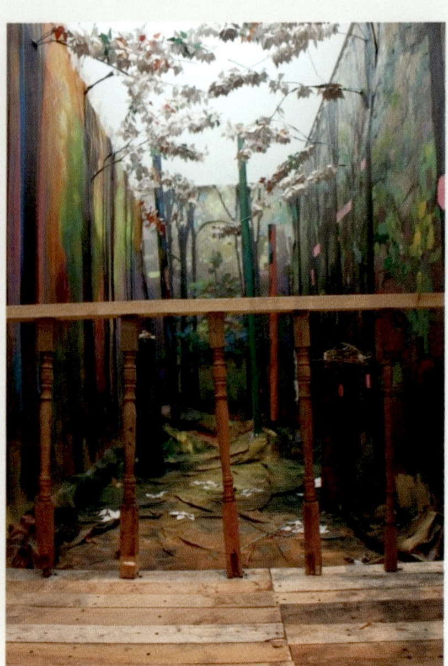

a rigorous building of a common identity rather than individual concerns. It is easy to conjure catch phrases that may begin with words like "pop", "nostalgic" or "childhood" in describing their practice, but the delicate pencil lines, neon flecks and ink washes cannot be pinned down so easily. What seems most significant in the consideration of their work, particularly within the context of their new installation "Axis Mundi", is how Team Macho work with one another to create new mythologies, how they kick-start and push their work along as a collective, and how their system of working informs their identity and practice as a whole.

The need to create a kind of survival system in order to foster art-making is by no means a new one. The last few decades have certainly seen changes in how and where artistic communities are established, and clear migratory patterns can be drawn towards particular urban centers that have allowed for fertile creative development. Under the influence of political and social upheaval, we saw for example the fall of the Berlin wall in 1989 give way to the rise of a vibrant art and music scene supported by access to an affordable cost of living. Photographs of revelers partying along the rubble of the fallen wall aptly capture a moment in history where Europe felt unified not only politically, but culturally as well. In an interview with Bob Nickas for Interview magazine, German photographer Wolfgang Tillmans refers to this moment as a time when "…there was a new language in music and a nonhierarchical socializing that seemed radically new. (T)his coincided with the fall of the Berlin Wall and Europe coming closer together, and nightlife and techno and ecstasy culture seemed like a very powerful pan-European movement." With the opening up of the east and the vacating of factories and commercial buildings as businesses moved from the city, Berlin literally had more accessible space for artistic production and studios, so the artists moved in.

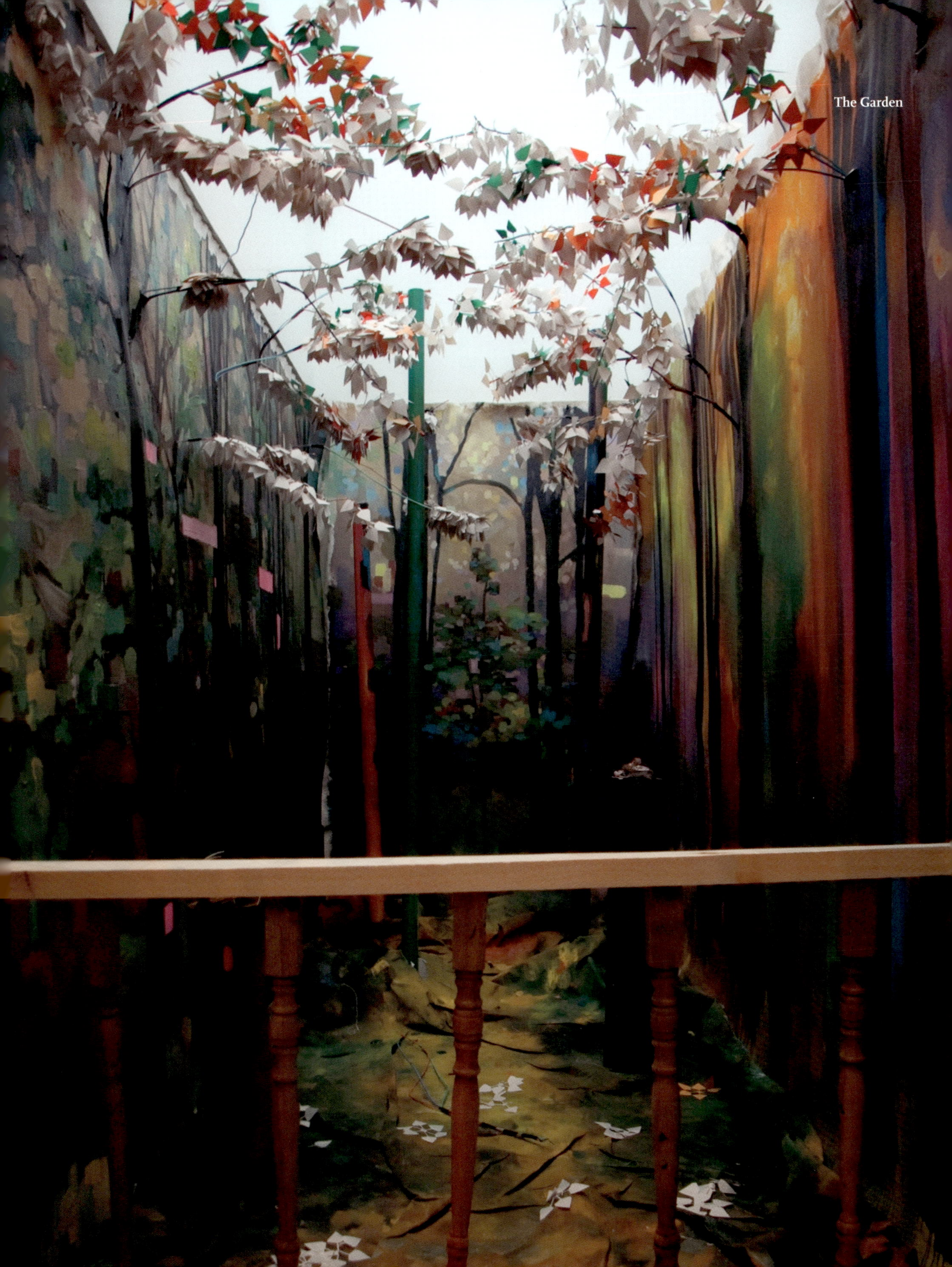

The Garden

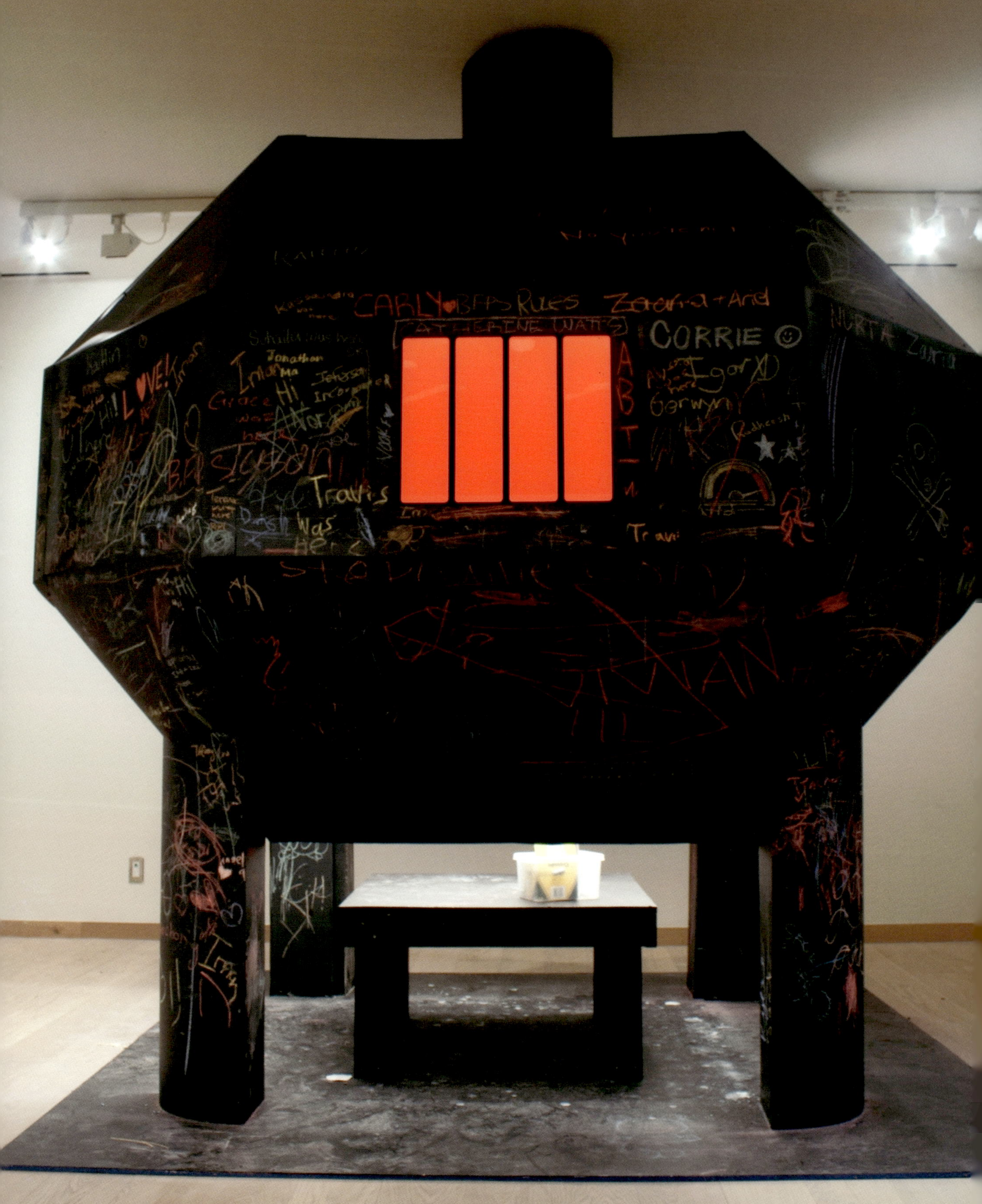

The Furnace

Similarly the end of last century saw the east end of London become an energetic mecca of cultural cross-pollination - fashion, music, artists and new strips of galleries morphed and expanded along-side one another as they poured through the neighborhoods of Hoxton and Bethnal Green, and more recently through Dalston and further into Hackney. New kinds of galleries opened on side streets alongside taxi repair garages and off-license liquor stores, while young artists like Tracey Emin and Sarah Lucas opened spaces like "The Shop" in 1993, a now infamous store and studio space on Bethnal Green Road that was for only six months, selling such items as ashtrays that allowed smokers to butt cigarettes out onto an image of Damien Hirst's face. In previous decades these working-class neighborhoods had been characterized by the erecting of low-income apartment blocks where Second World War bombs had left vacant lots, they were made famous through the violent folklore of infamous residents such as the Kray brothers. Quickly in the 1990s however this changed.

Expensive Mayfair galleries were no longer the sole commercial tastemakers of the London art world, and affordable rents empowered fresh dialogues which allowed new kinds of galleries such as Counter (now Carl Friedman Gallery) and later Modern Art to establish themselves. The Paris district of Belleville is only one of many other examples of an outer borough of a European city that has undergone a similar transformation.

Beyond Europe we also see new communities being established in urban centers like Lagos, as ex-pats return to Western Africa on the wave of a fresh oil and financial boom. Project and studio spaces are emerging in what were previously no-go zones within the context of contemporary art, and spaces such as CCA (Centre for Contemporary Art Lagos) flourish and churn with curatorial rigor. For its part Toronto has established its own idiosyncratic community-based manner of functioning as a city, framing itself along cultural groupings such as Chinatown, Greektown or

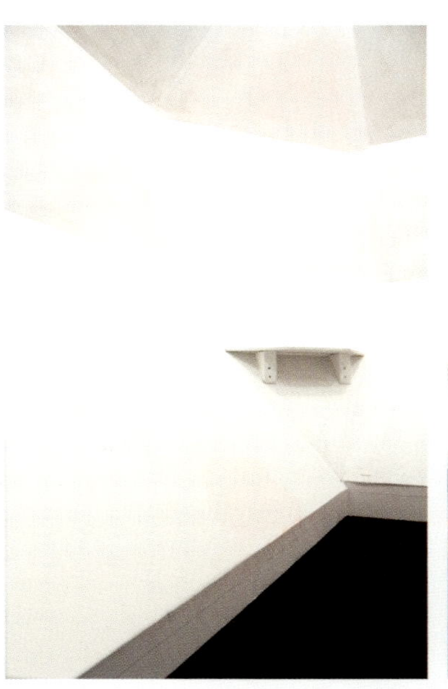
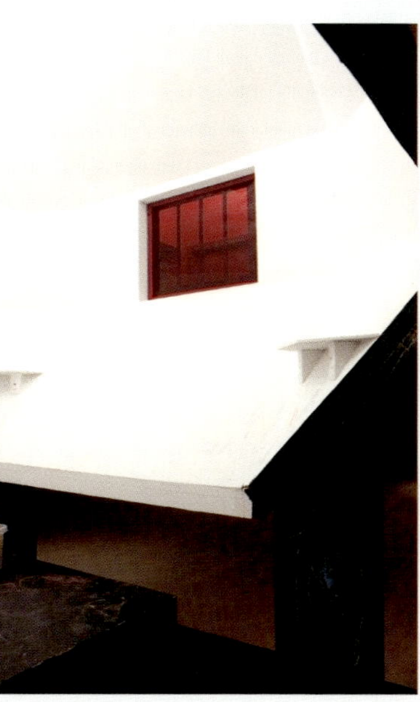
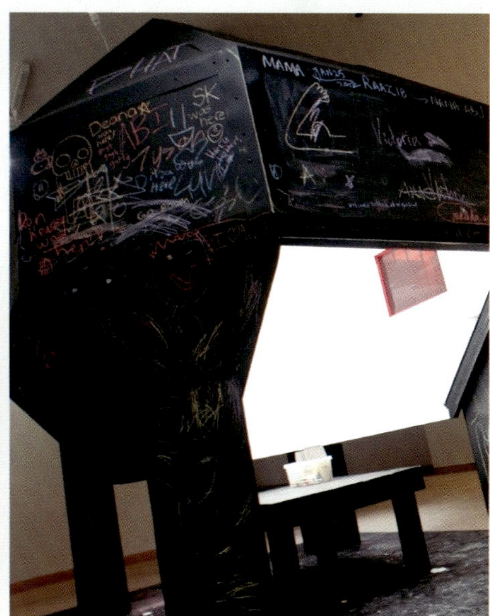

Little Portugal, as well as more functional and aspirational identities like "the Art and Design District" or the former garment district of Kensington Market. Within these artist communities established themselves wherever there was affordable space suitable for living and establishing studios – in the 1990's this was the going south-west towards the neighborhood Parkdale, and more recently movement seems to push further north toward the Junction, a former outskirt of the city that, as the name implies, grew alongside the junction of four railway tracks.

the Rosedale area, spear-headed and funded by painter Lawren Harris. The first purpose-built studio complex in Canada, here artists like Tom Thompson, Franklin Carmichael and A. Y. Jackson could live and work alongside one another in more or less ideal conditions while paying an affordable rent. Beyond providing physical space for one another, the Group of Seven artists were also able to use their collectivity to create and communicate a specific vision about art within their contemporary scene that elevated discussion and form beyond standard commercial art

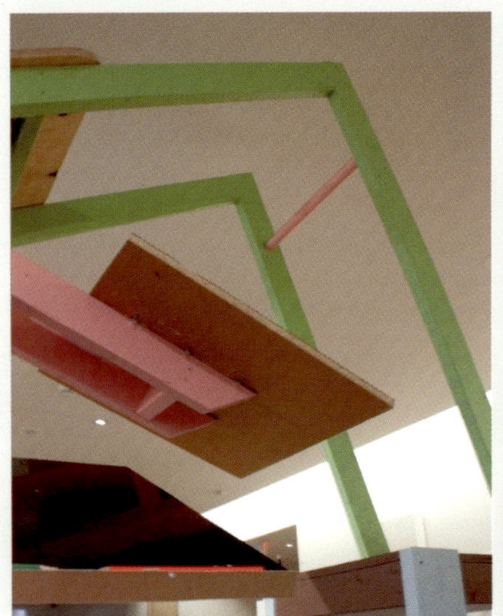
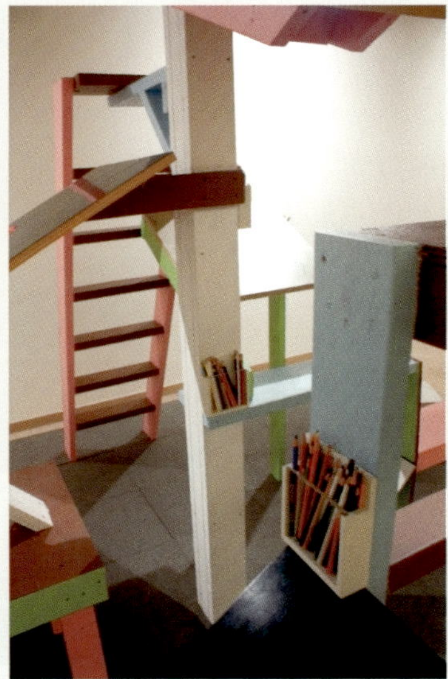
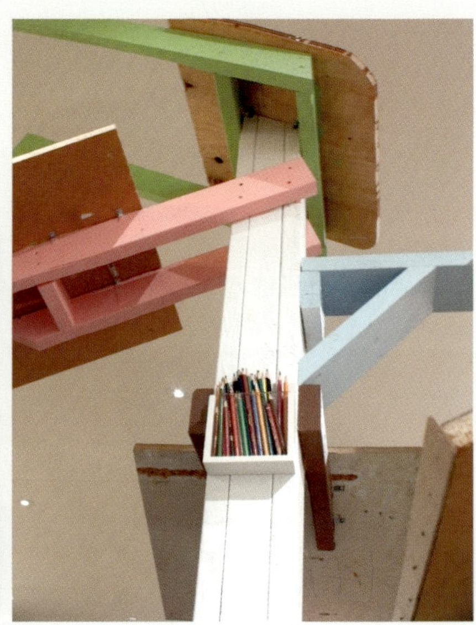

Deeper within this neighborhood construct, Toronto also has a lineage of more specific artist-led support systems from which Team Macho's collaborative effort draws heritage. Looking back to early last century, we see artists that would eventually become associated with the Group of Seven forge pathways for other practitioners by working supportively alongside each other. There was for example in 1913 the construction of The Studio Building in

practices. By establishing themselves along collective lines, they were able to organize exhibitions, publish about their work, influence teaching in art colleges, and debate their particular political and geographical vision of Canadian art. This vision became a platform for informing cultural policy deeper into the century, and continues to be an influential (albeit at times controversial or even misrepresentative) marker of Canadian identity today.

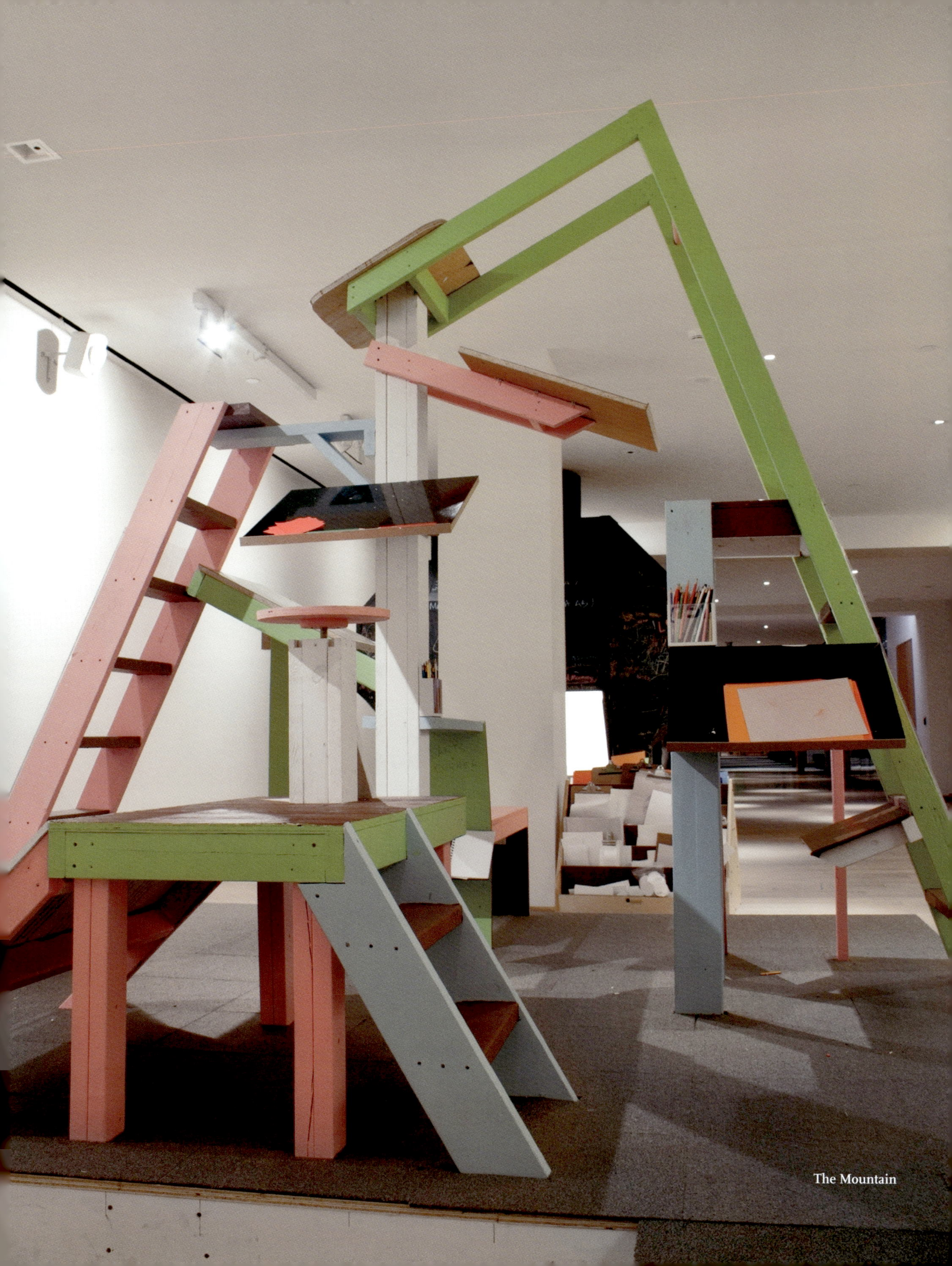

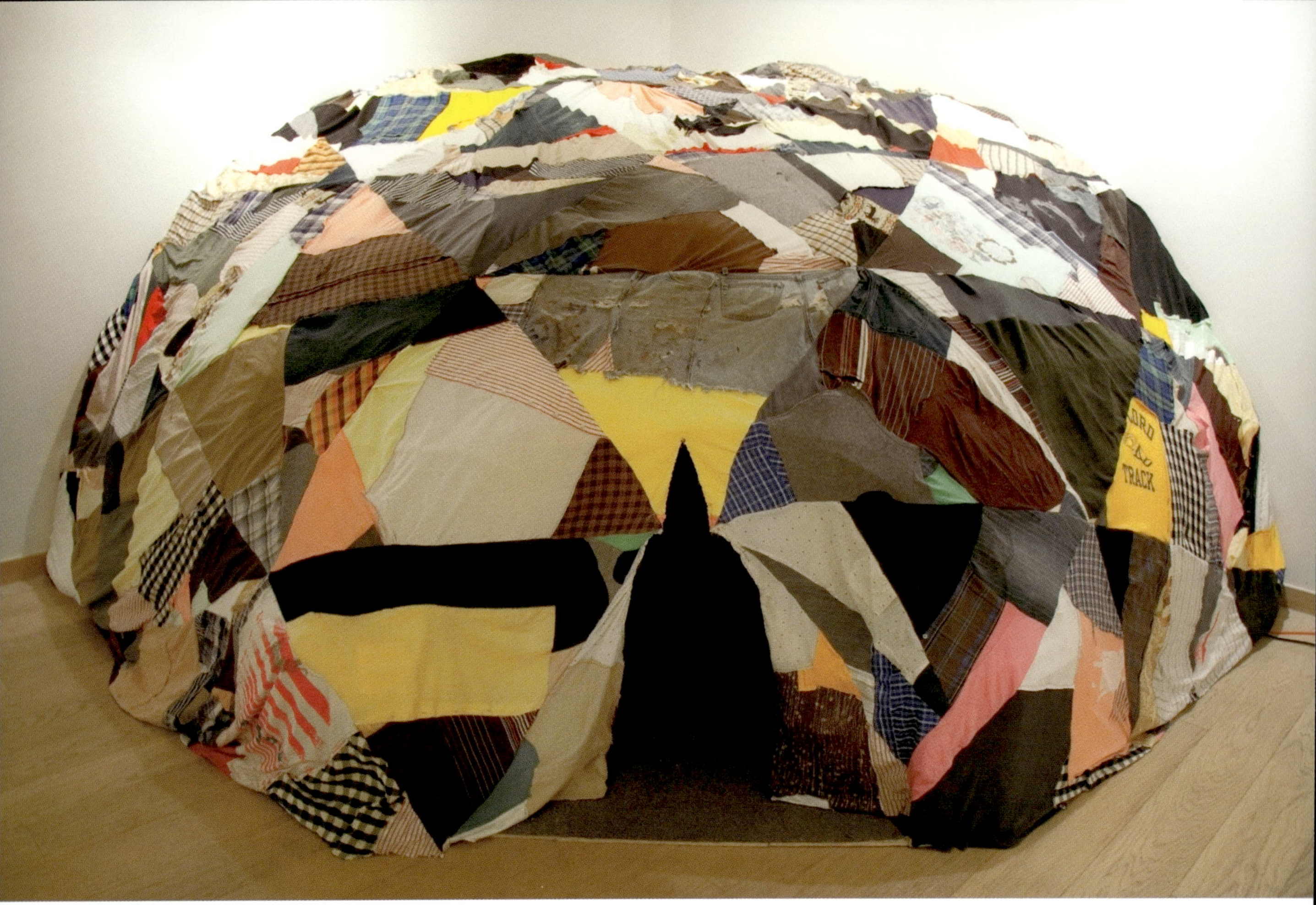

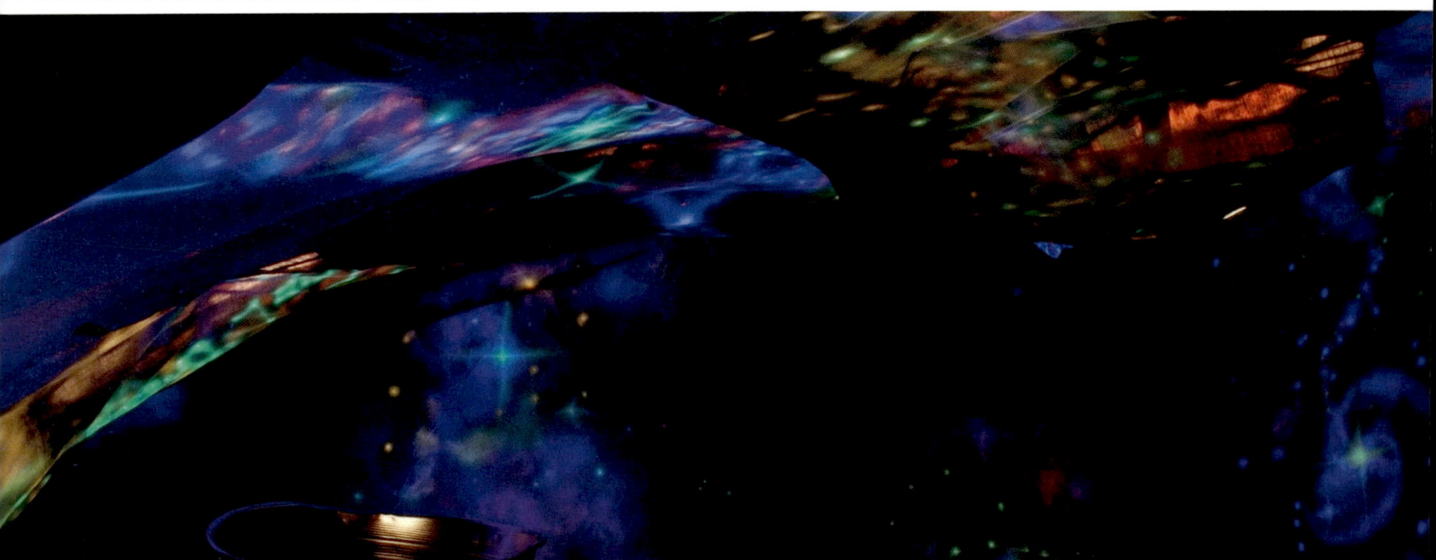

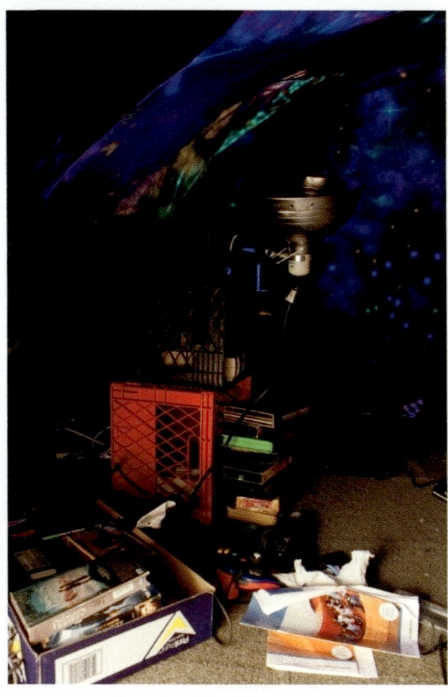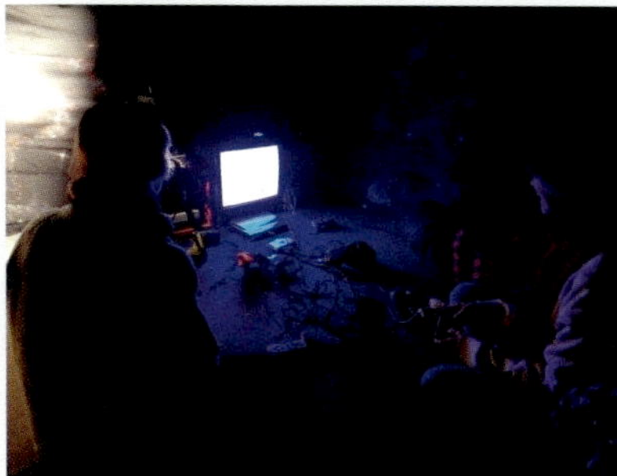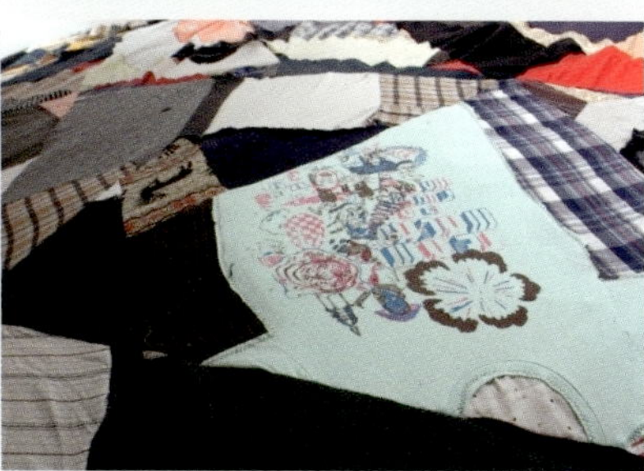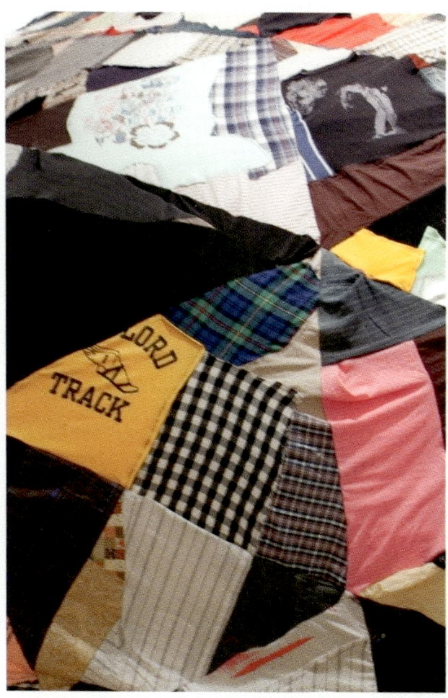

In the 1970's artist group General Idea continued pushing strategies for reaching wider audiences for their work and that of their peers, both within Toronto and beyond. When they established Art Metropole, a gallery shop and archive set up in 1974, the artists began to play with distribution systems in inventive ways that would provide platforms for artists that were not previously accessible. In one project "Ads by Artists" (1987), Art Metropole commissioned artists to create artworks that would appear as advertisements in international art magazines, while through other projects the artists focused on developing ephemeral artworks, publishing artist books, and with the help of Penny Gale established ground breaking distribution systems for artist videos.

From this lineage, the romance of what Team Macho is trying to achieve with Axis Mundi takes root. In considering the problematics of space within the city, the artists wanted to create an artwork that would literally convert a museum space into a solution that responds to the lack of accessible affordable studios for other practitioners and their communities. Rather than create an exhibition that would more traditionally present their work framed and hung on the gallery walls, Team Macho have created four sculptural spaces which their peers and the public can enter and use - for as long as they choose, and more importantly without having to worry about rent. The structures take their inspiration from Team Macho's own communal work environment where they live and work alongside one another in a series of rooms and spaces that include (in addition to studios) an area used for sleeping made from tents and wooden structures, a kitchen and a woodshop. As a sculptural installation Axis Mundi follows the same DIY aesthetic to this live/ work space, using materials such as plywood, metal sheeting and quilting made from their own clothes to create the environments.

The artists take their title and starting point from Northrop Frye's notion of the Axis Mundi which forms "a vertical line running from the top to the bottom of the cosmos"[1], symbolically unifying and holding together our very existence in this world. Here Team Macho interpret and apply Frye's idea of the Axis as an organizational system, using his descriptive and metaphorical subdivisions– *the Cave, the Mountain, the Furnace* and *the Garden* - to literally frame their own concept of idealized and accessible space. Frye's idea of a layered universe here becomes the structure through which Team Macho decipher and mythologize their own process, giving the public an entry point into their world. For the Cave, the artists have sewn together clothes to create a soft, igloo-like structure that can be entered by crawling on all fours through a flap. Inside sit monitors, a VCR, stacks of 1980s and 90s video tapes, and flickering game consoles, creating a somewhat claustrophobic refuge for those needing a place to hide away. Alongside stands the Mountain, a structure reminiscent of an elaborate tree fort or wooden playground structure outfitted with drawing tables and seats. Through a series of ladders and platforms you can climb the mountain, a visual metaphor that can be read either as a journey to artistic enlightenment, or more cynically as a path of ascension through the pitfalls of the art-world ranks. Coated in black chalkboard paint that can be scrawled on and erased, the Furnace is a large imposing structure that is purposely uncomfortable and overly warm to sit in, especially when sitting alongside others. By contrast the final piece of the Axis, the Garden, is contemplative and beautiful. Entering through a rustic cabin-like door, the space inside is composed of long canvases of unfinished forests and delicate paper tree structures complete with fluttering leaves.

Traveling through and experiencing all four components, Team Macho draw reference to the different states of consciousness that they themselves experience in the making of art, as well as the interconnectedness of their – and by extension our - common experience. Like their peers before them, Team Macho highlight art-making as a heroic yet precarious pursuit, made stronger when others partake in the process. Through Axis Mundi they ask only that we join them on their journey, so let's go along for the ride.

[1] Frye, Northrop "Words with Power; Being a Second Study of the Bible and Literature", p 151.

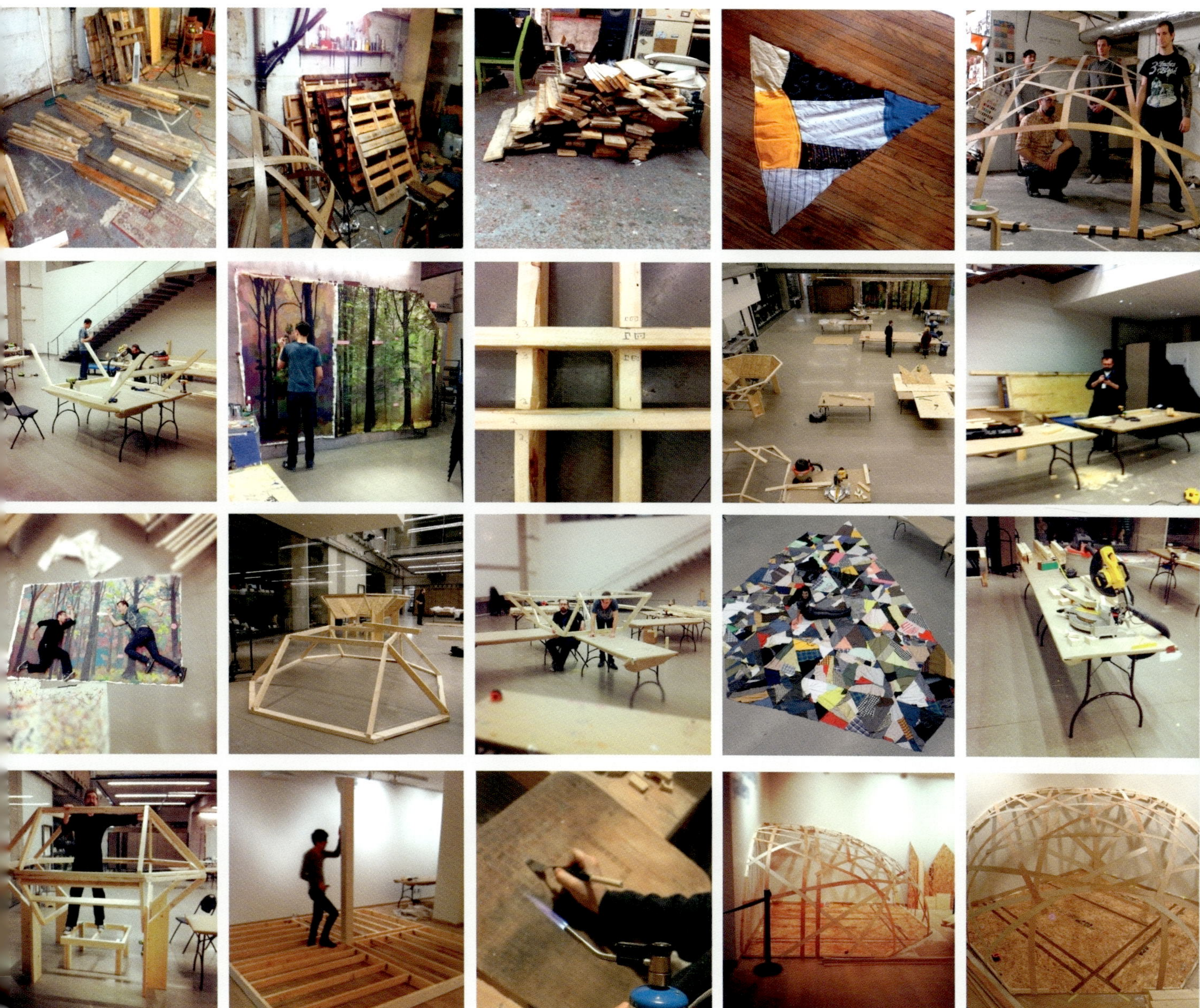

Images from the creation of **Axis Mundi**

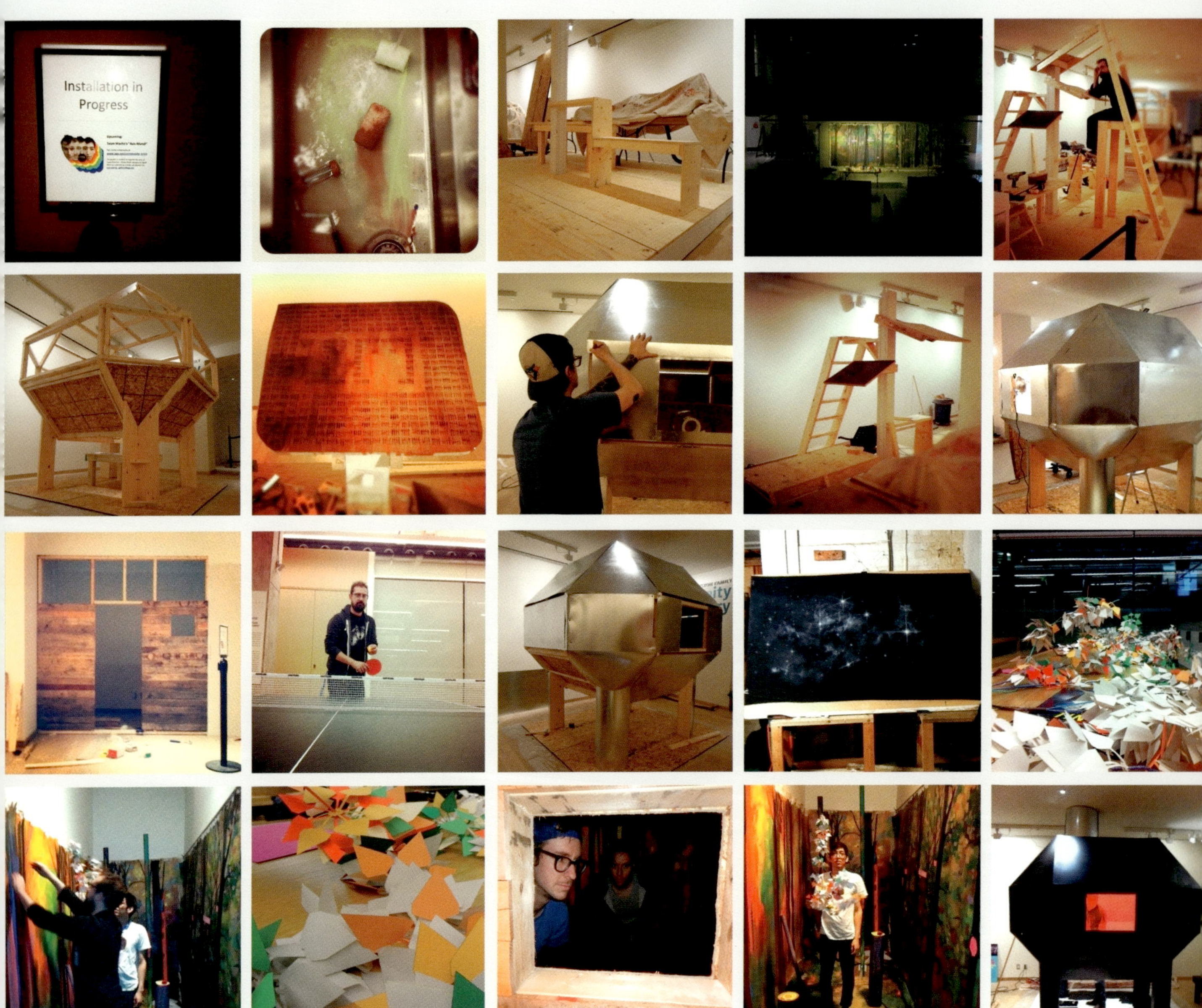
Installation in
Progress

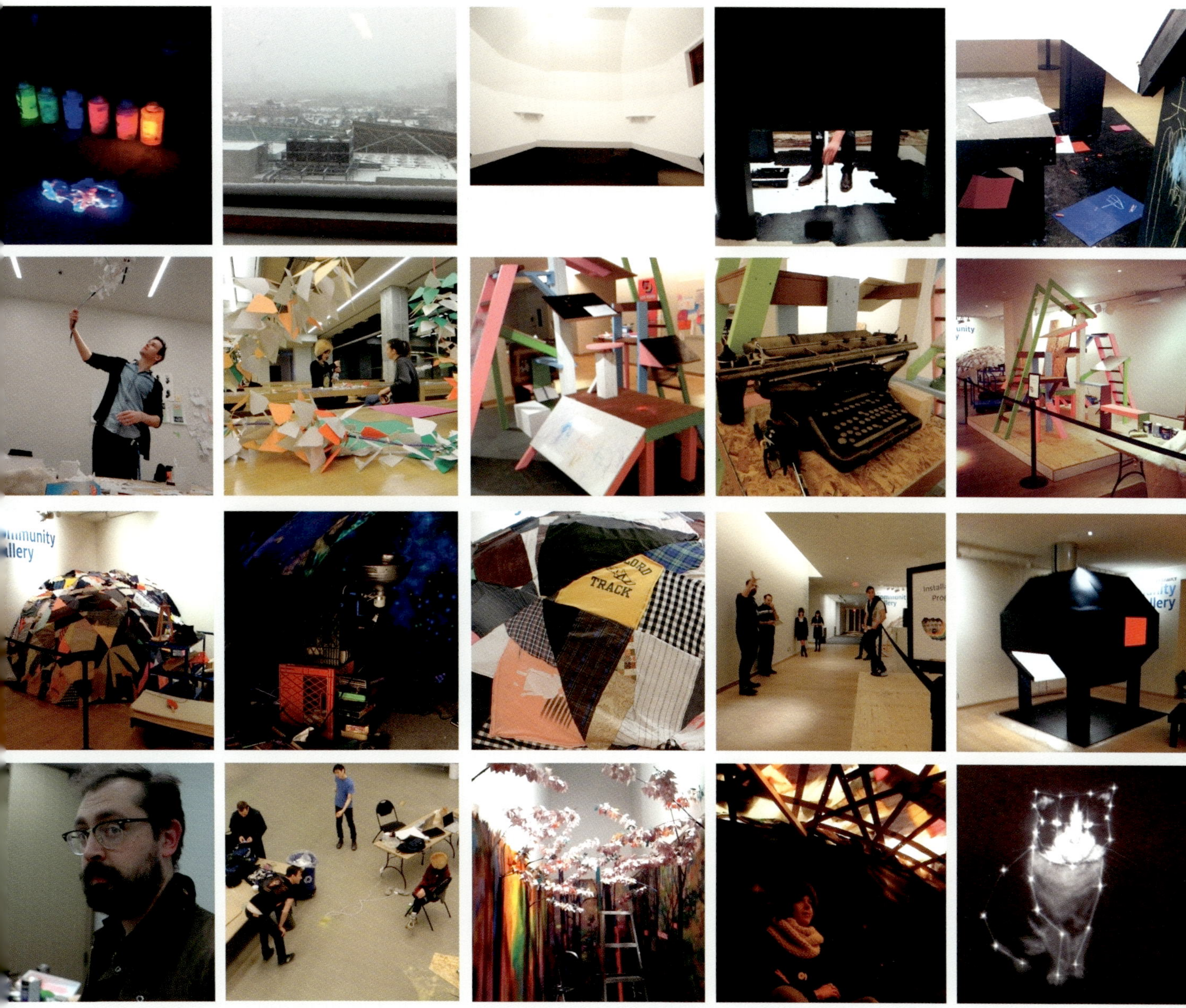

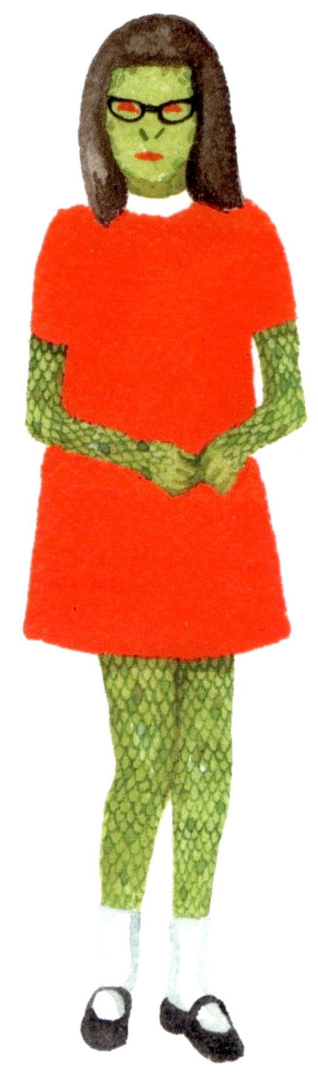

Demi-Orc 2008
Neon Wizard 2008

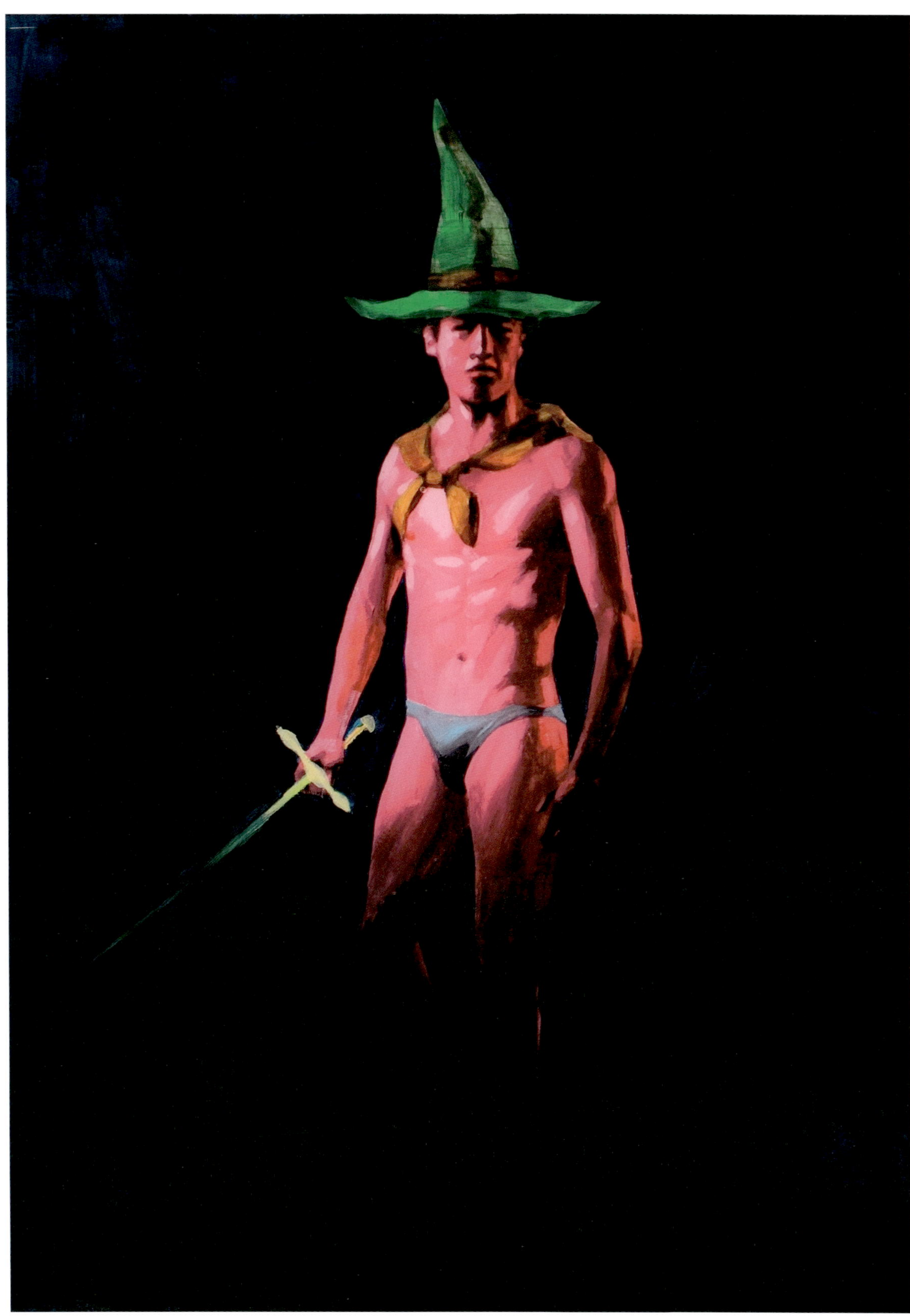

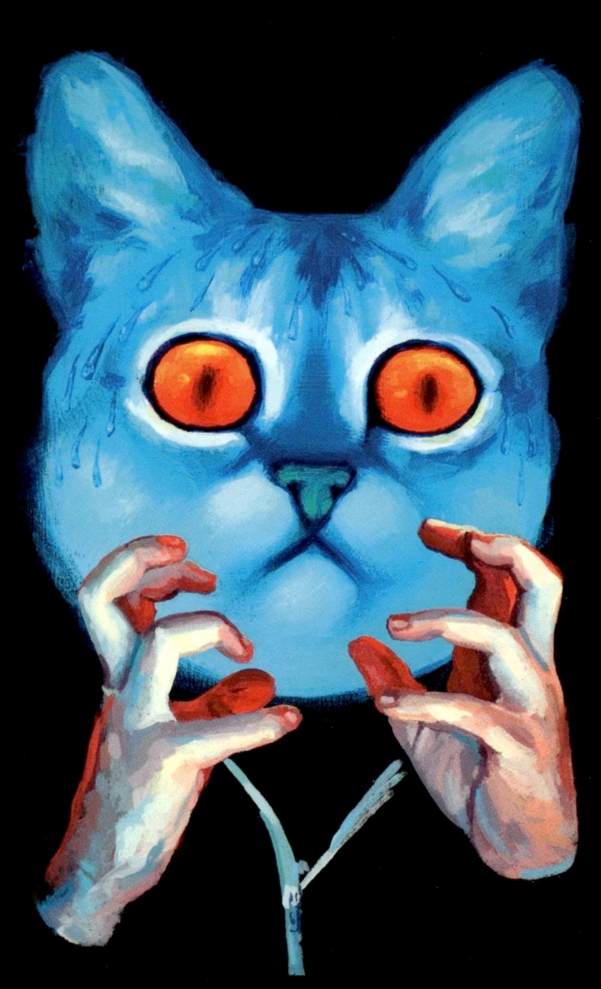

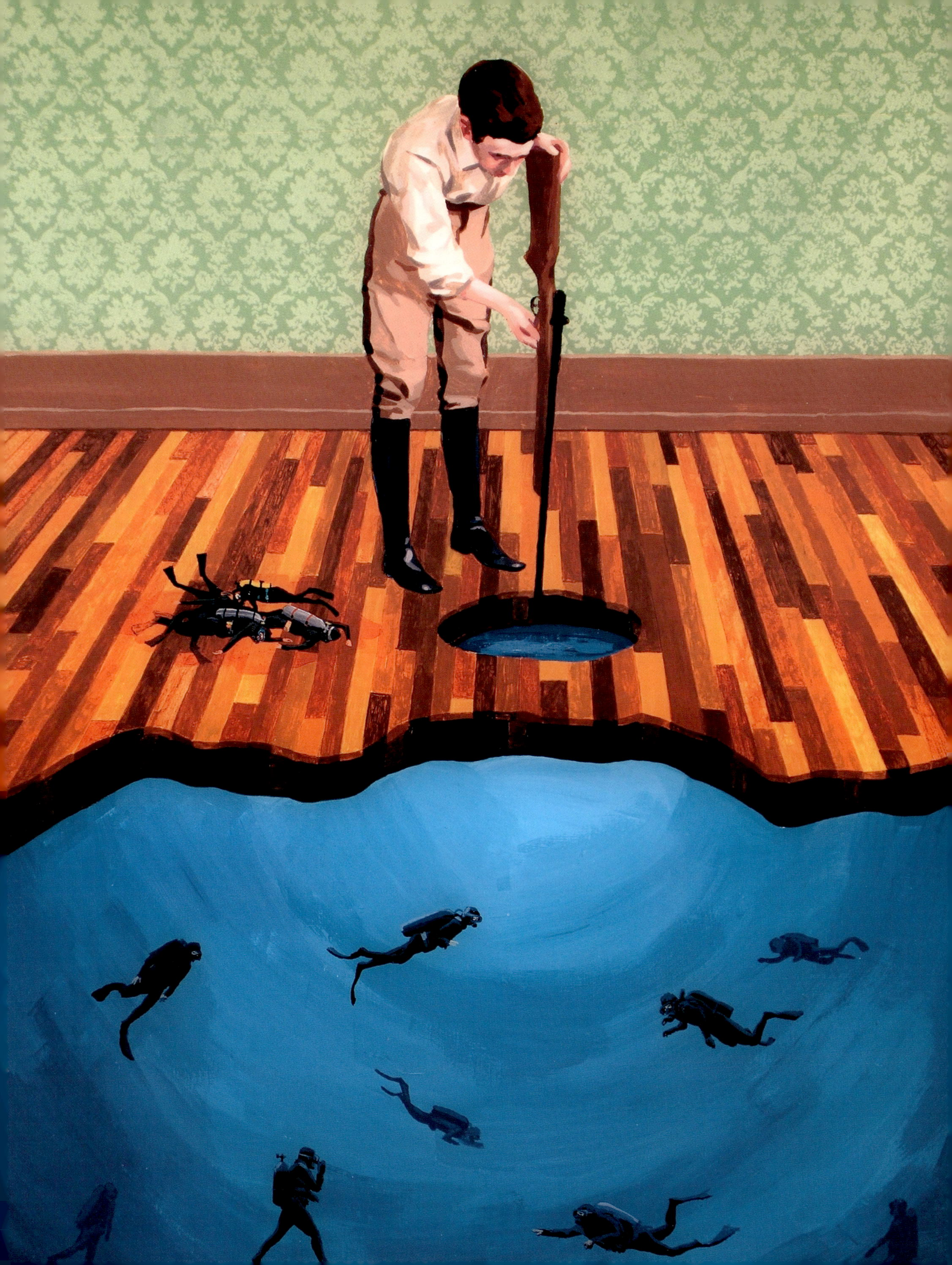

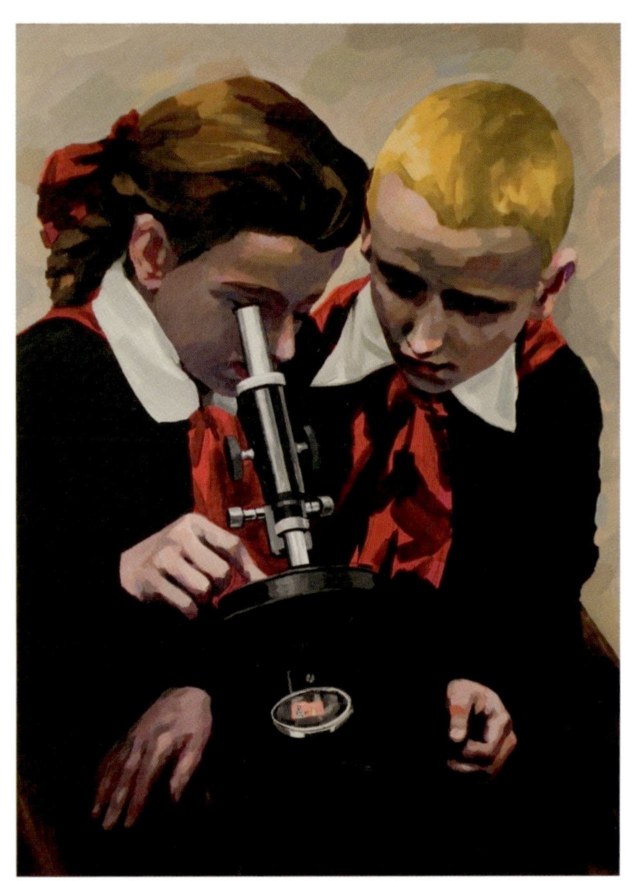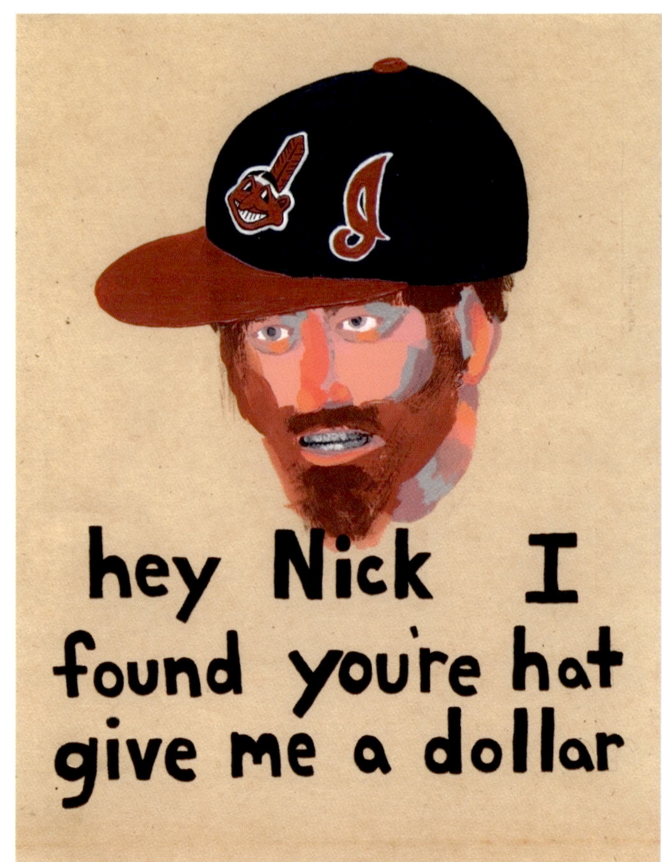

I Stared Into the Void And The Void Stared Back   2010 (previous)
Pest Control   2008 (previous)
Giant Science   2009
Hey Nick   2008

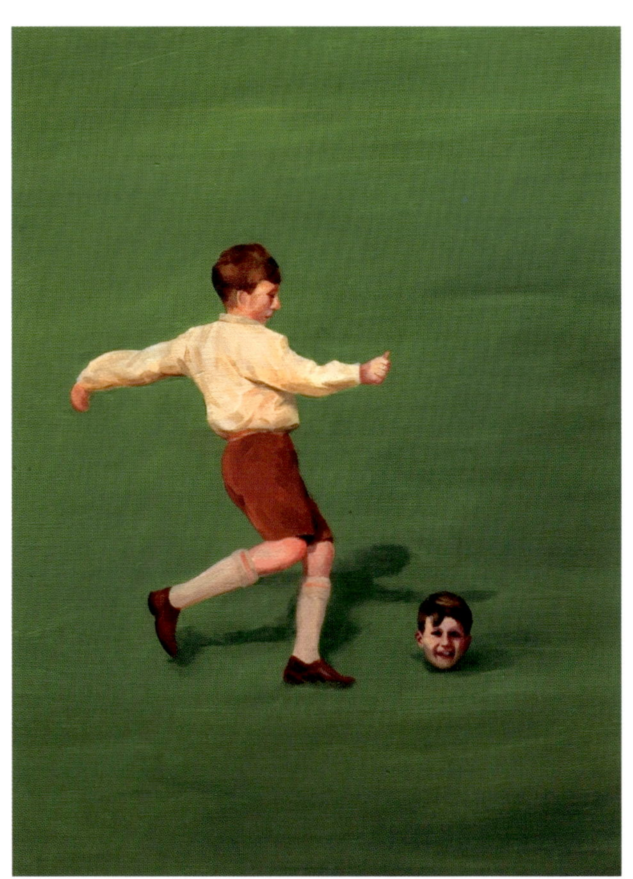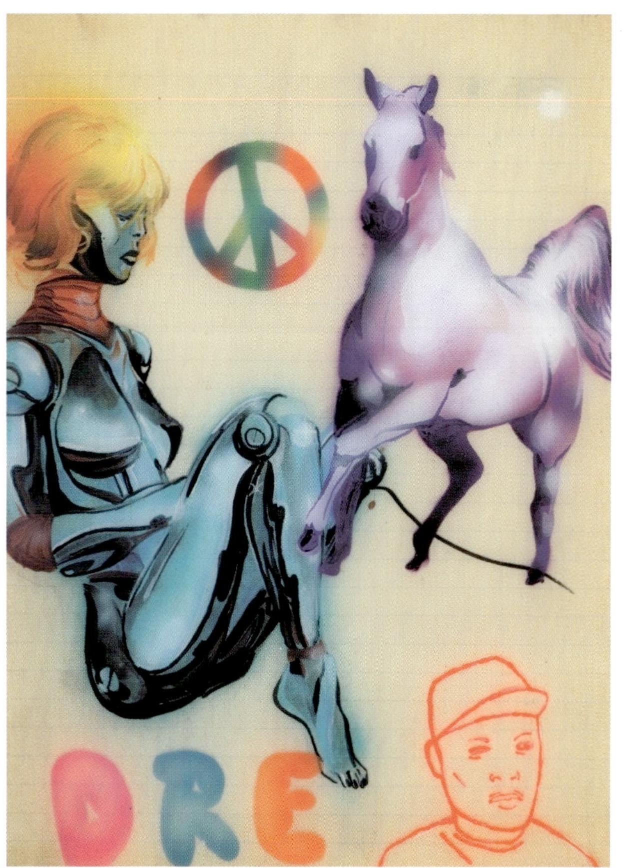

Royal Training 2008
DRE 2008

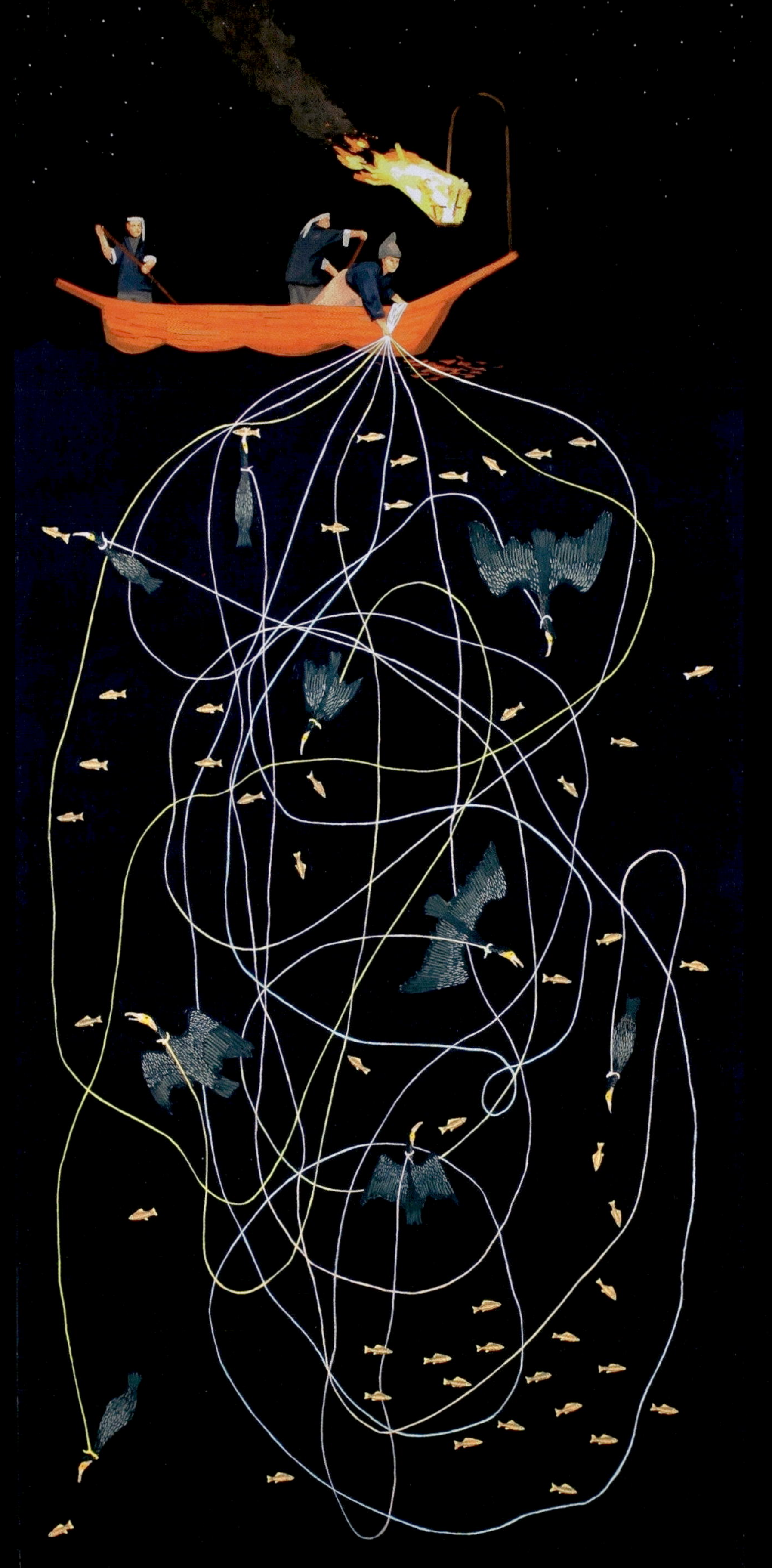

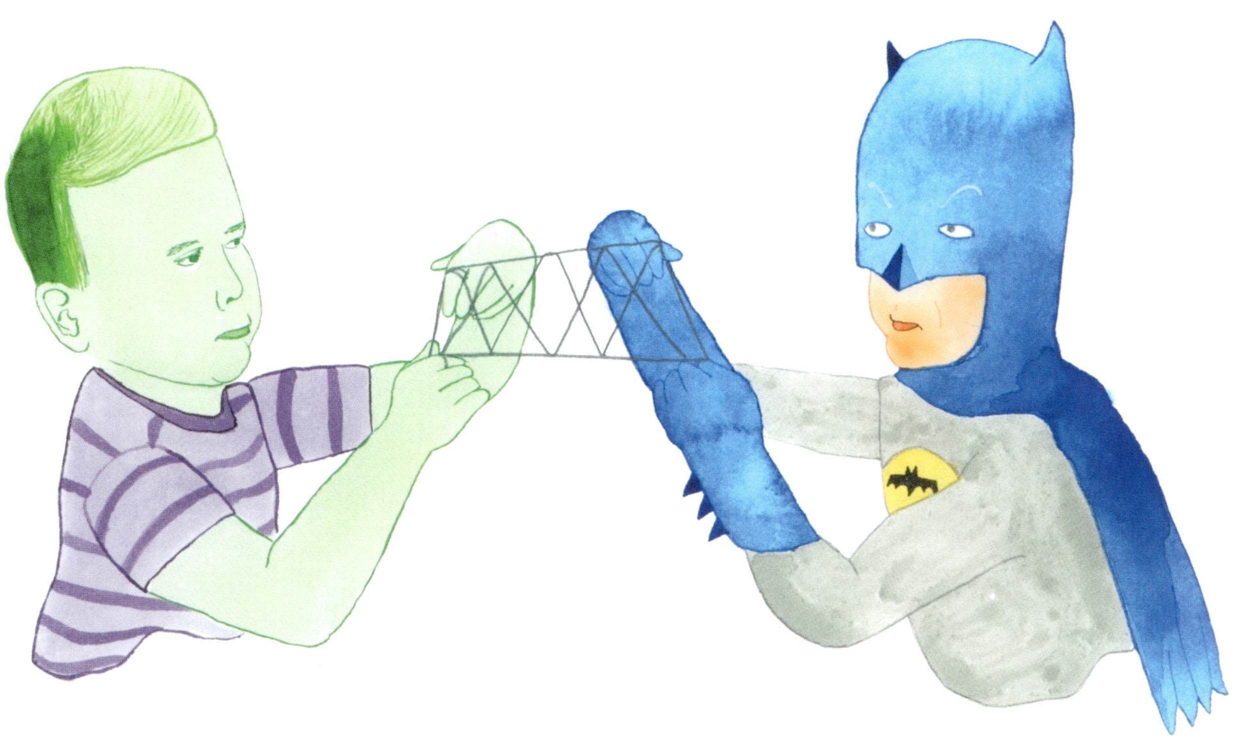

Ukai Dukai 2008
Superkidzzz 2008

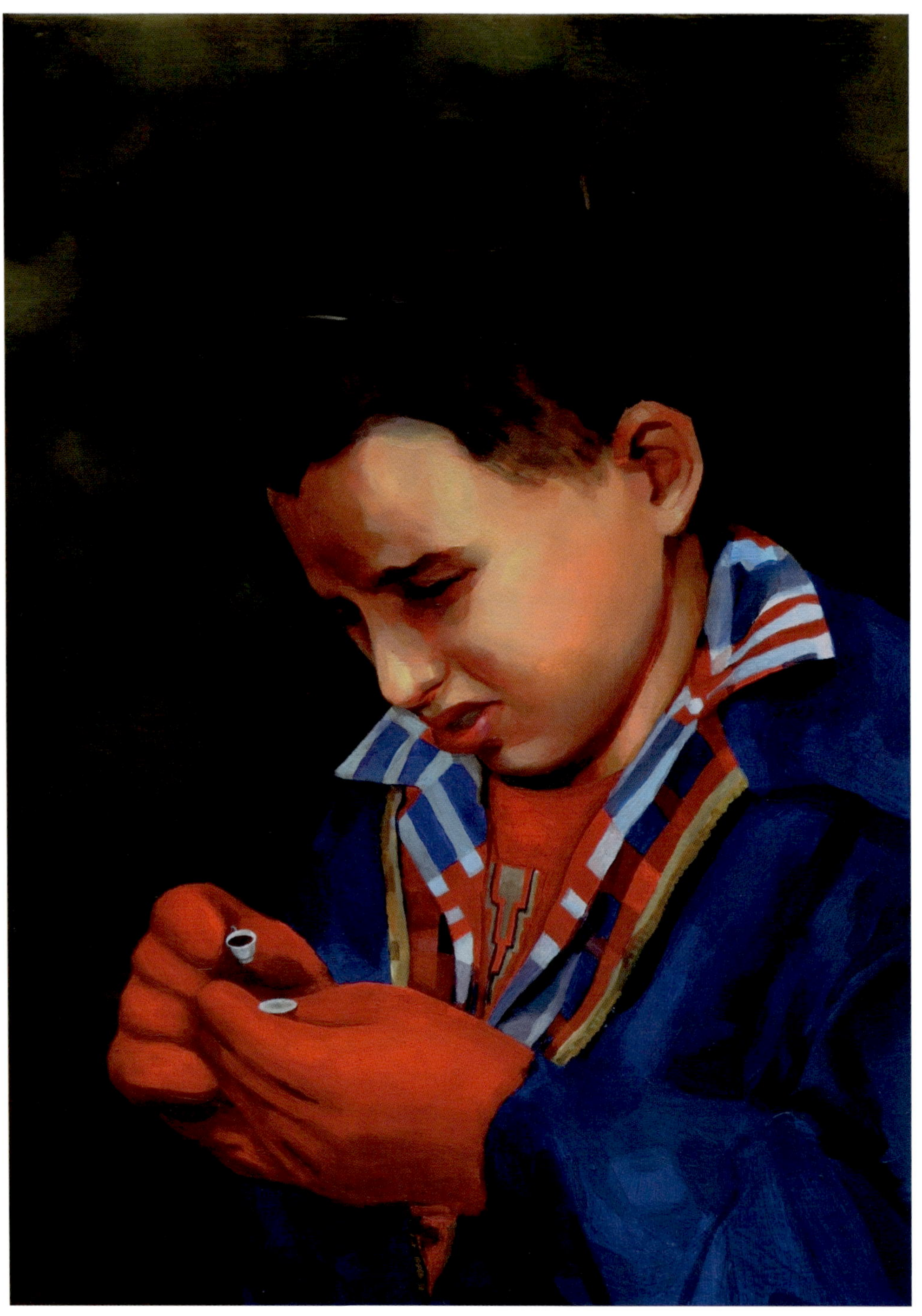

How To Be A Rock Hound   2009
Canadian Hopscotch   2008

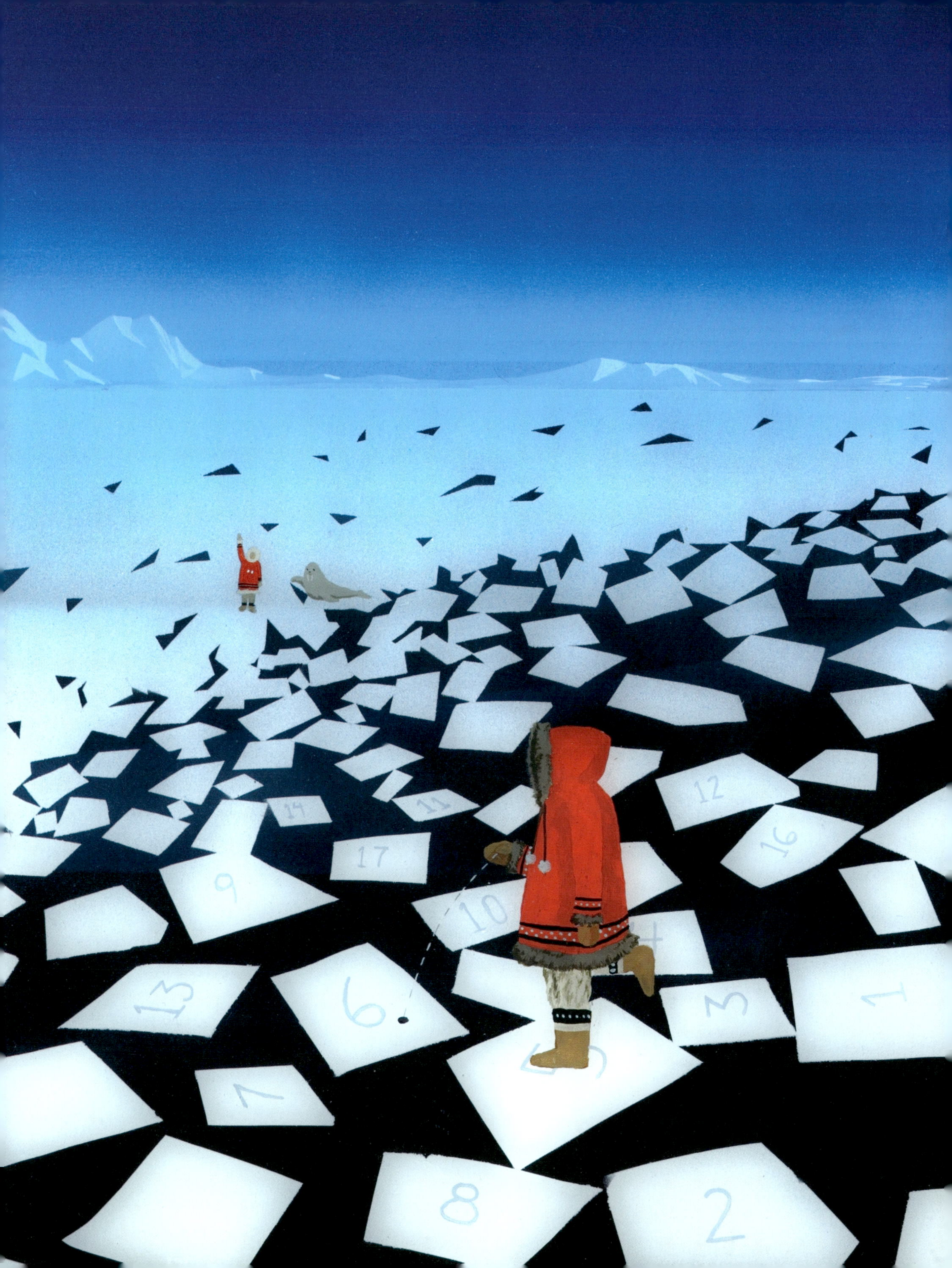

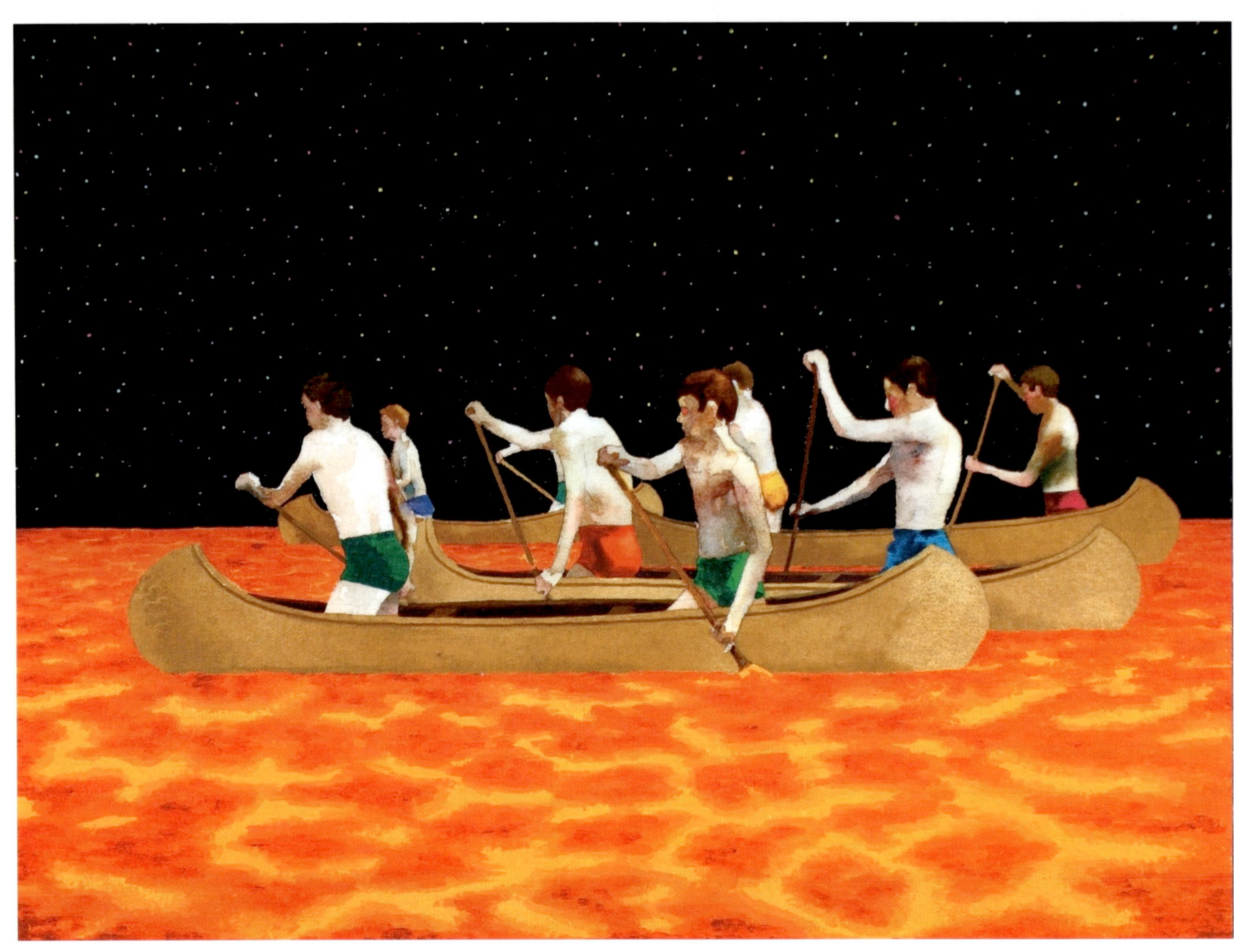

We Told You So   2008

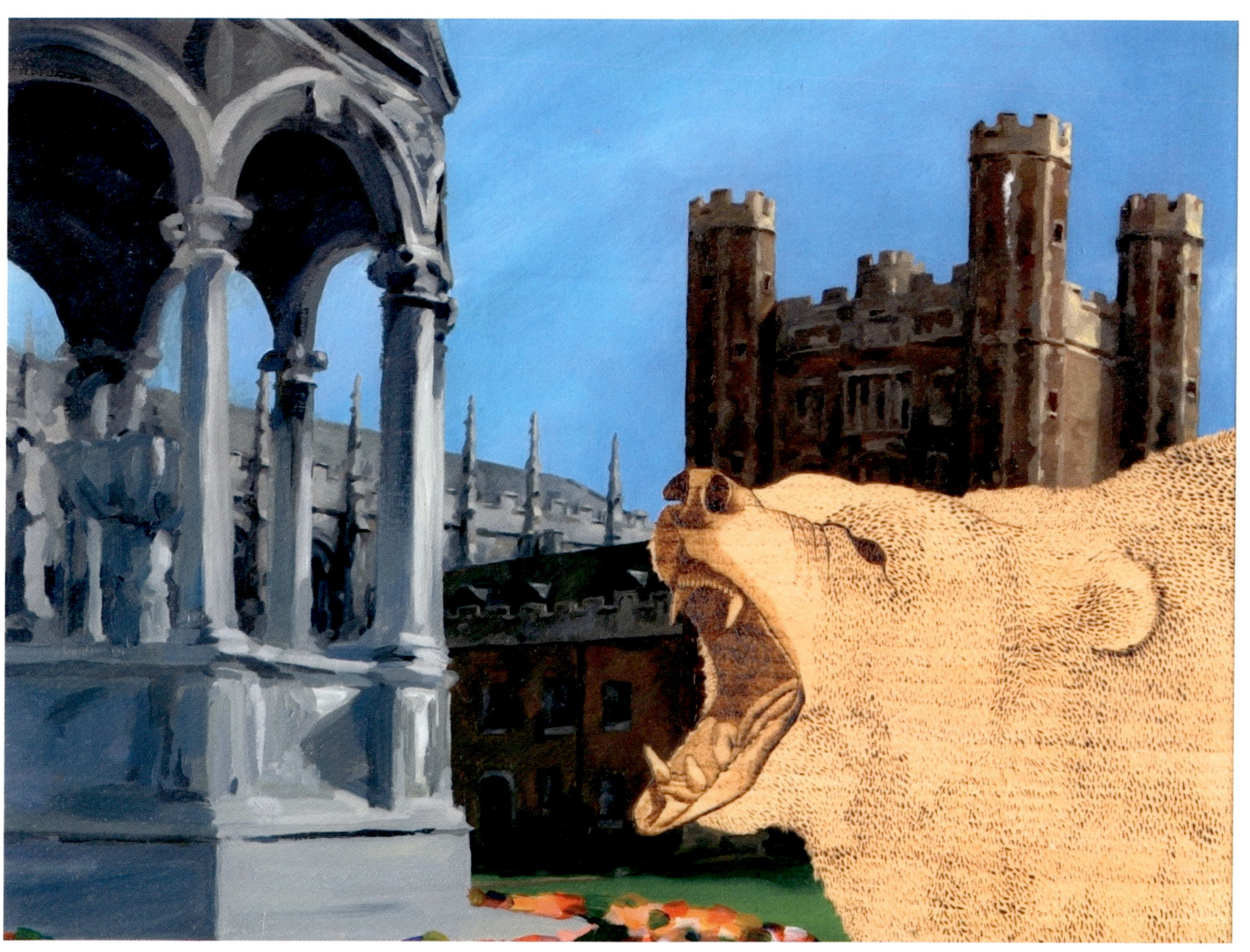

Byron's Revenge 2008

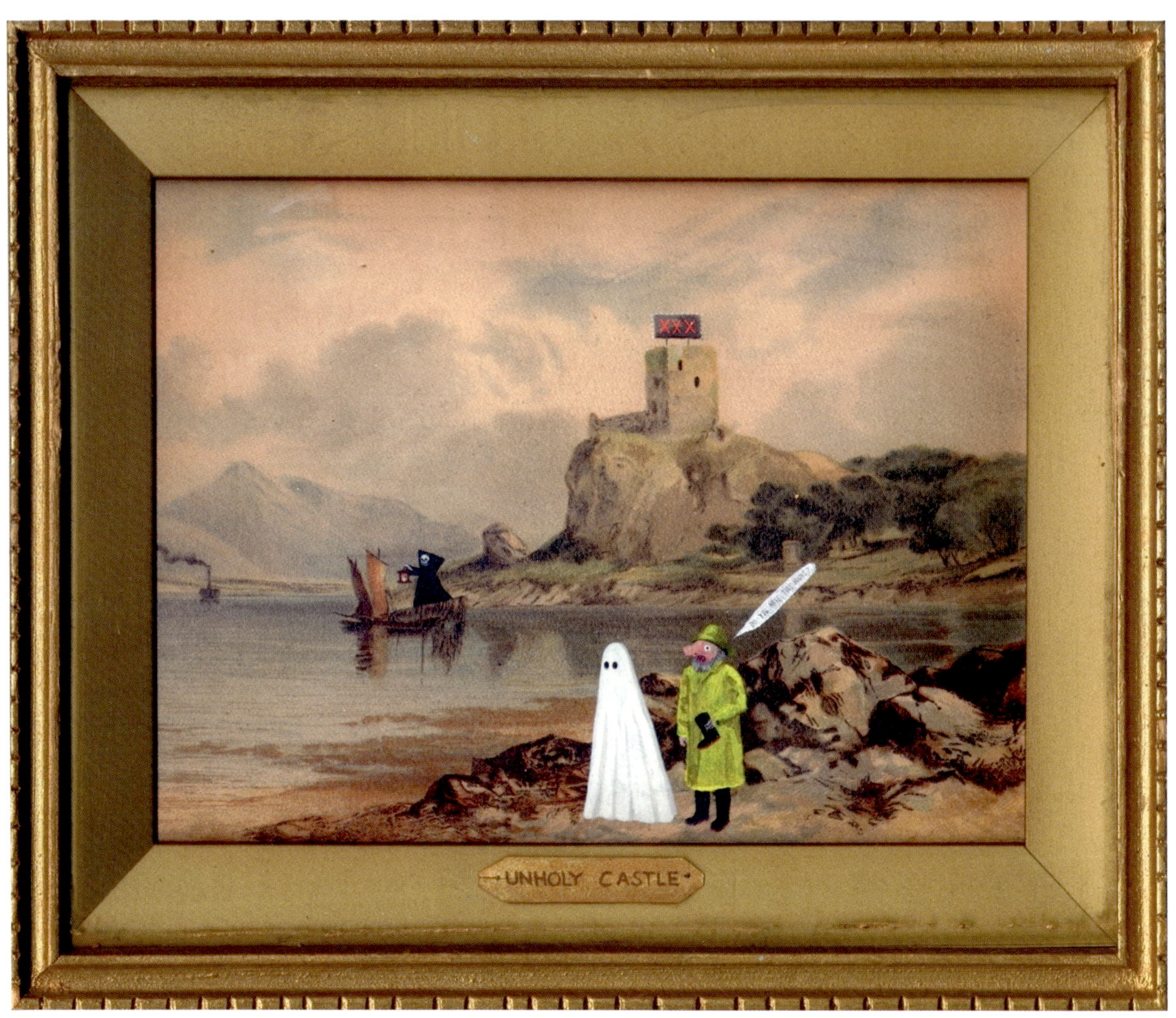

Unholy Castle   2008

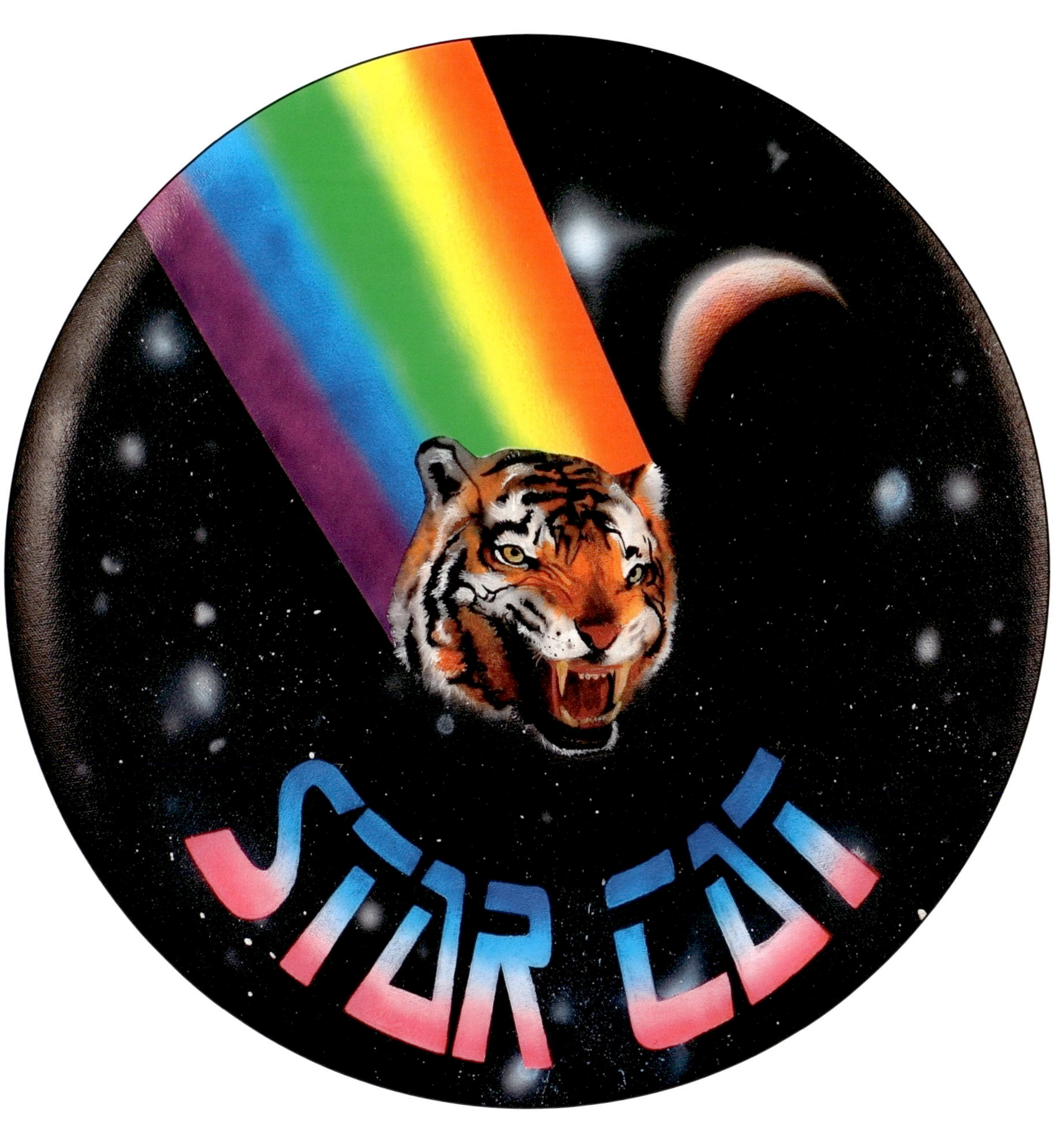

Star Cat 2008

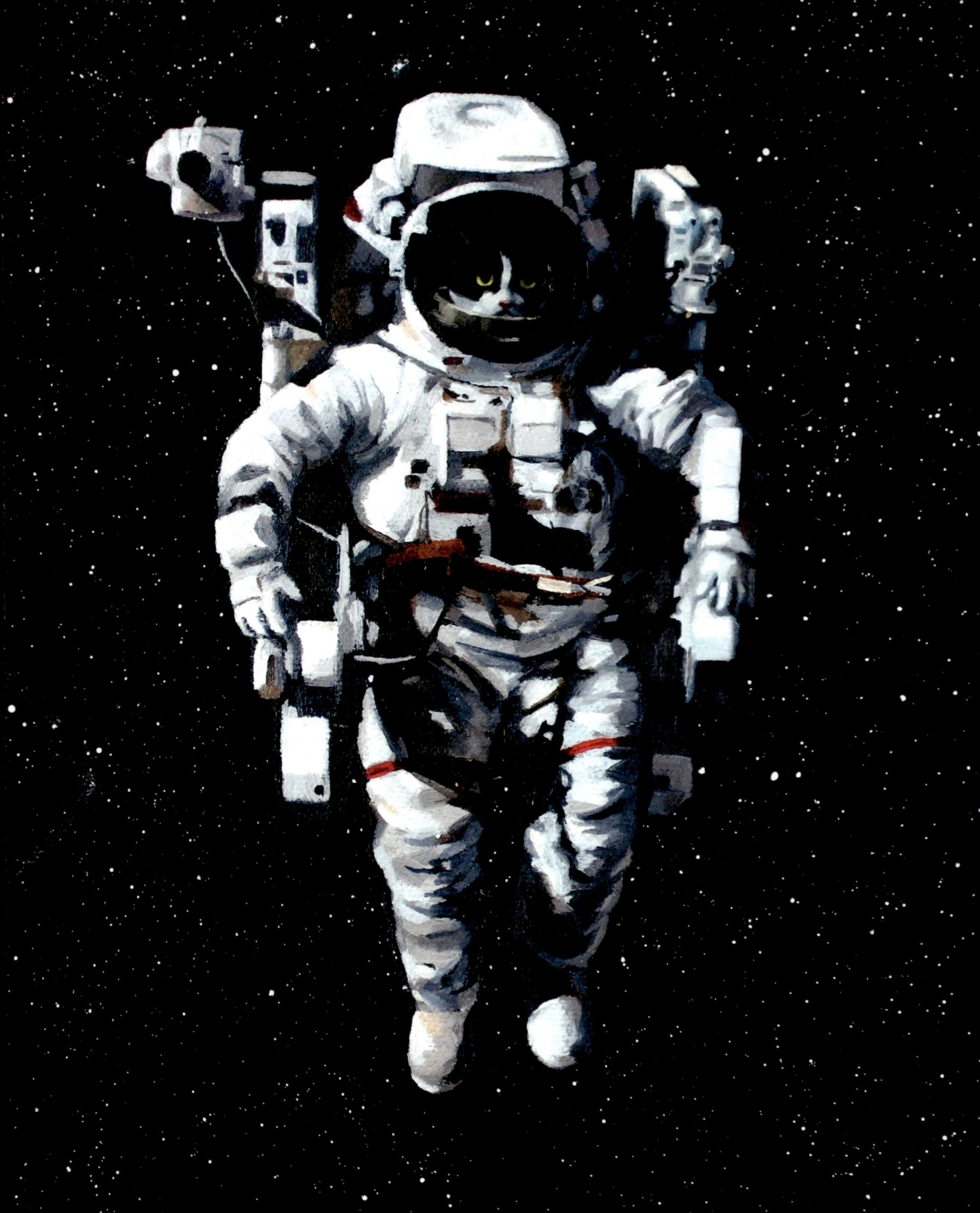

Space Catet   2008

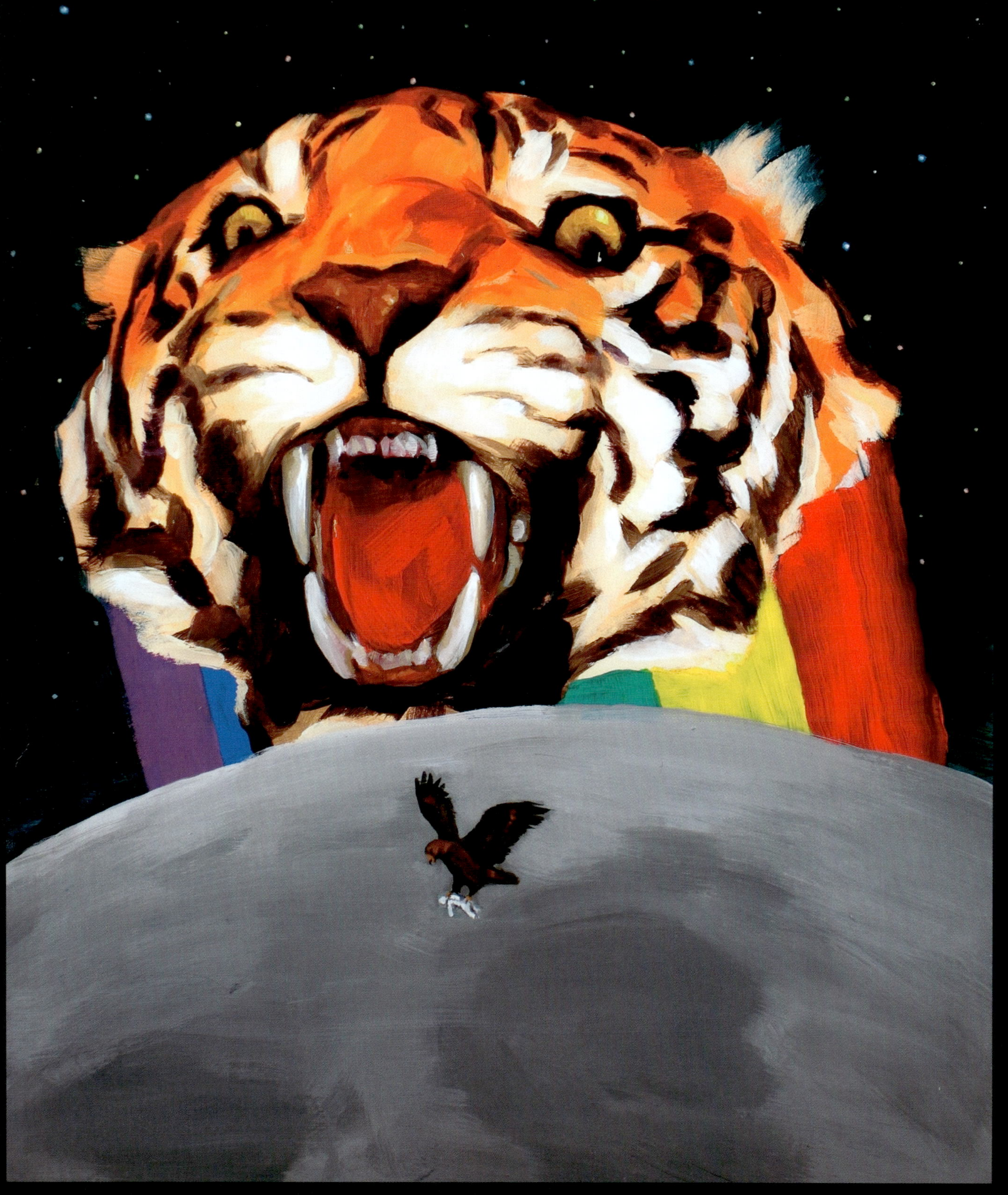

Star Cat Returns! 2010
SuperRadIronClad 2008 (over)

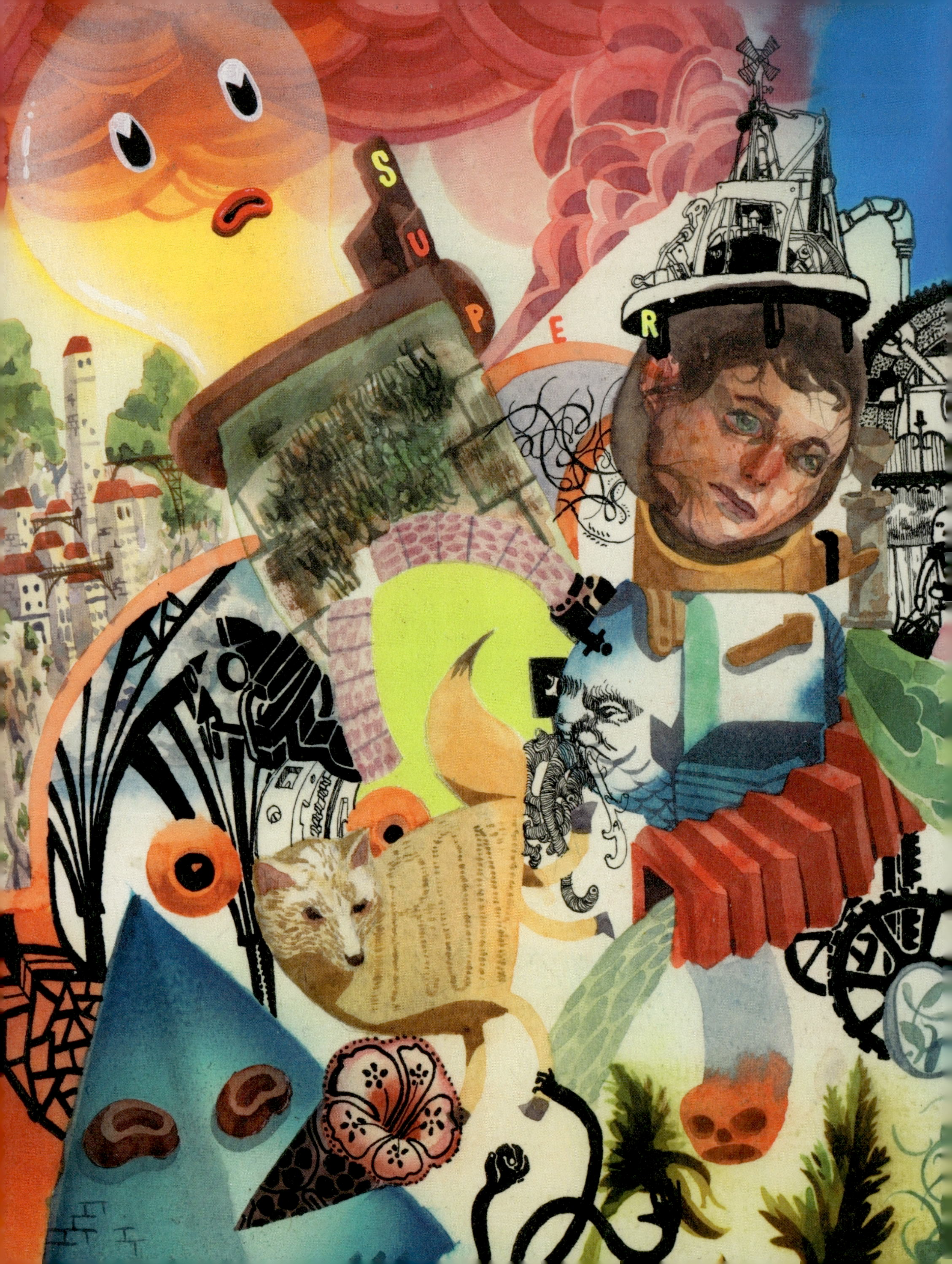

S
U
P
E
R

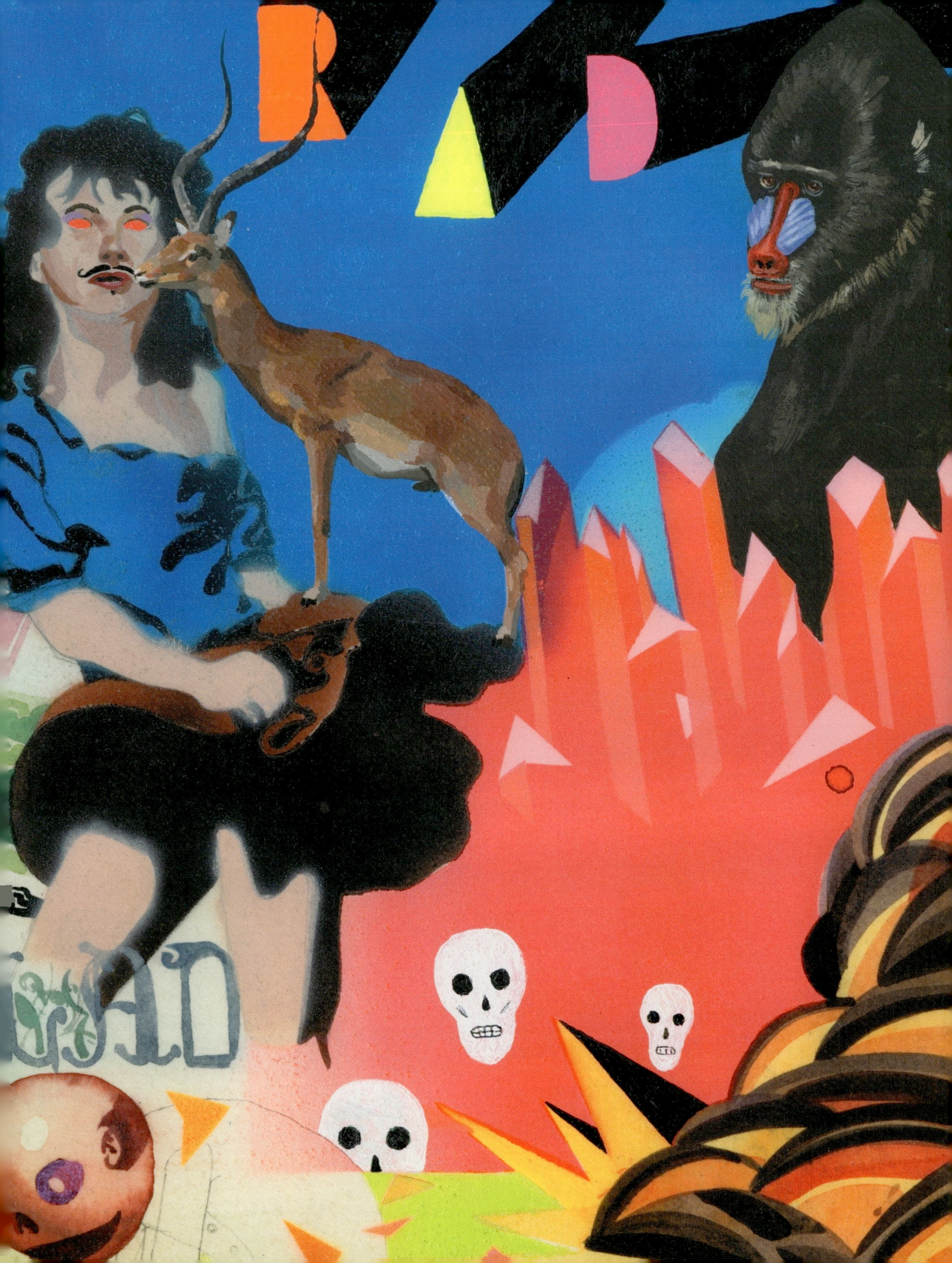

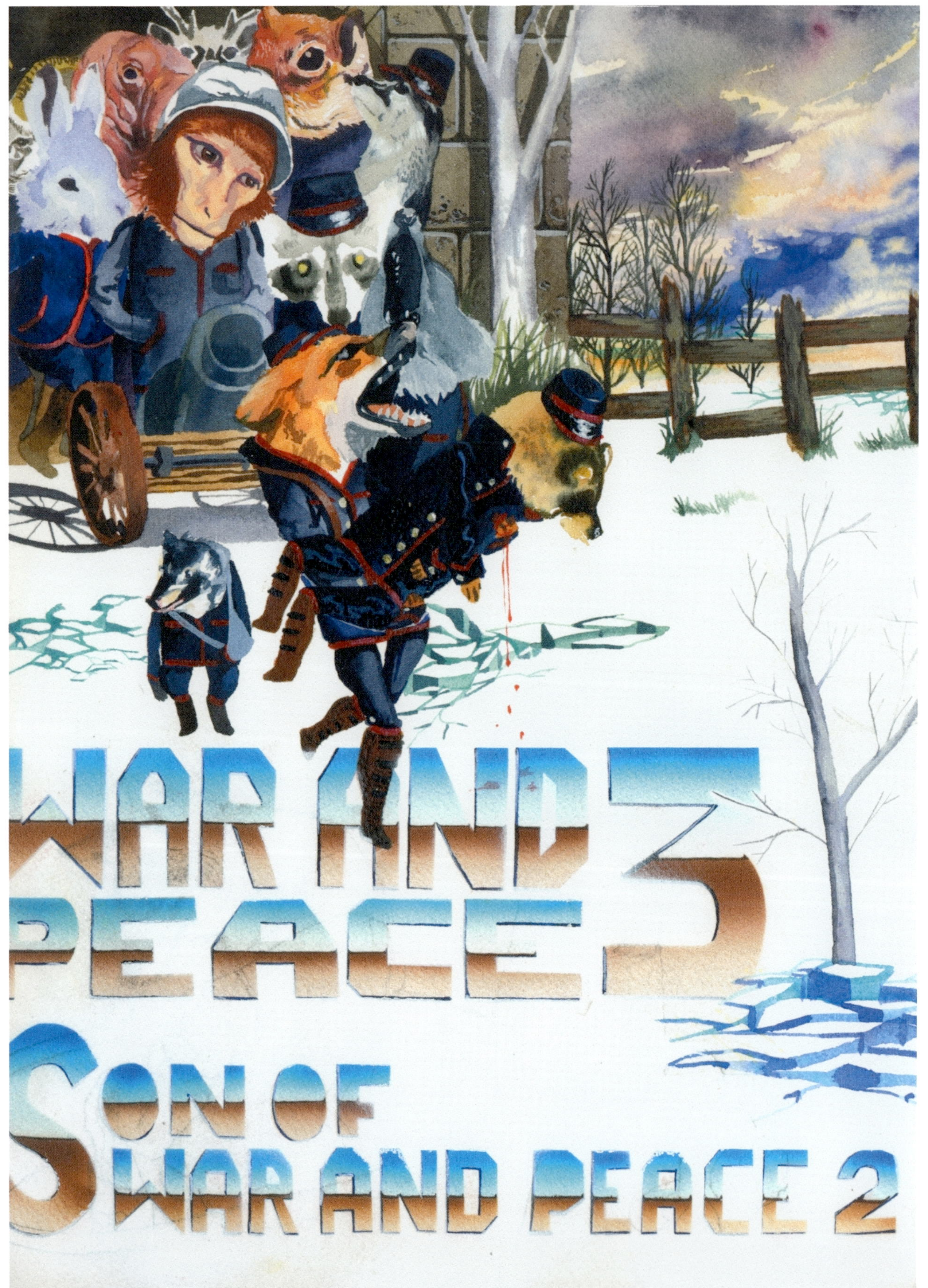

WAR AND PEACE 3
SON OF
WAR AND PEACE 2

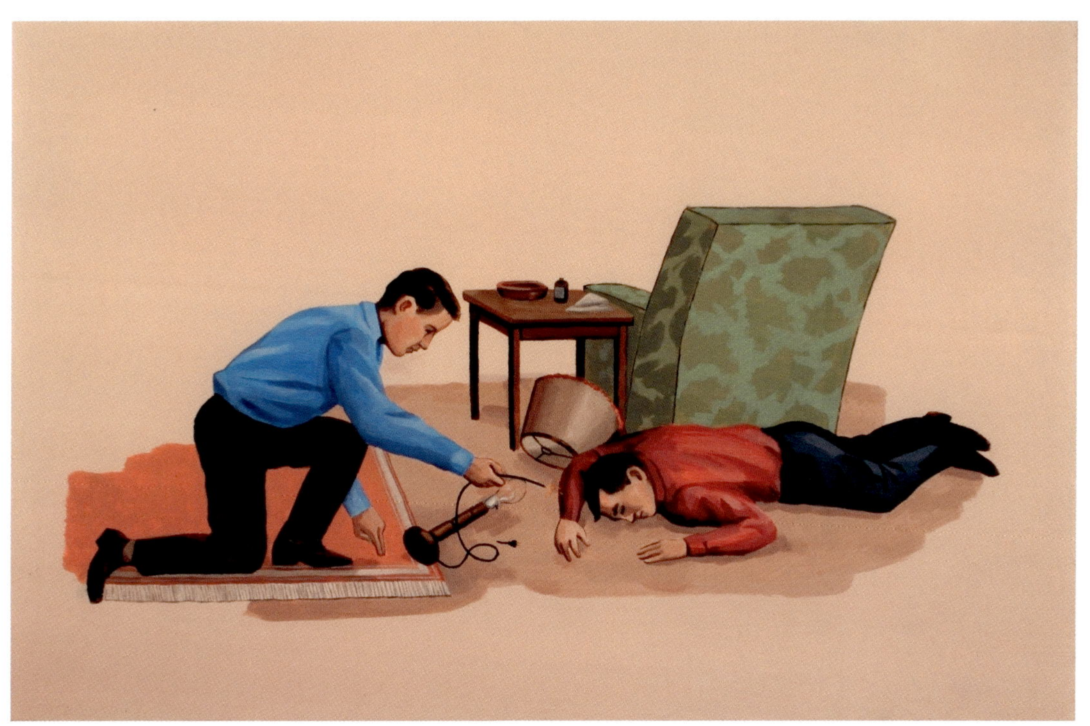

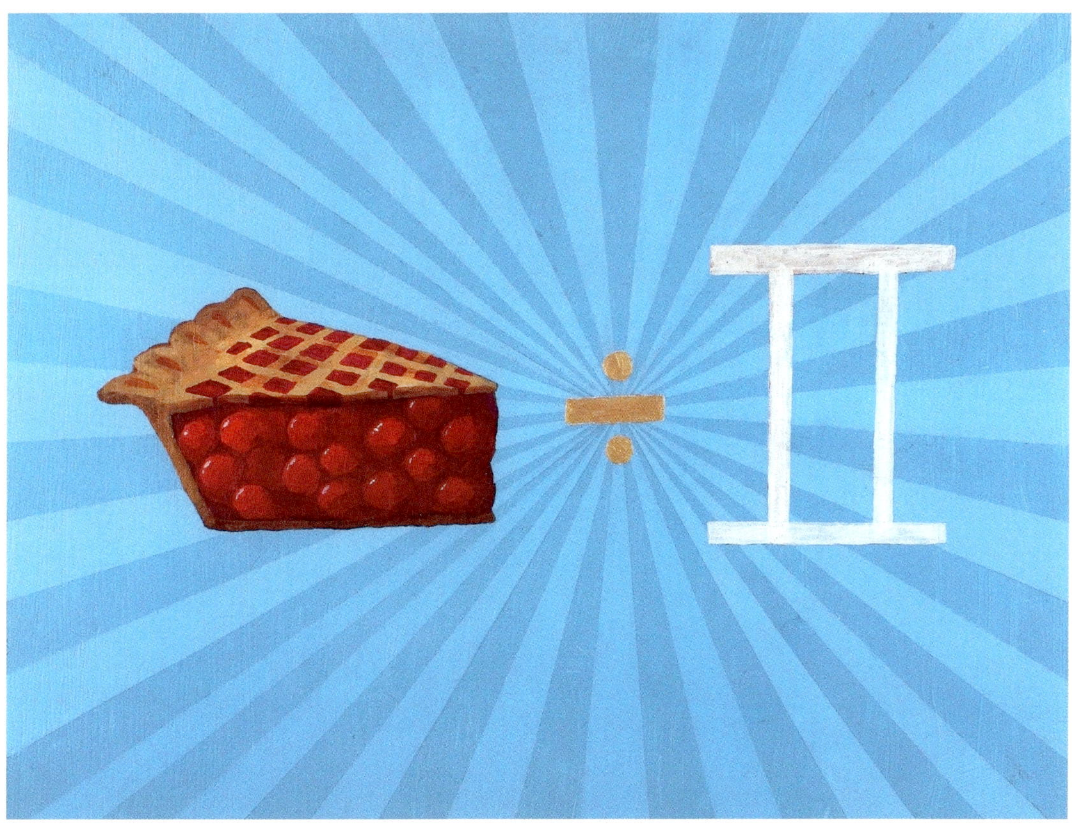

Nascent Practitioner 2010
Can I Have Some Of That? 2008
War And Peace 3 2008

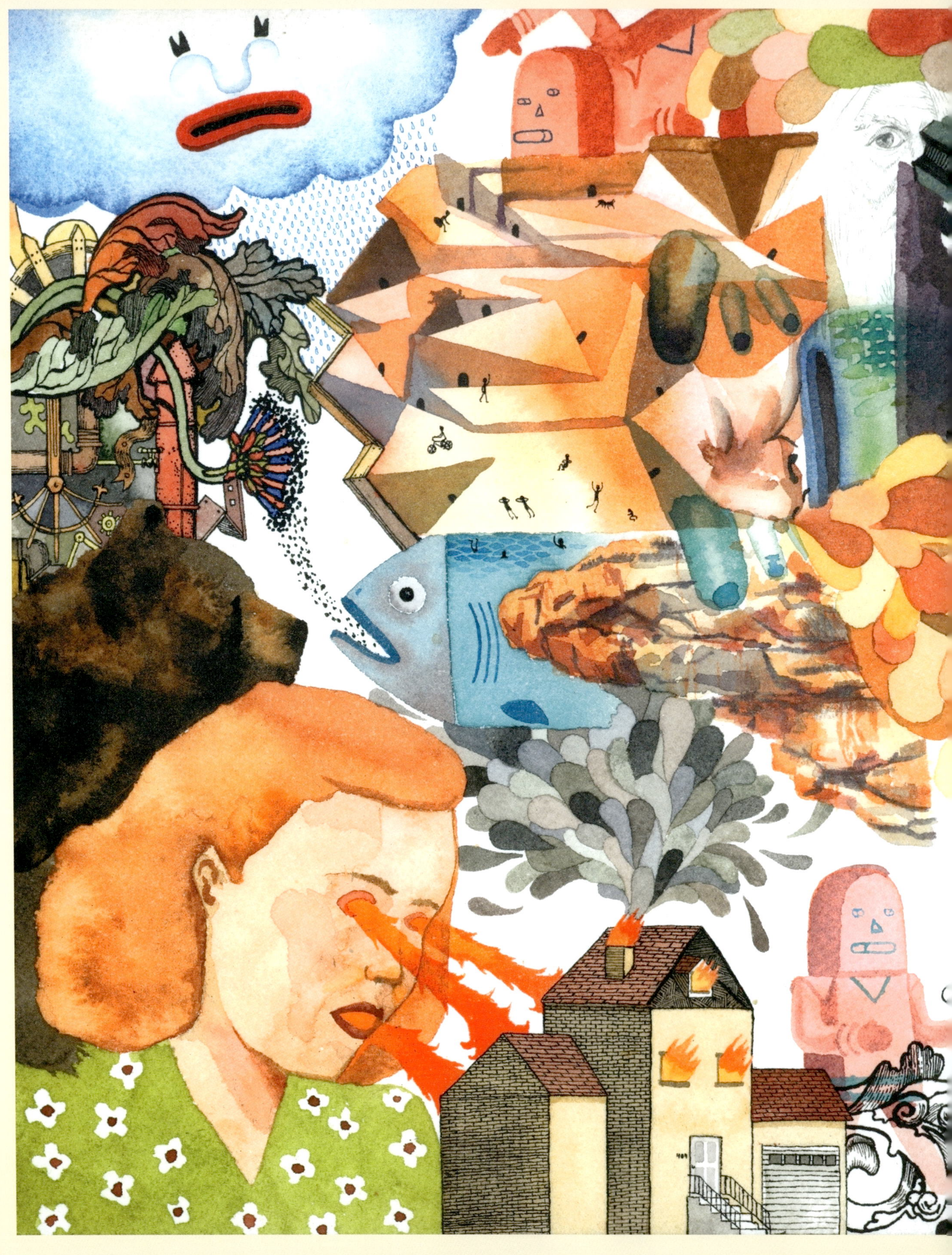

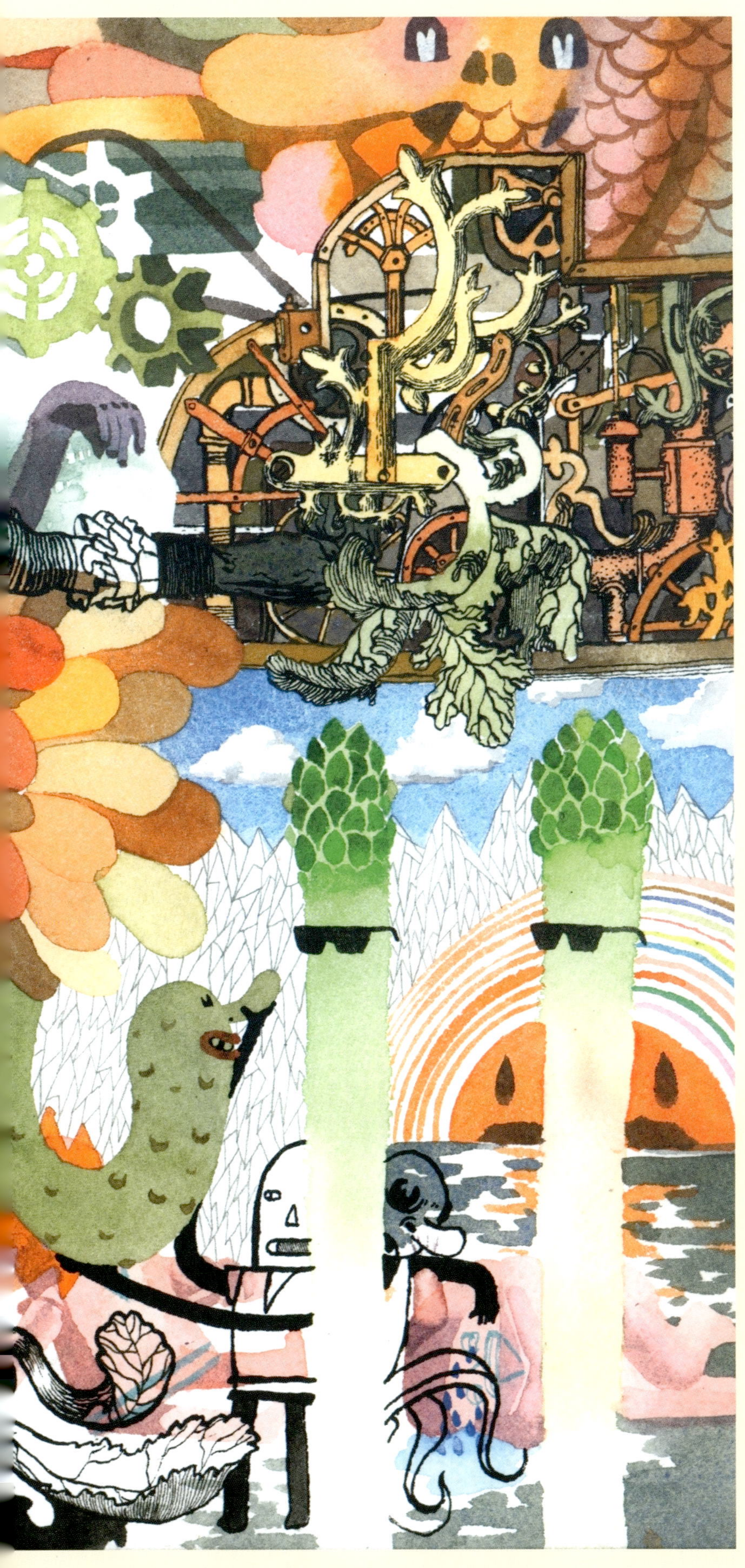

Asparaguys 2008

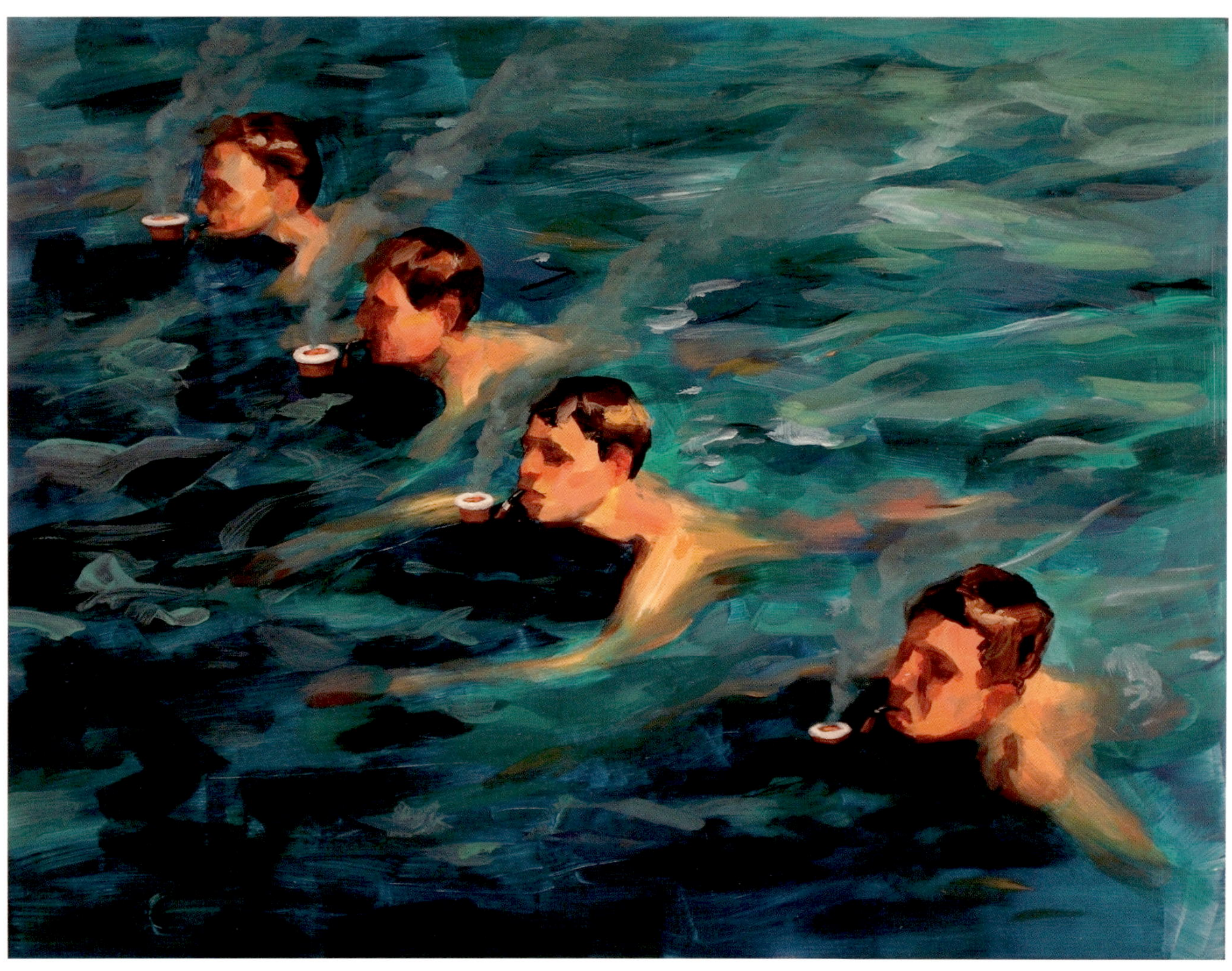

The Calabash dash   2010

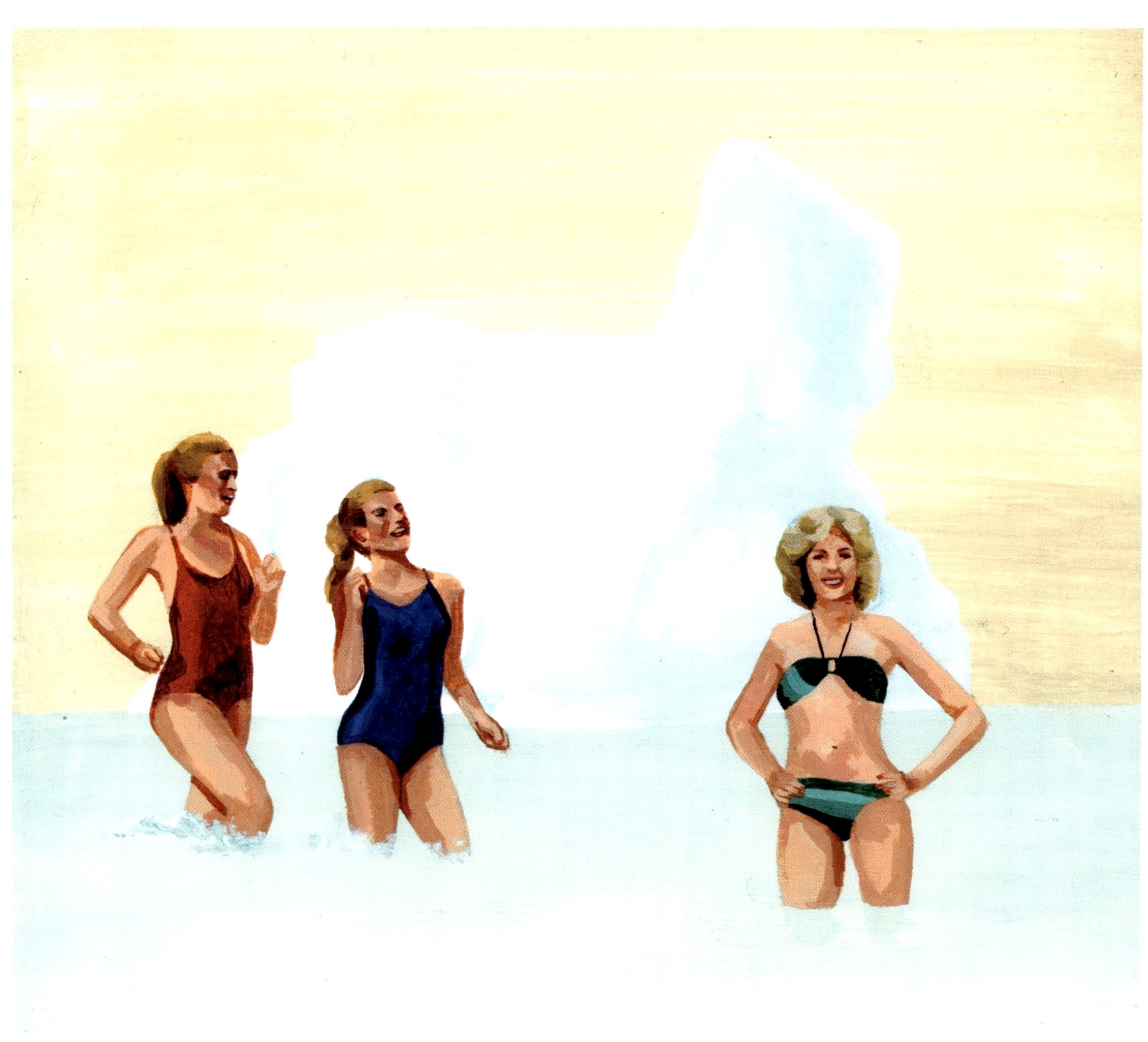

Ice Nymphos of the 49th Parallel 2008

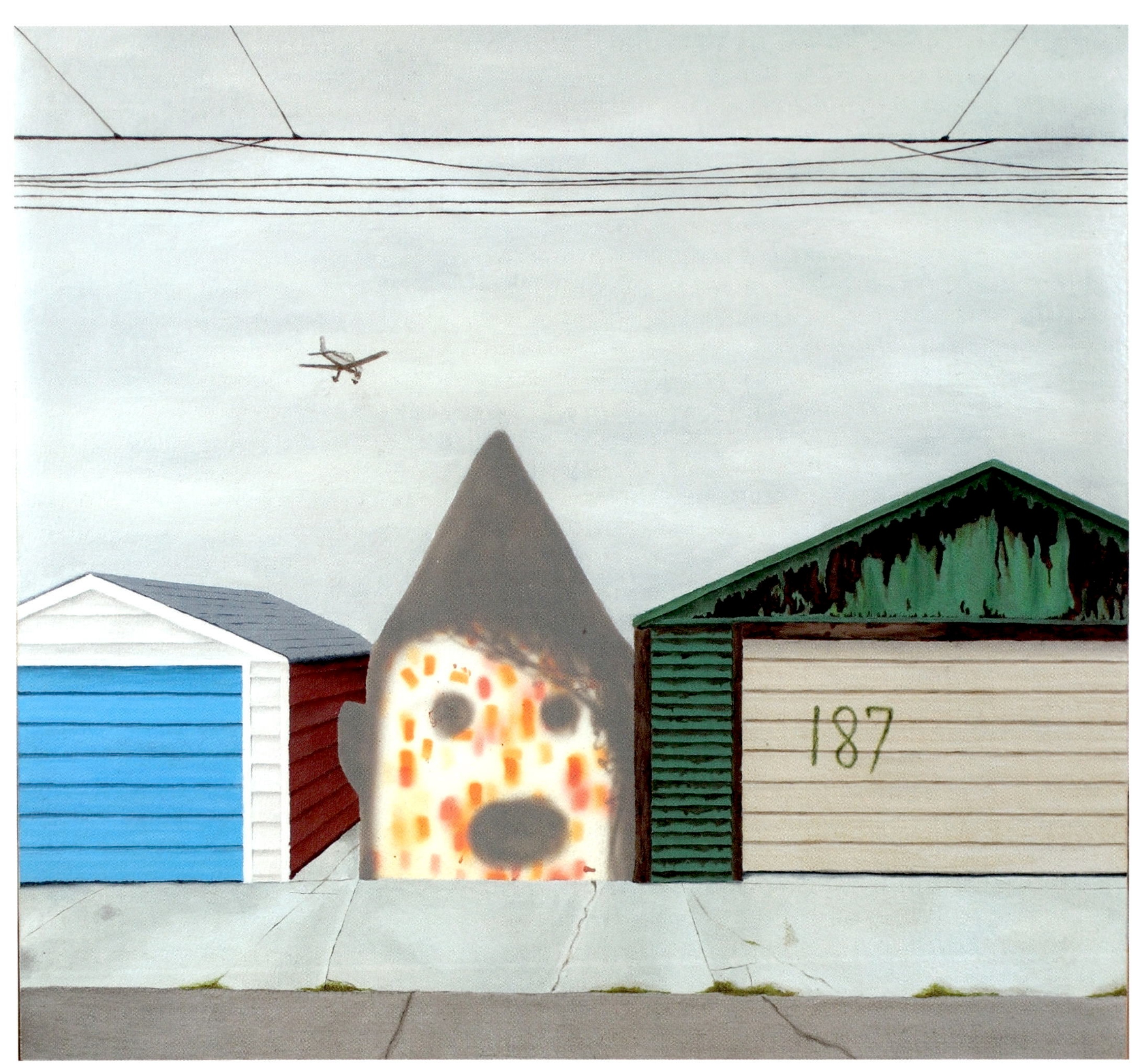

The Ugliest Garage on the Block   2010

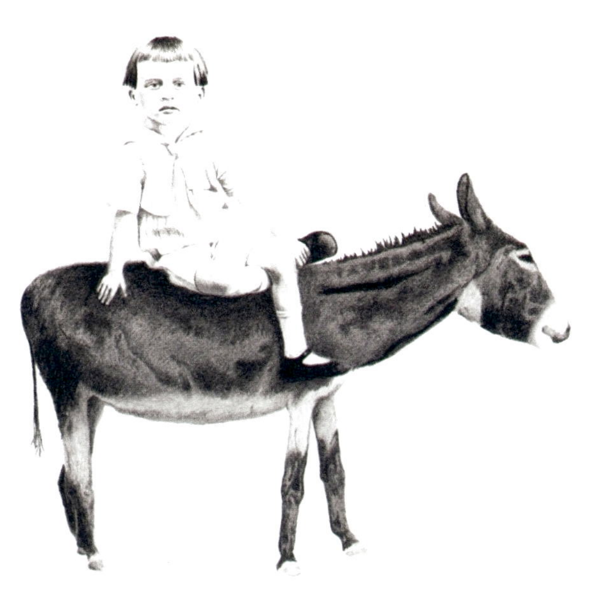

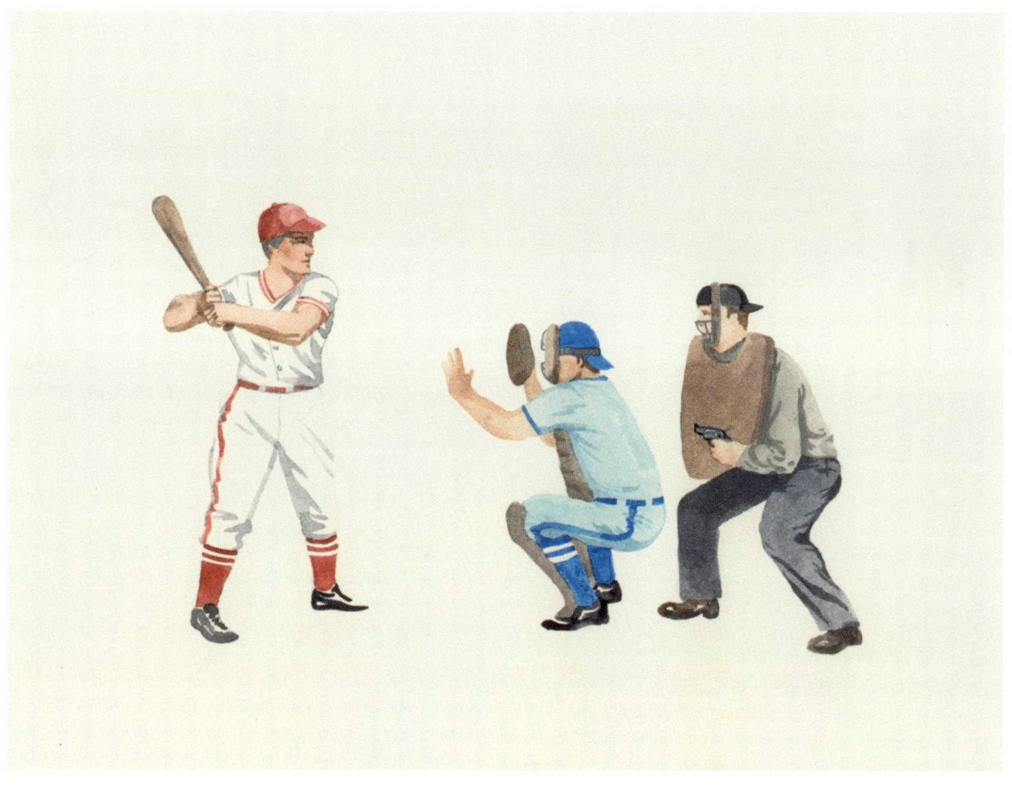

Donkey and Boy   2008
Baseball Is A Sport   2008

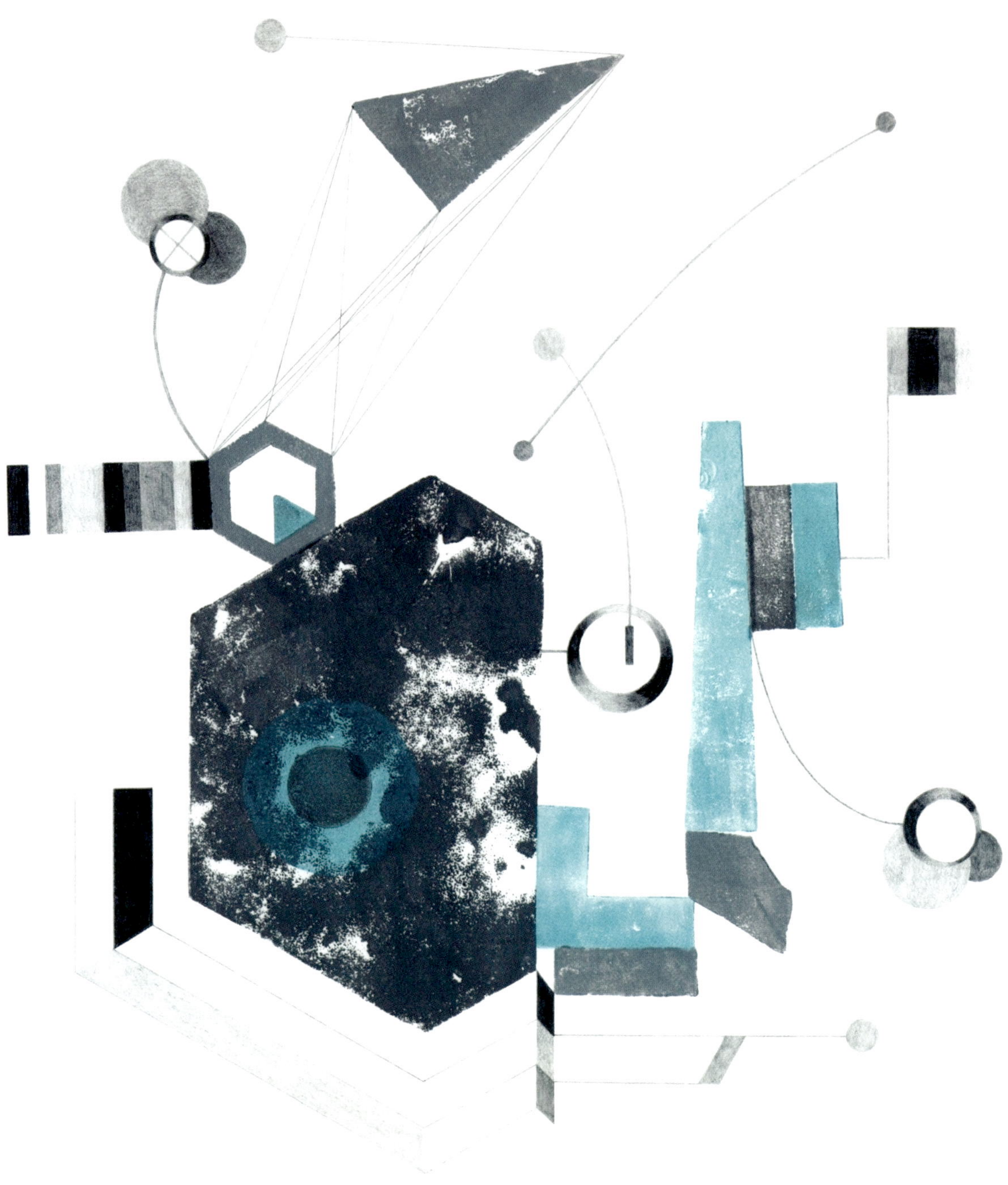

Intractable Tactical Jam   2009

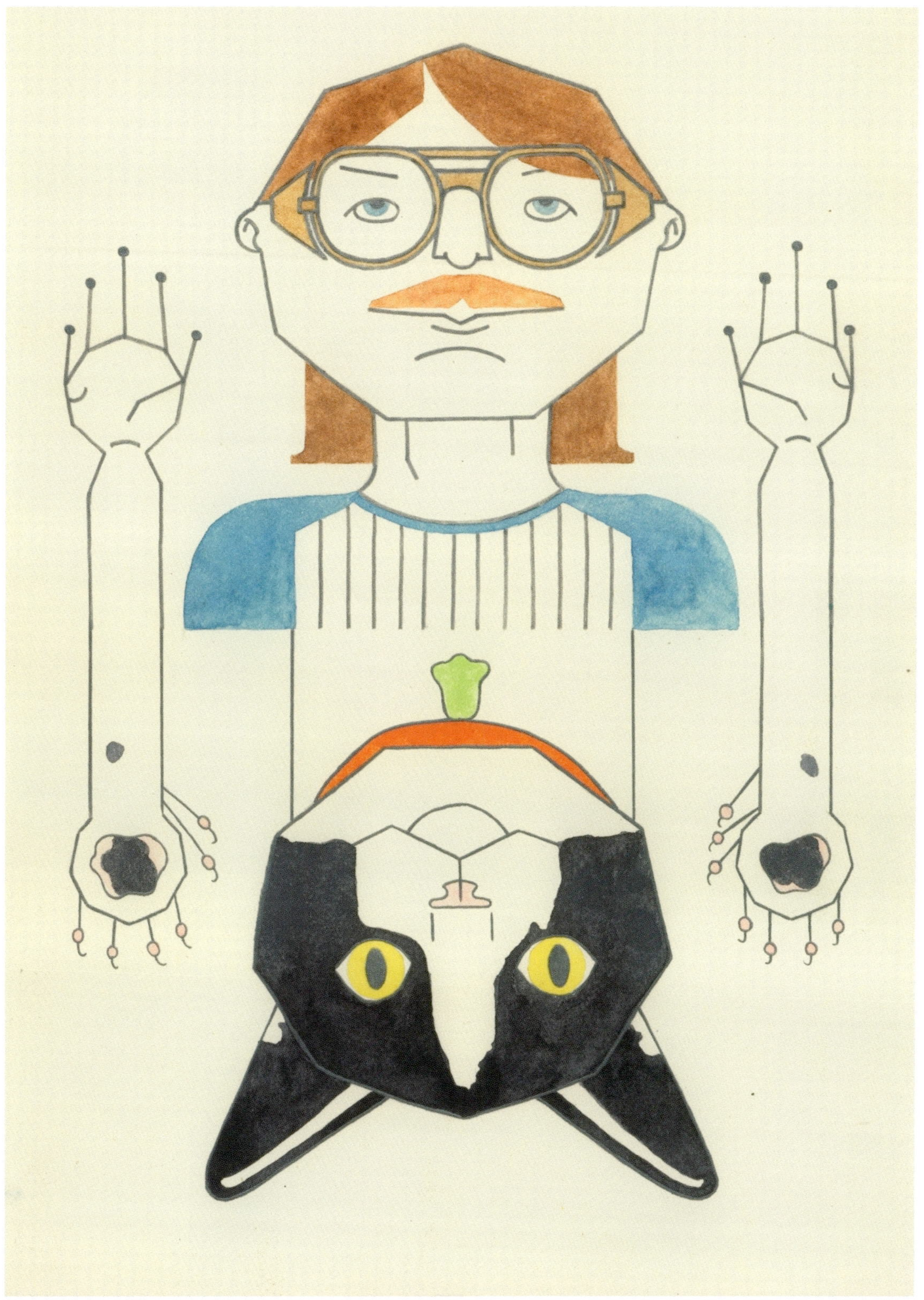

Budidies 2008

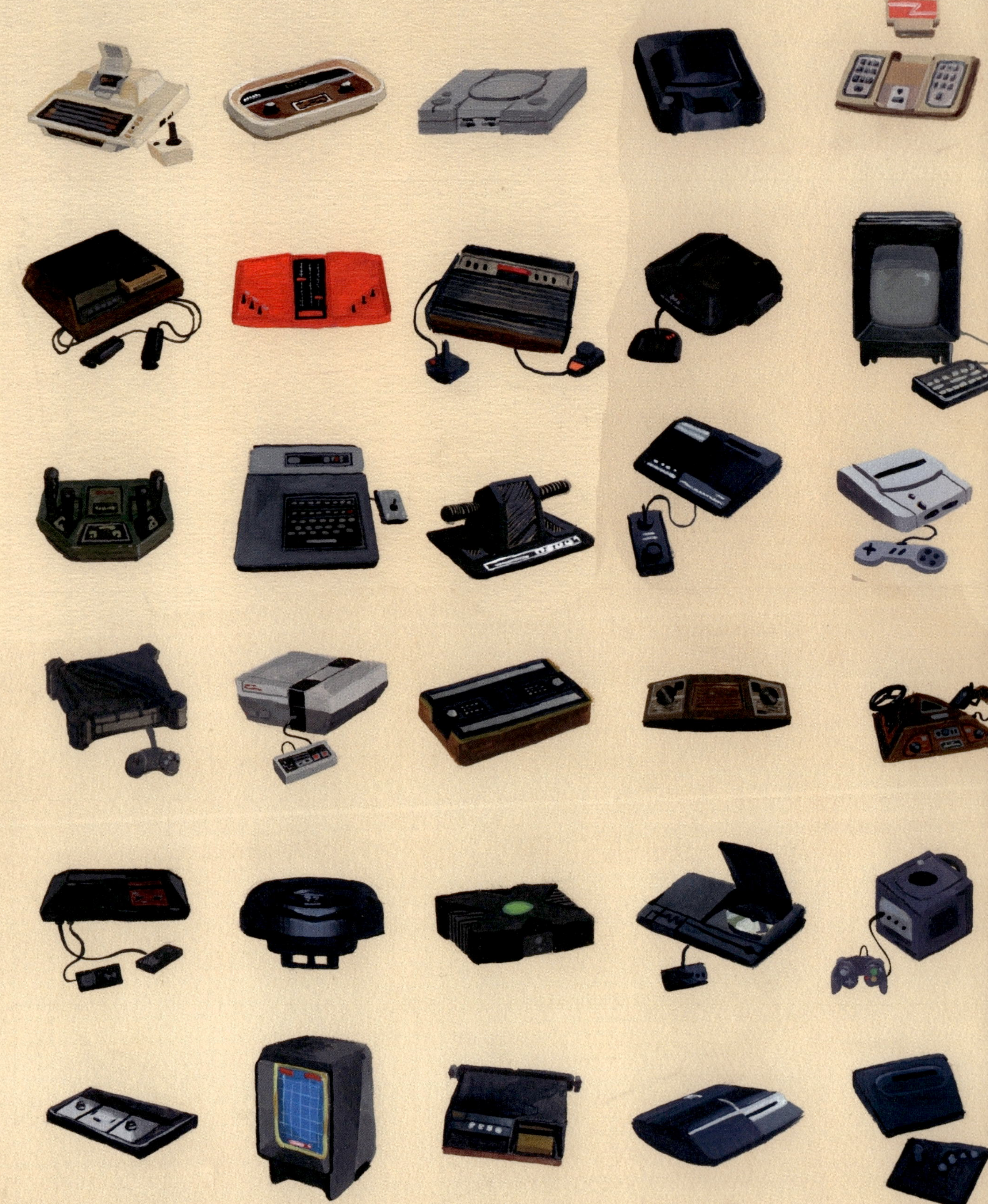

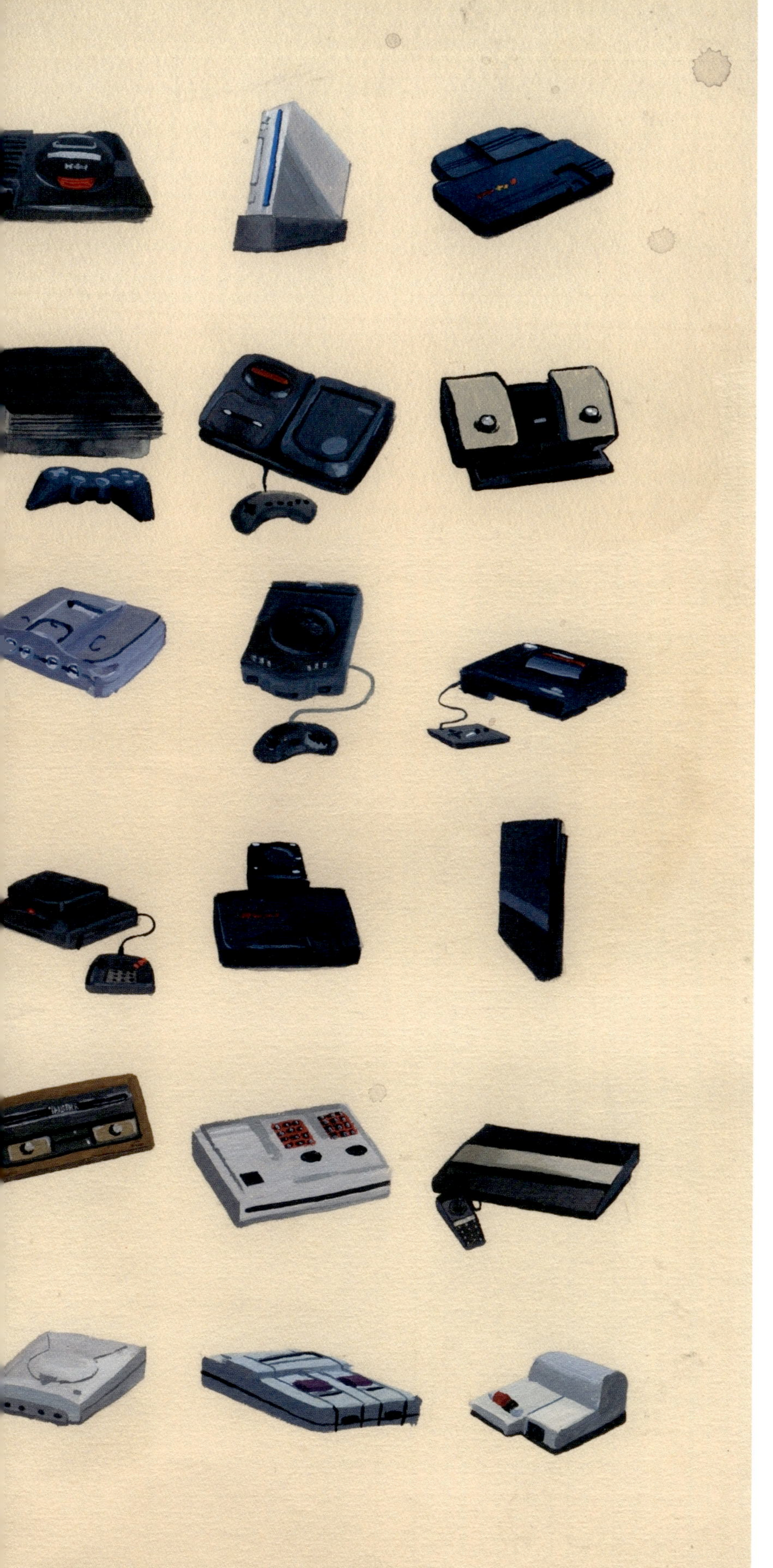

Holy Relics 2009

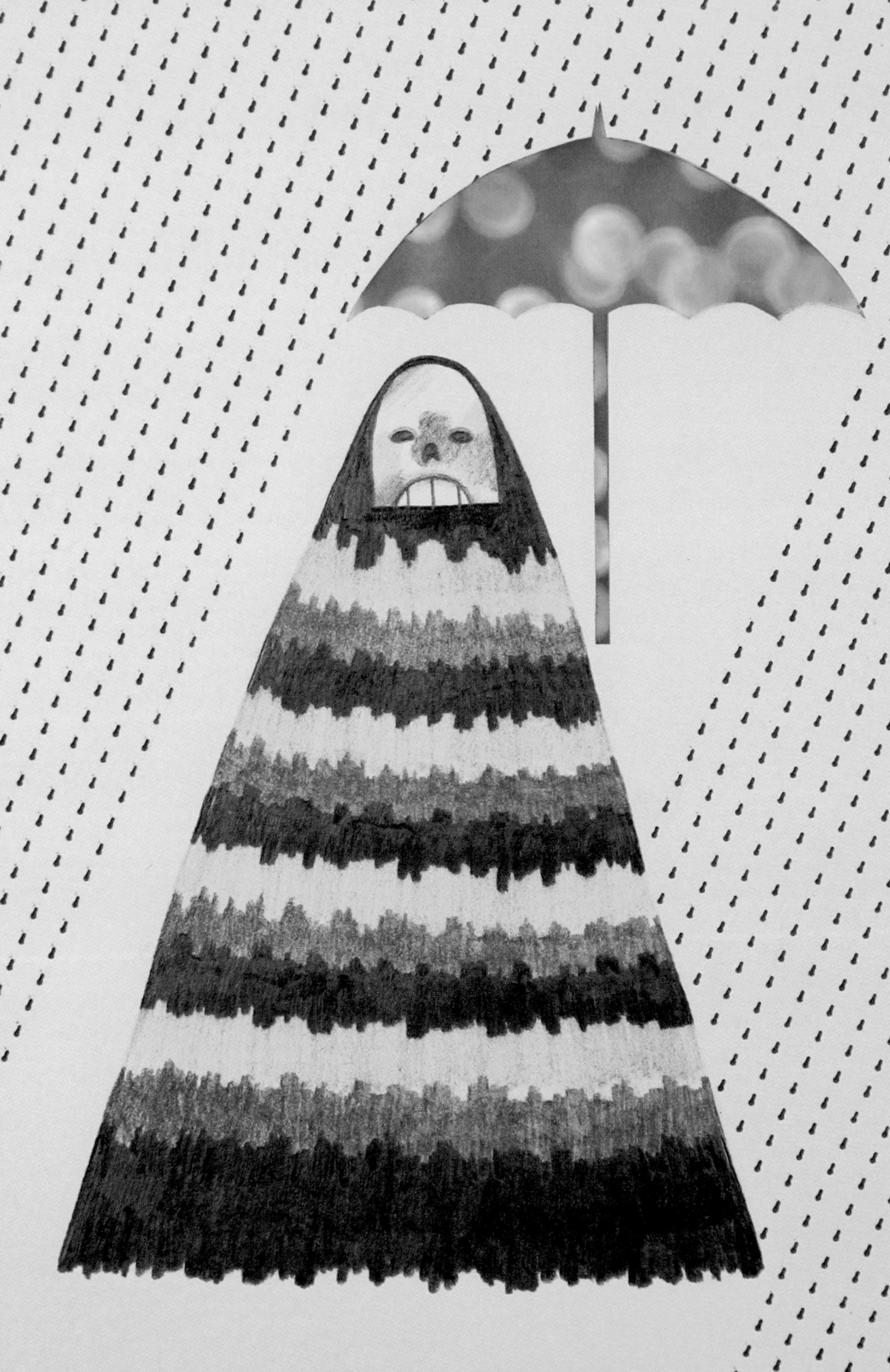

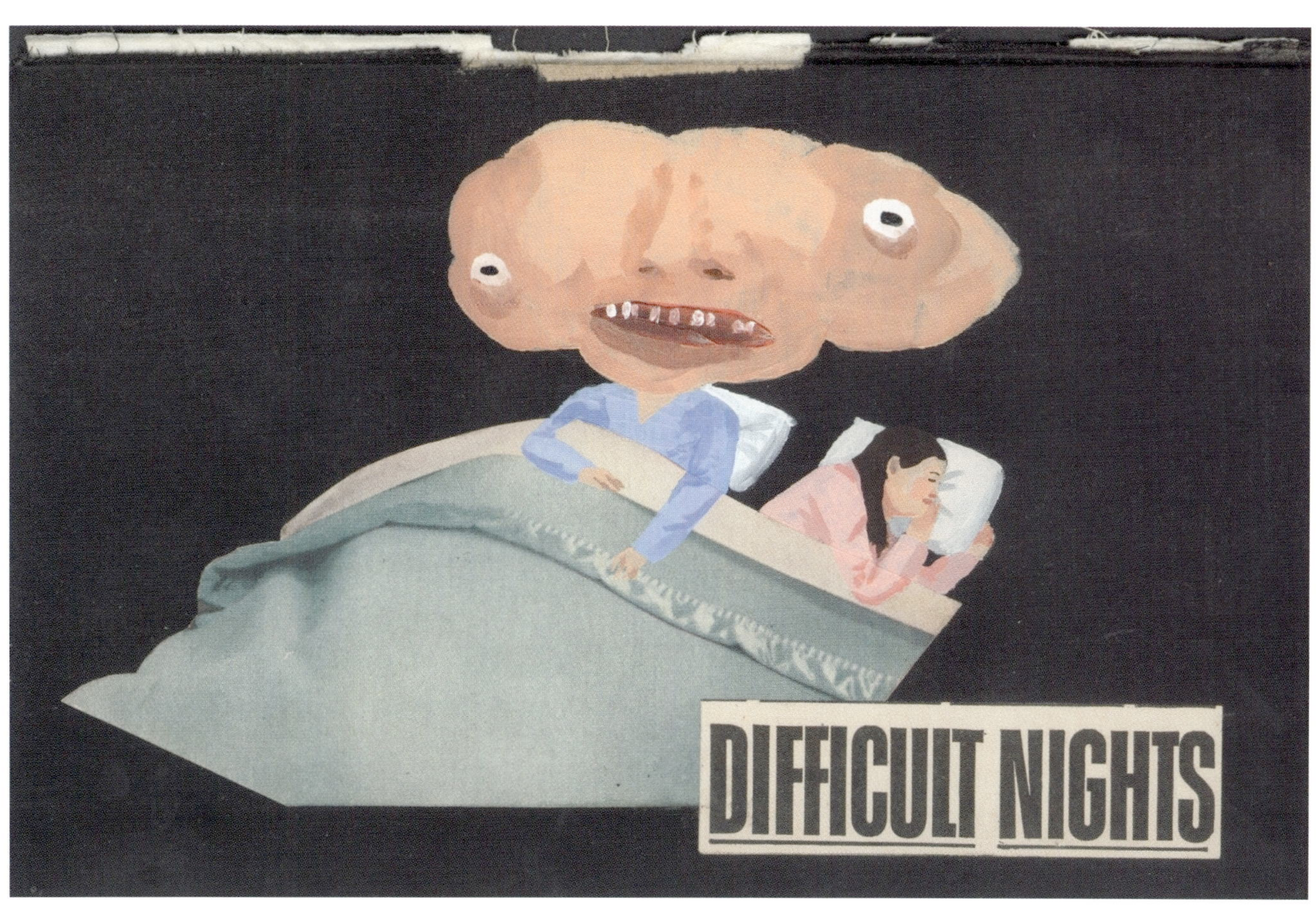

DIFFICULT NIGHTS

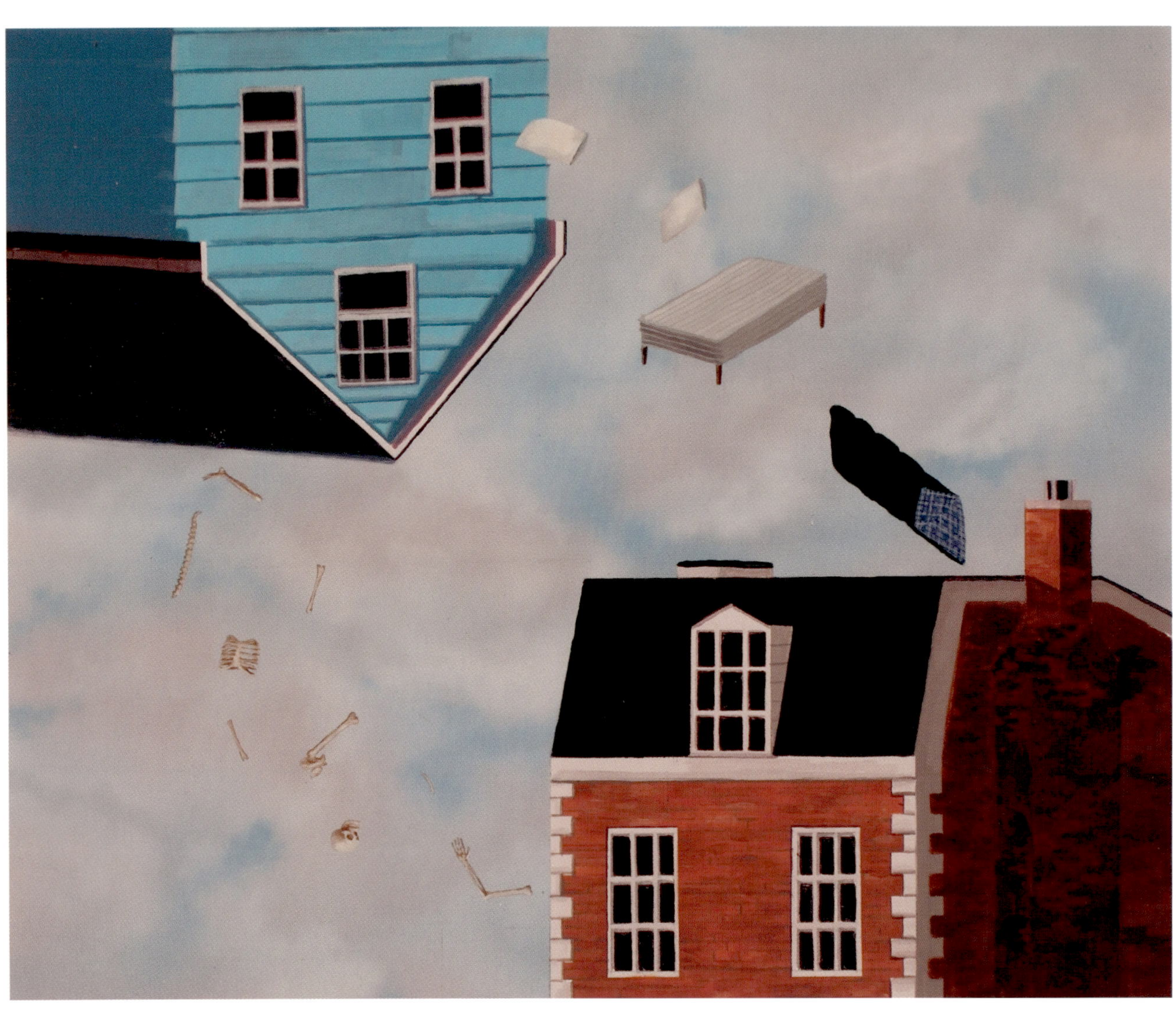

Vicious Cycle 2010
Nuclear Family   2010
A Splendid Day for Sabre Play 2010

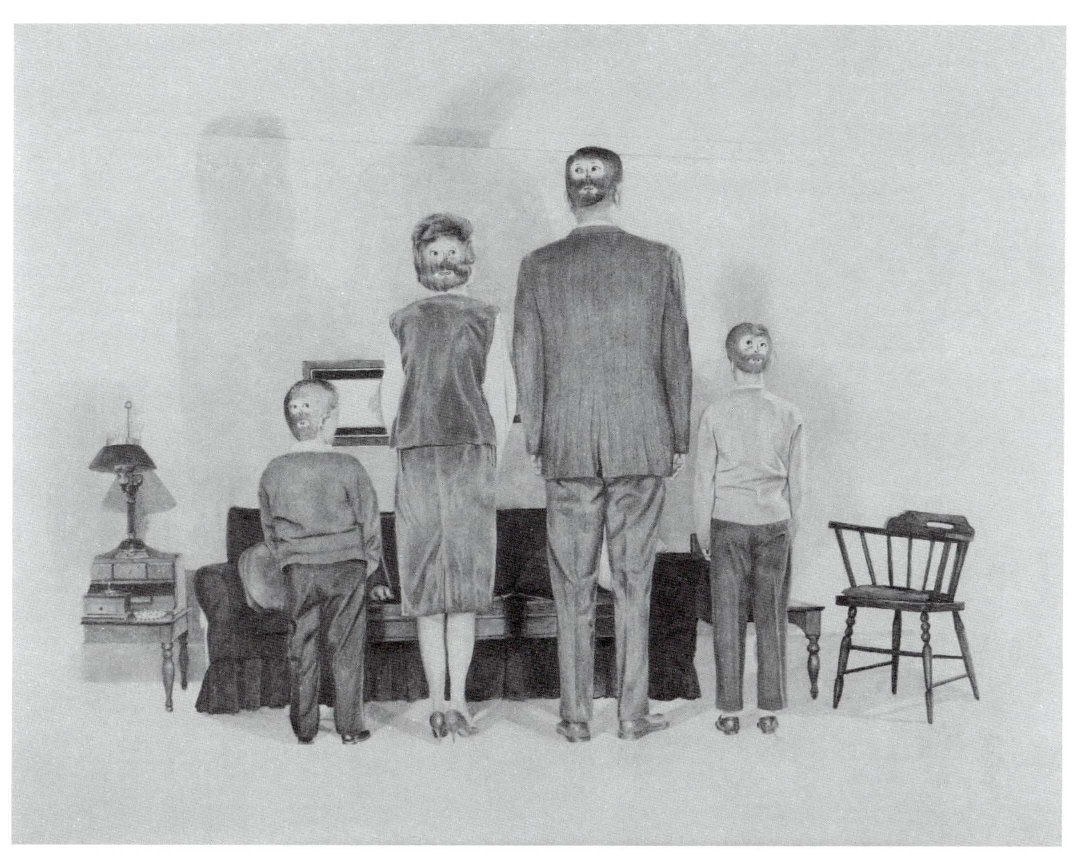

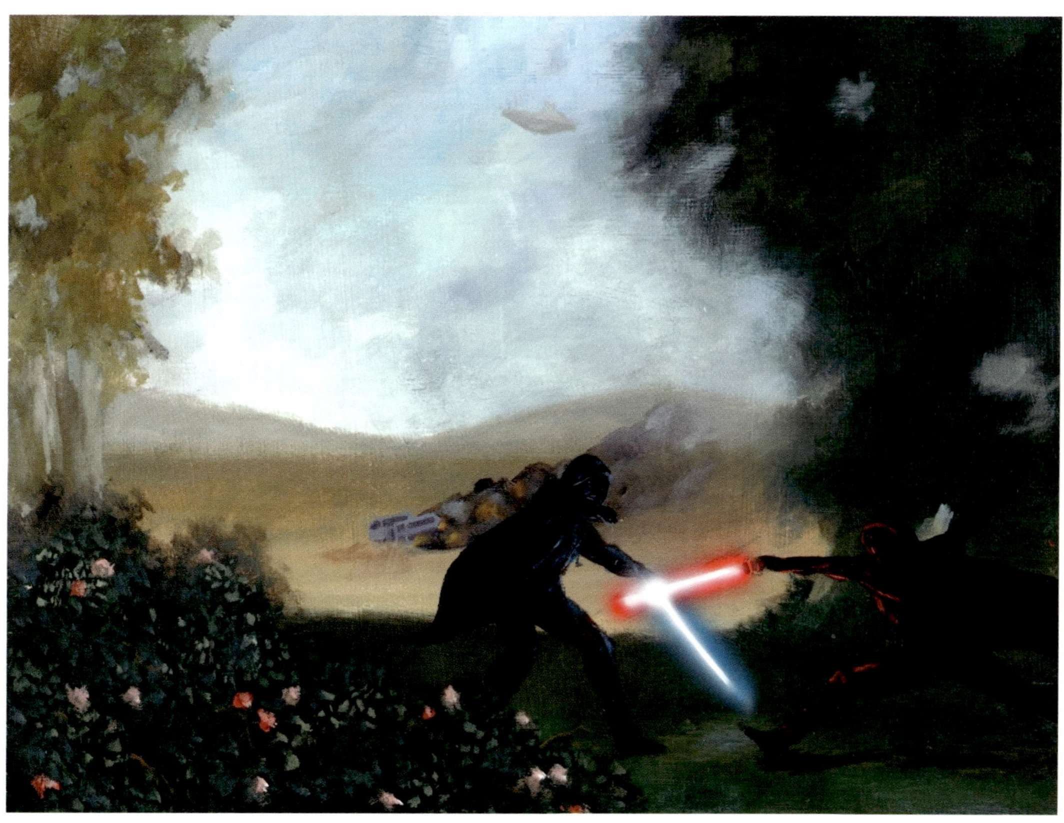

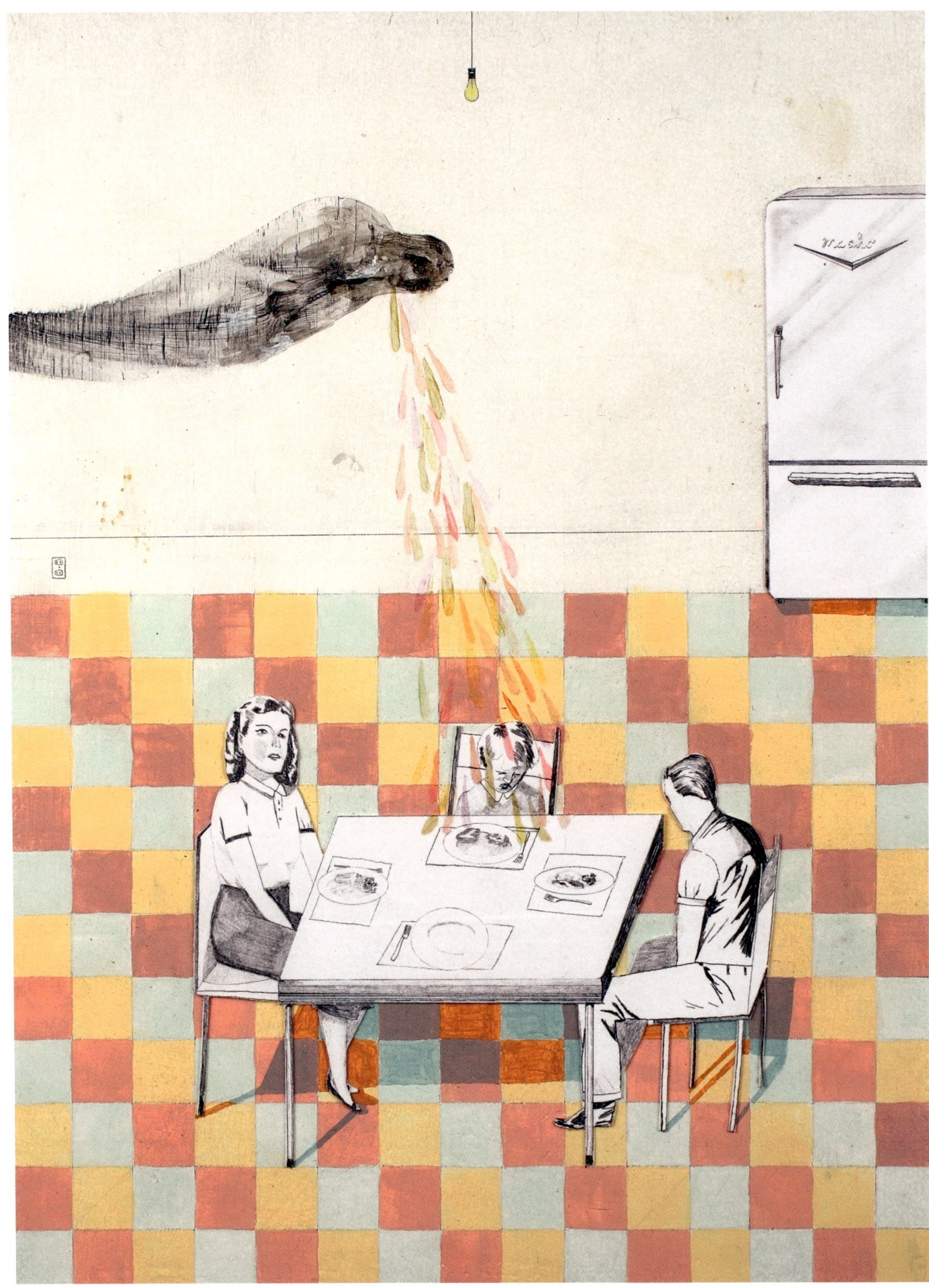

Ghost Dad 2008
ffffuuuuu 2010

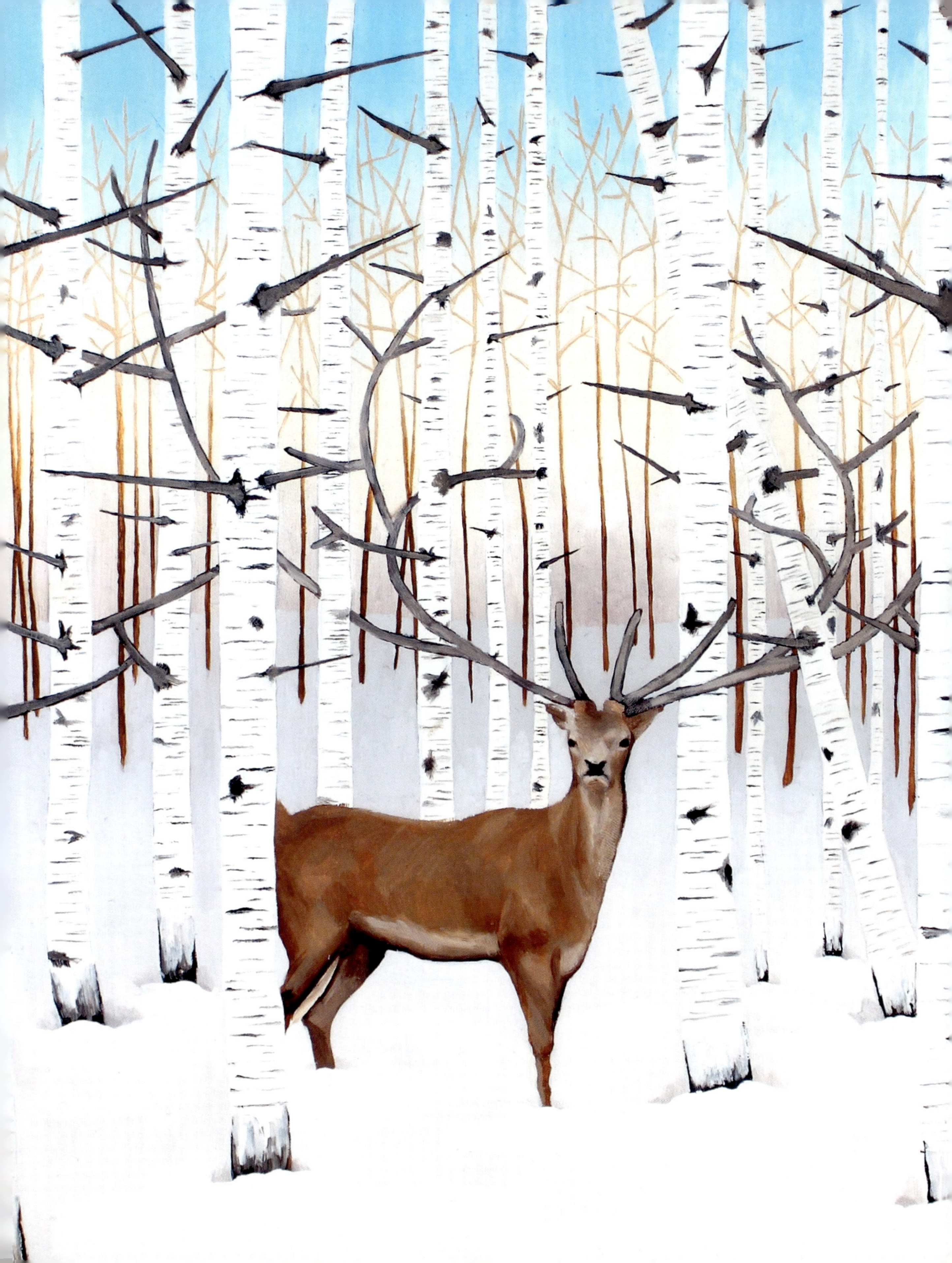

A Macho Oracle   2009
You Are Never Alone In The Bone Orchard   2008

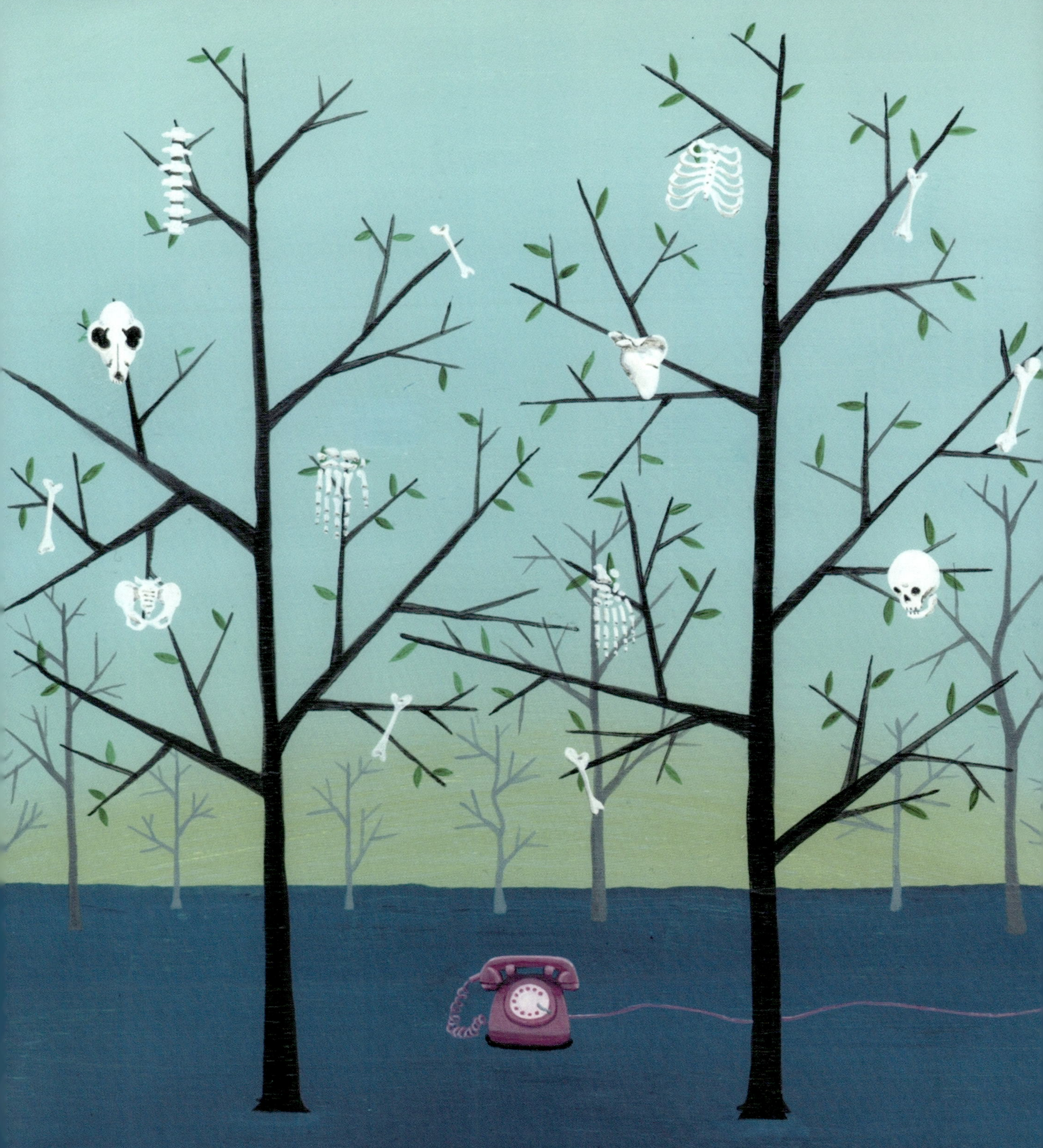

You are never alone in the bone orchard.

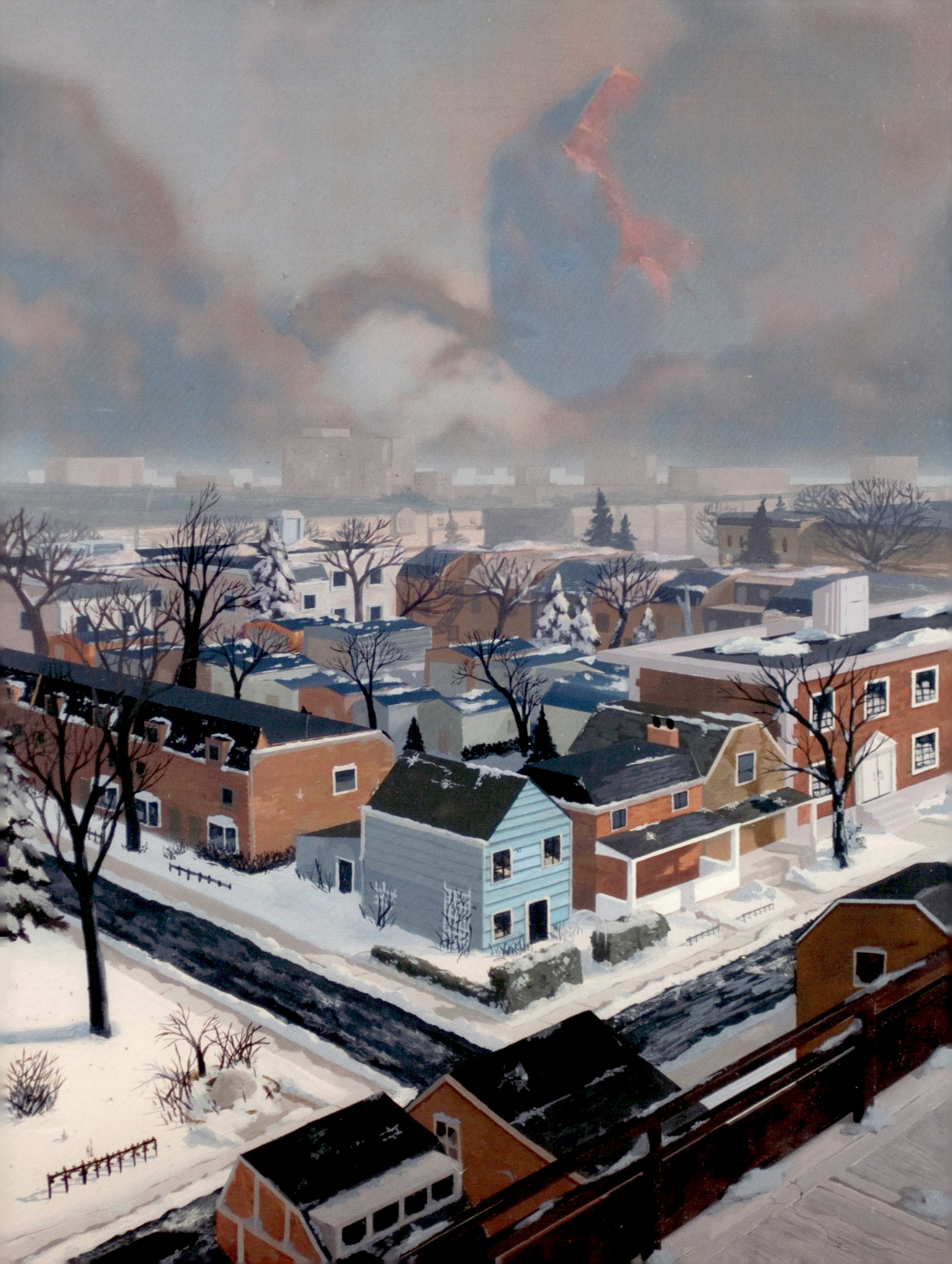

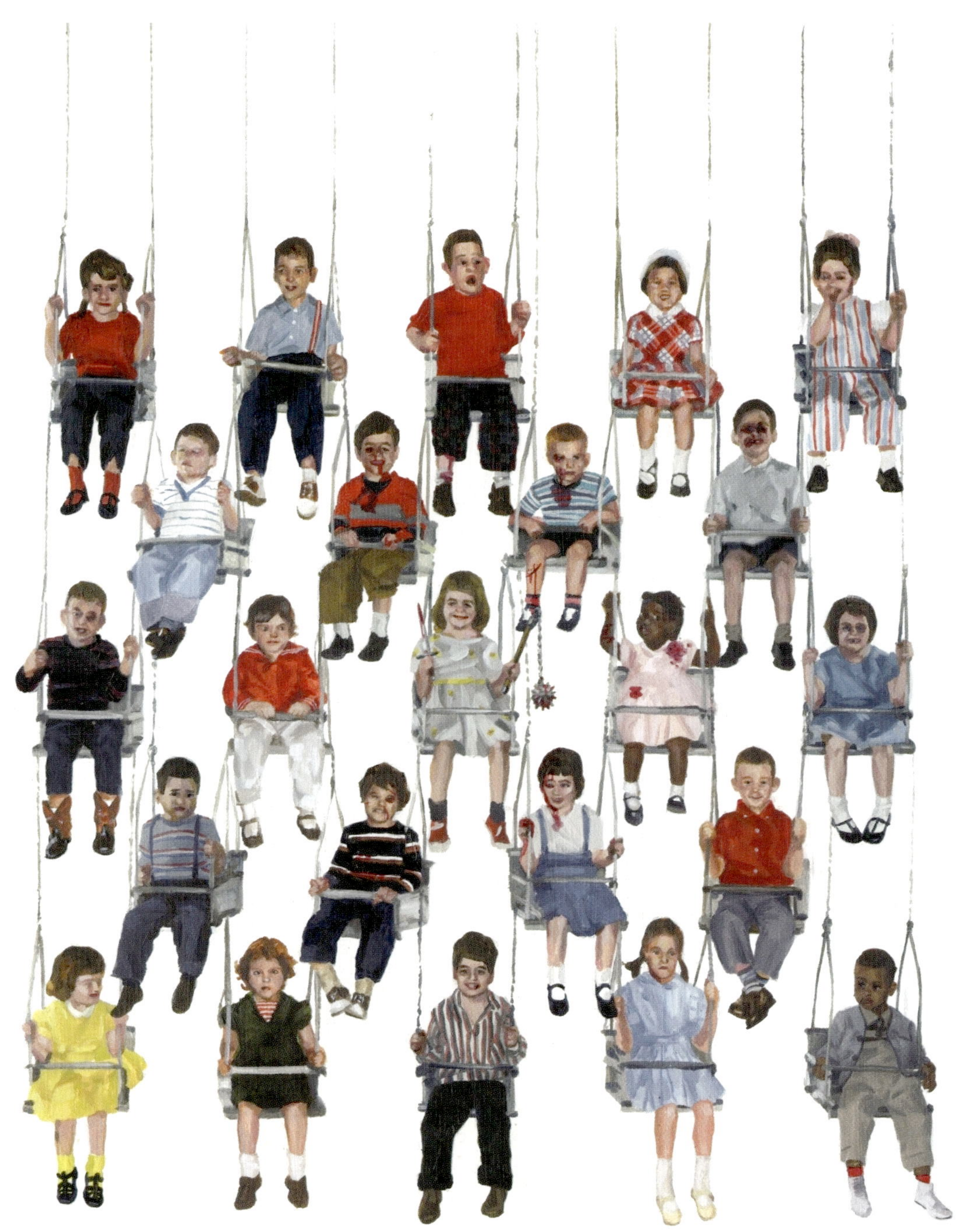

Our Heavenly Mansions 2010
Swing Kids 2008

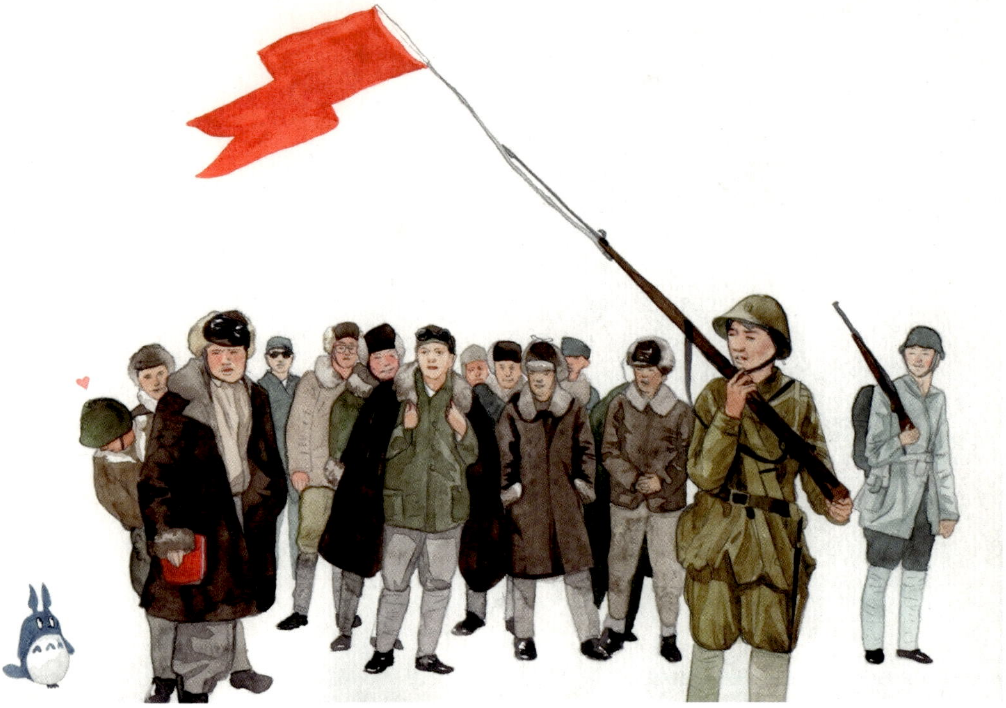

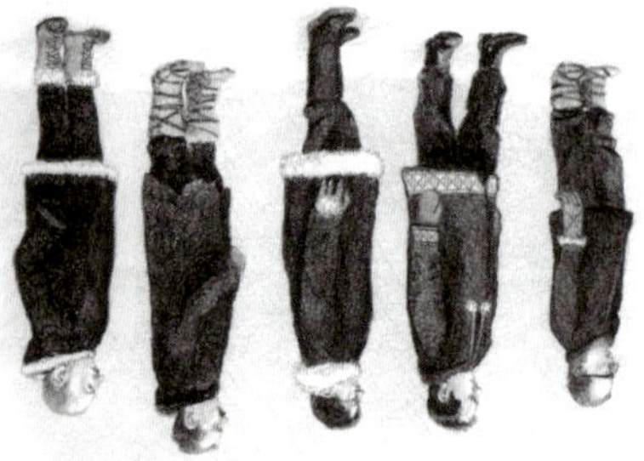

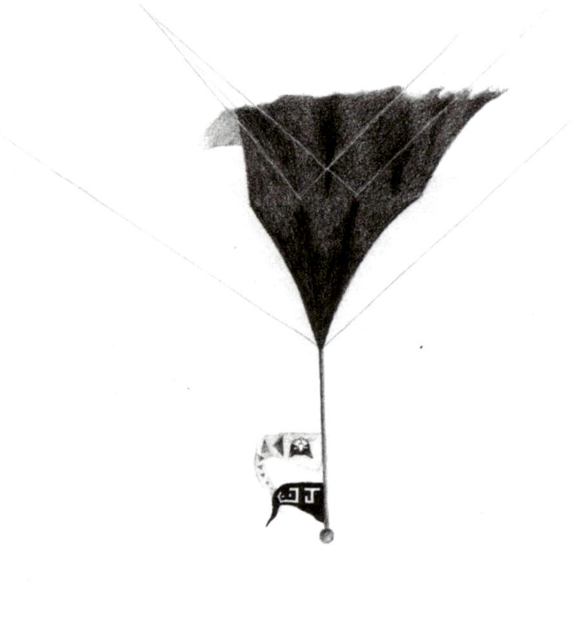

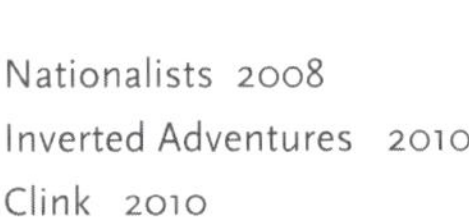

Nationalists 2008
Inverted Adventures 2010
Clink 2010

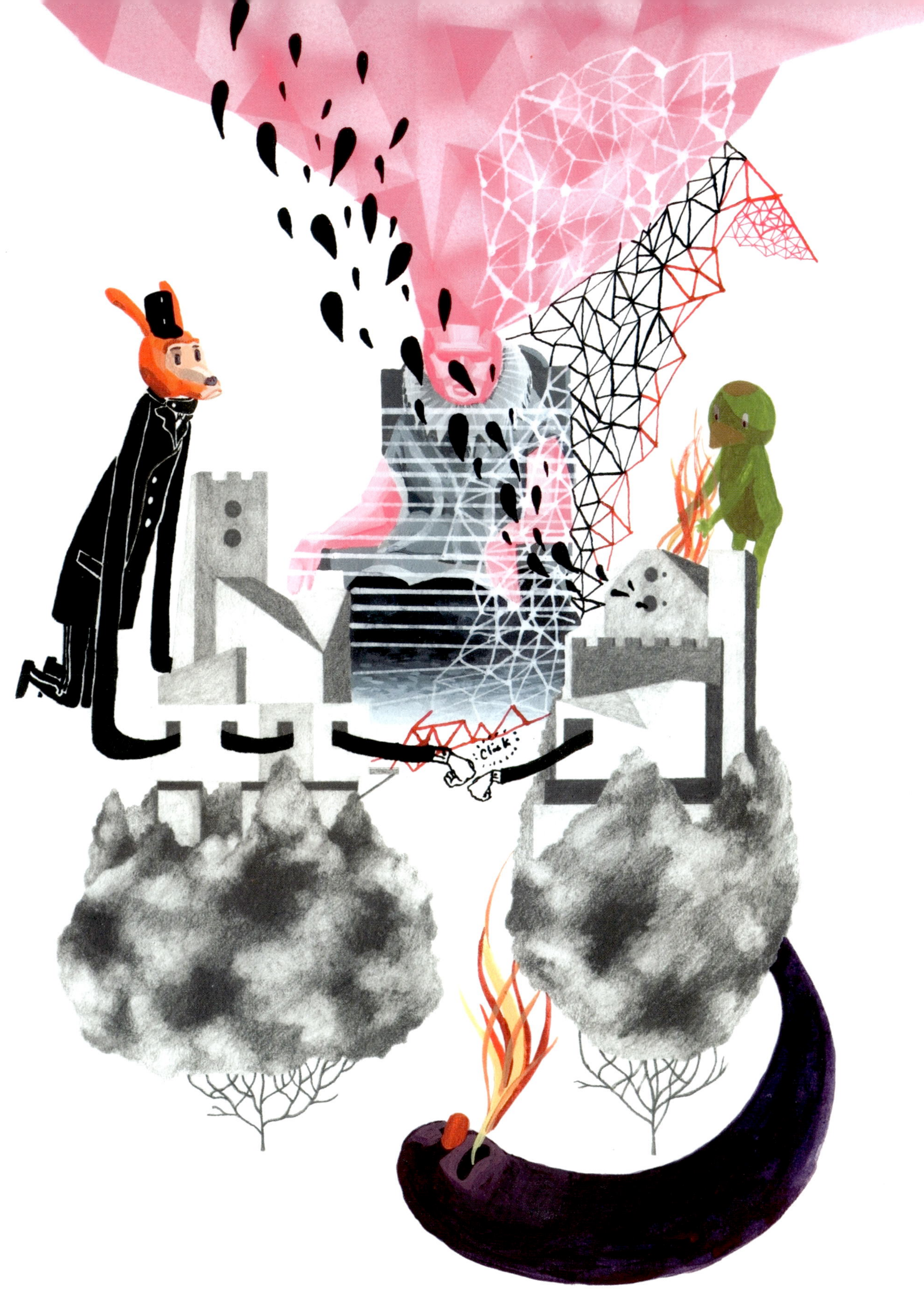
Click

The Dullest Boy There Ever Was   2008

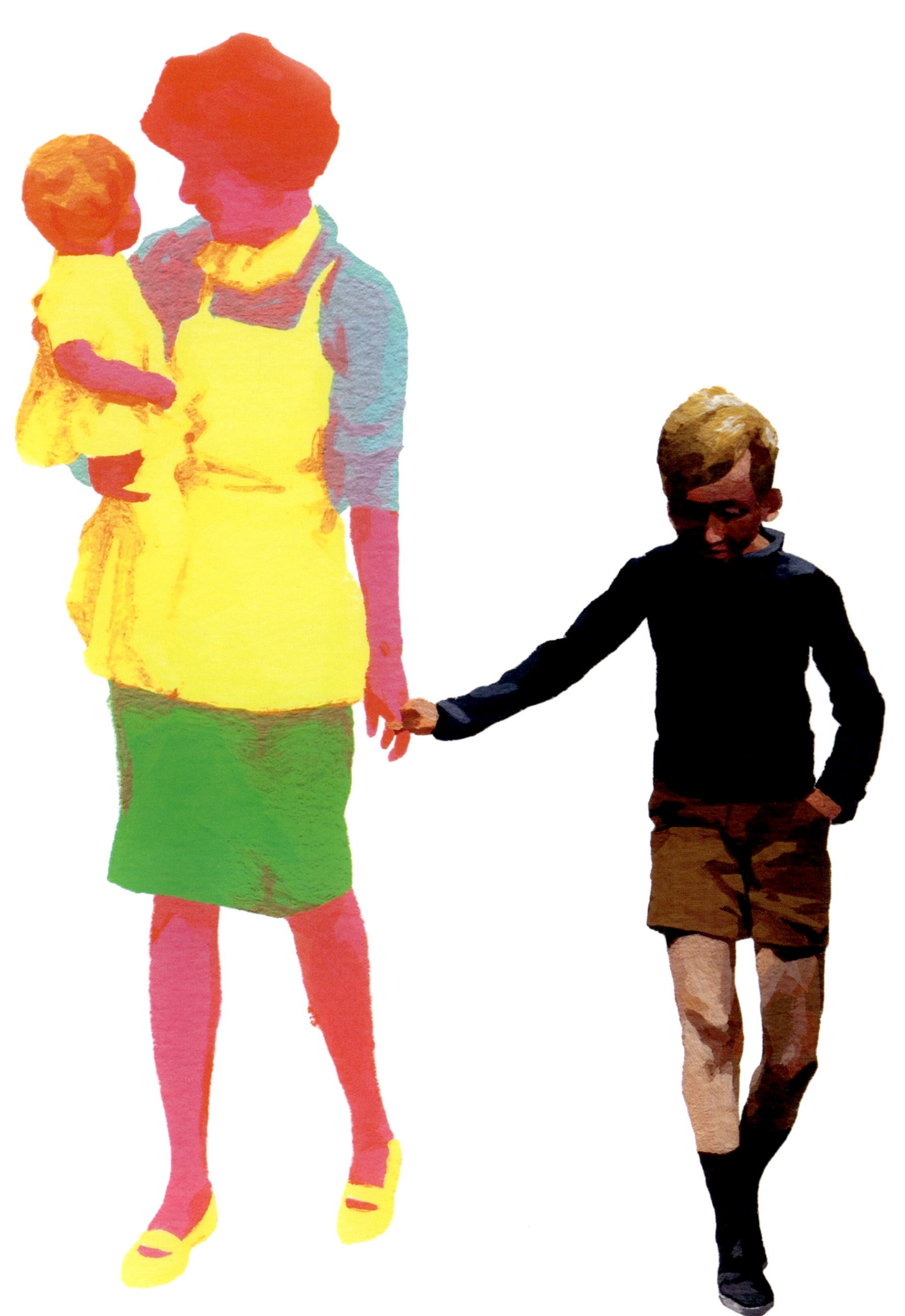

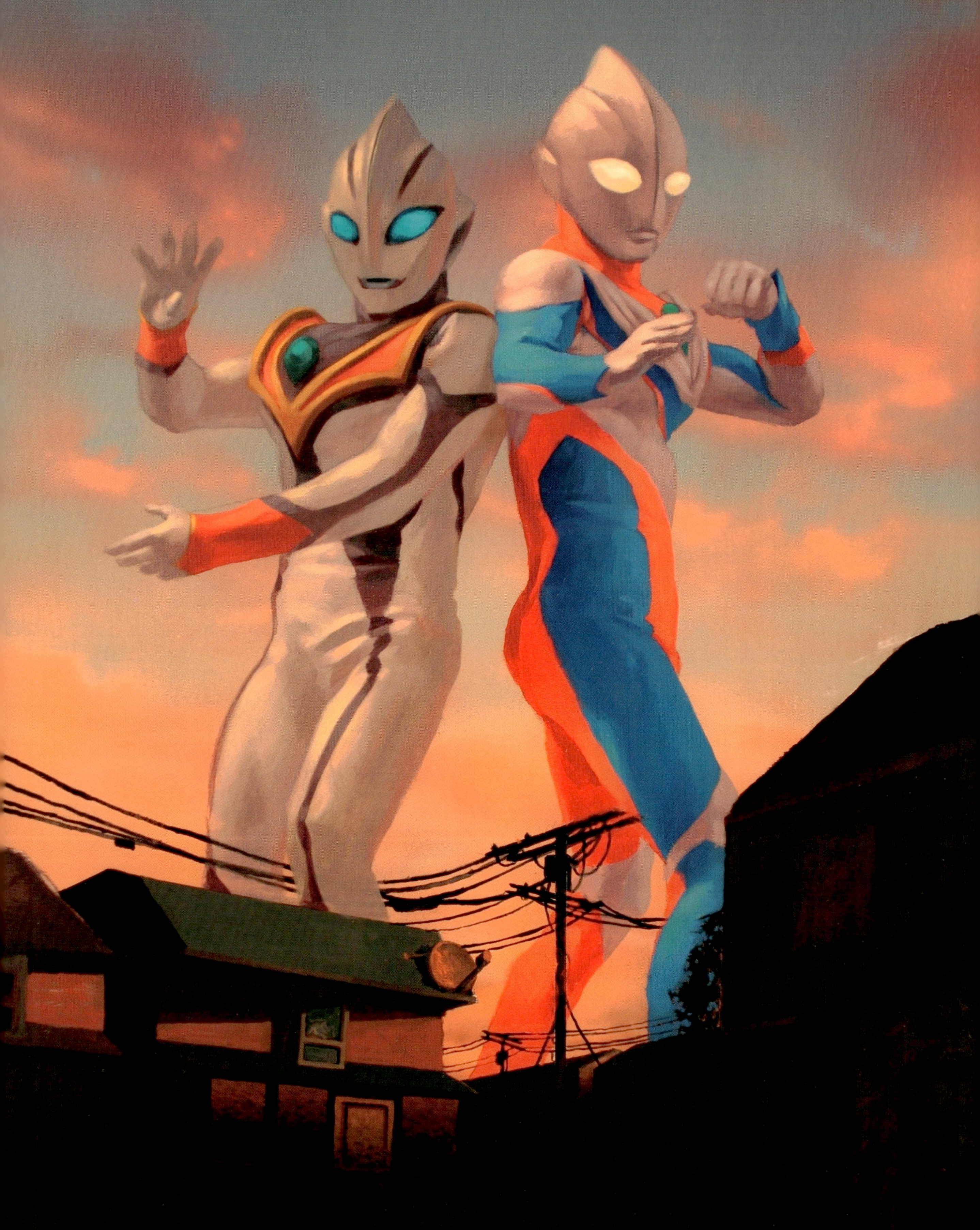

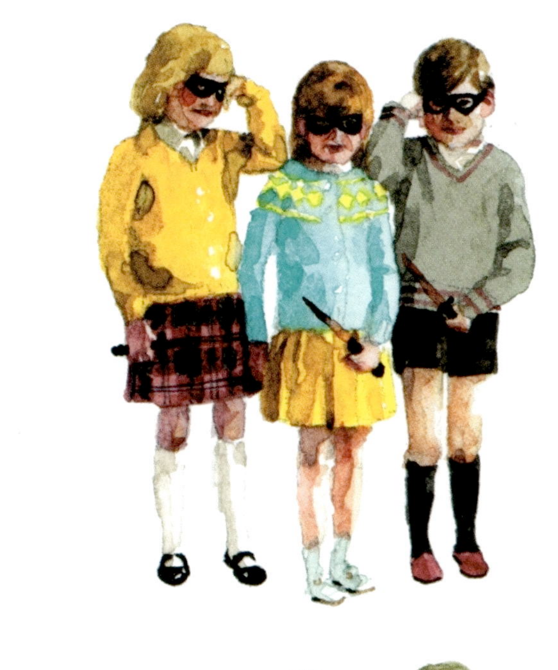

imperturbable little prodigies of
delightful, lovable goodness

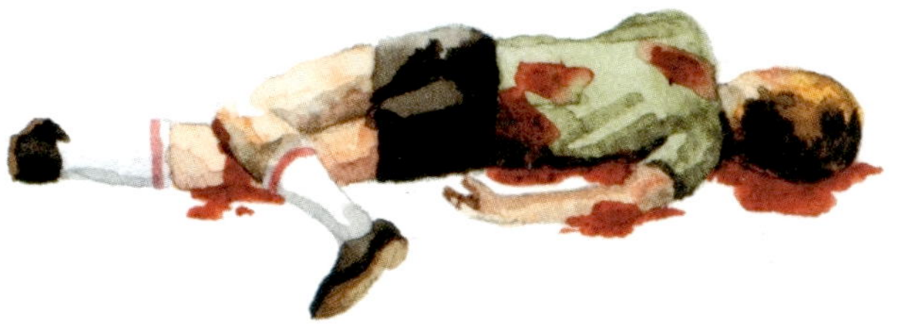

Little Prodigies 2008
Neighbourhood Watch 2010

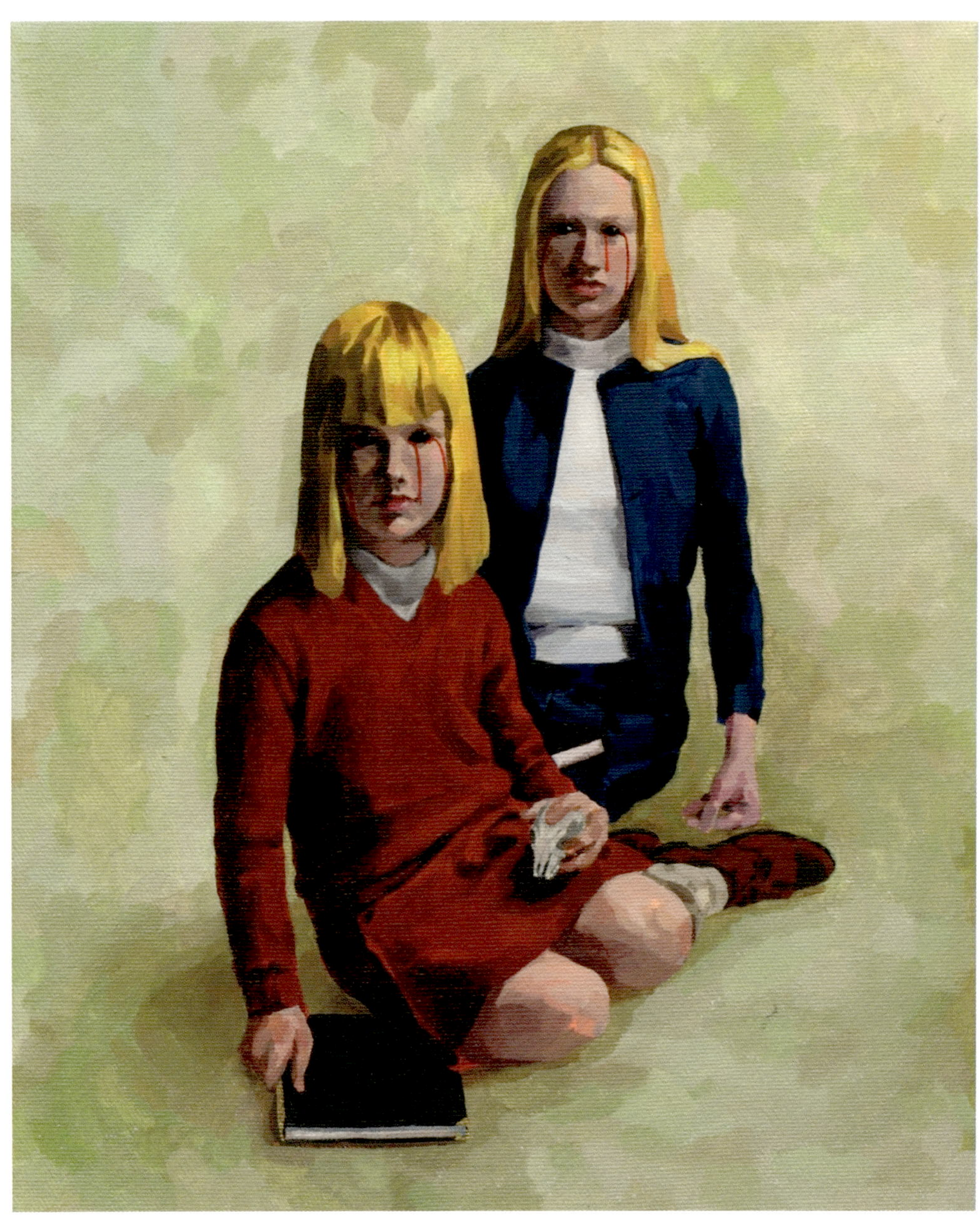

The Dunwich Sisters 2009
The Holy Mountain 2010

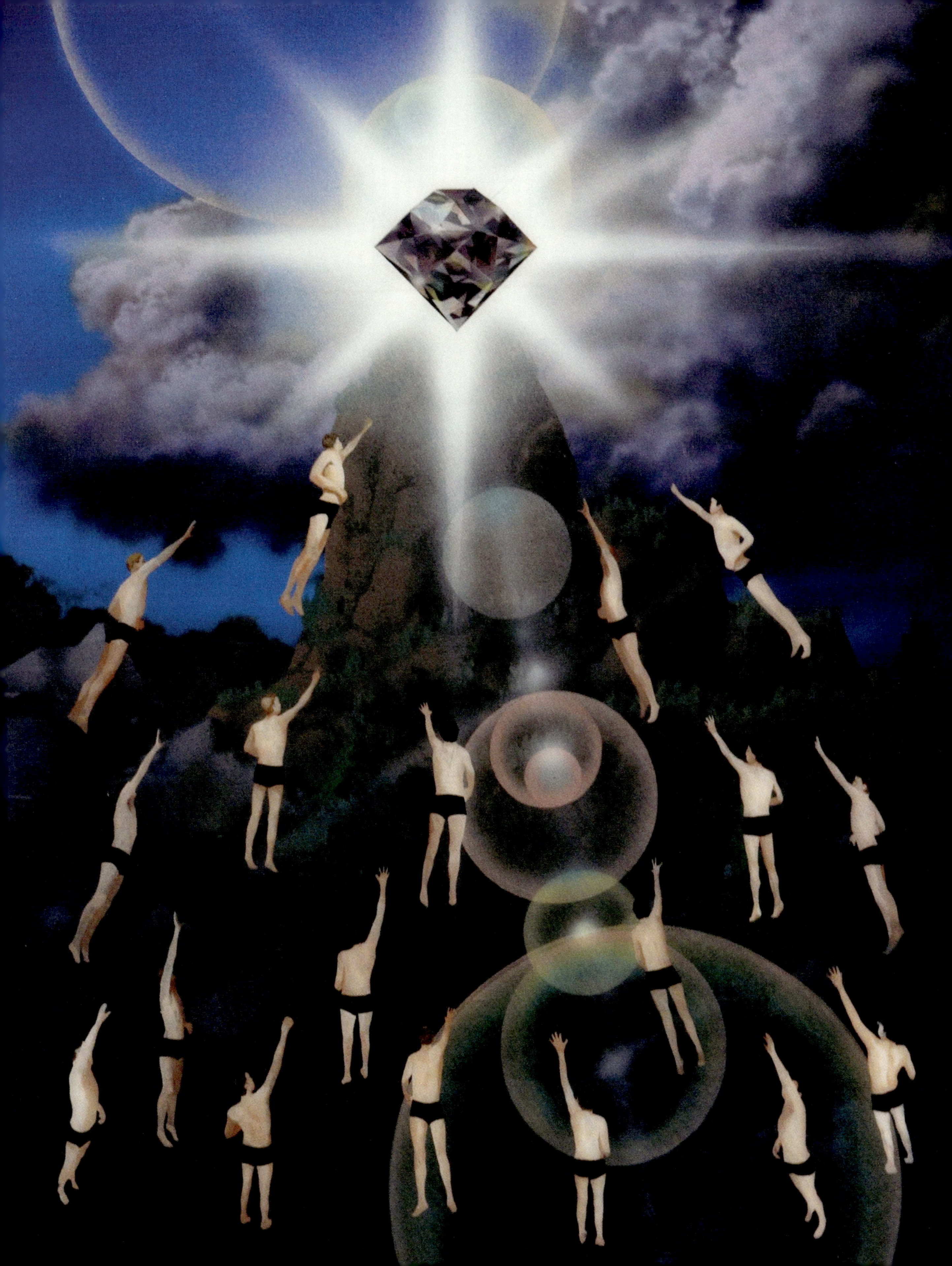

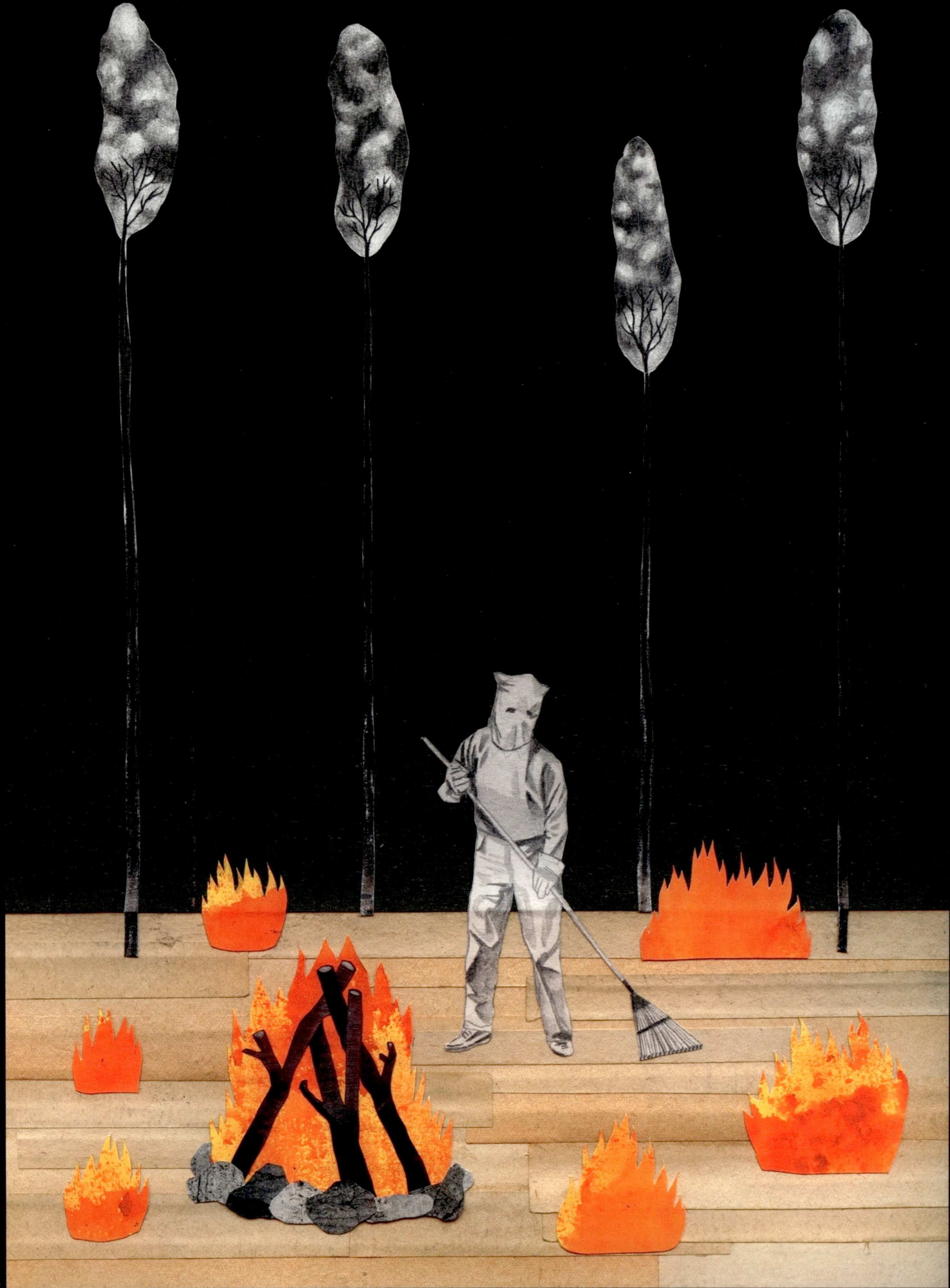

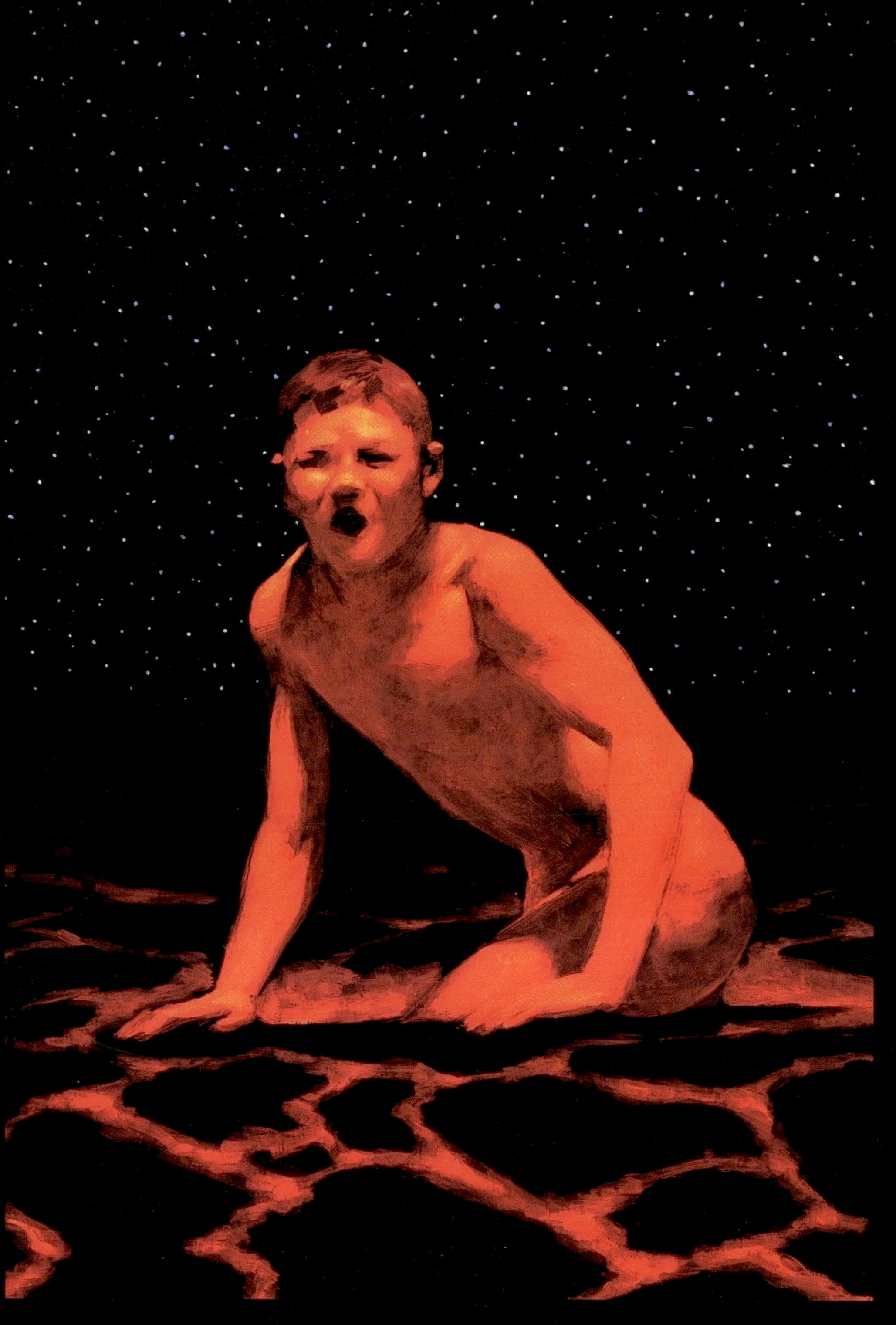

Harvest Time In The Fire Garden   2010
Good Old Fashioned Lava Boy   2010

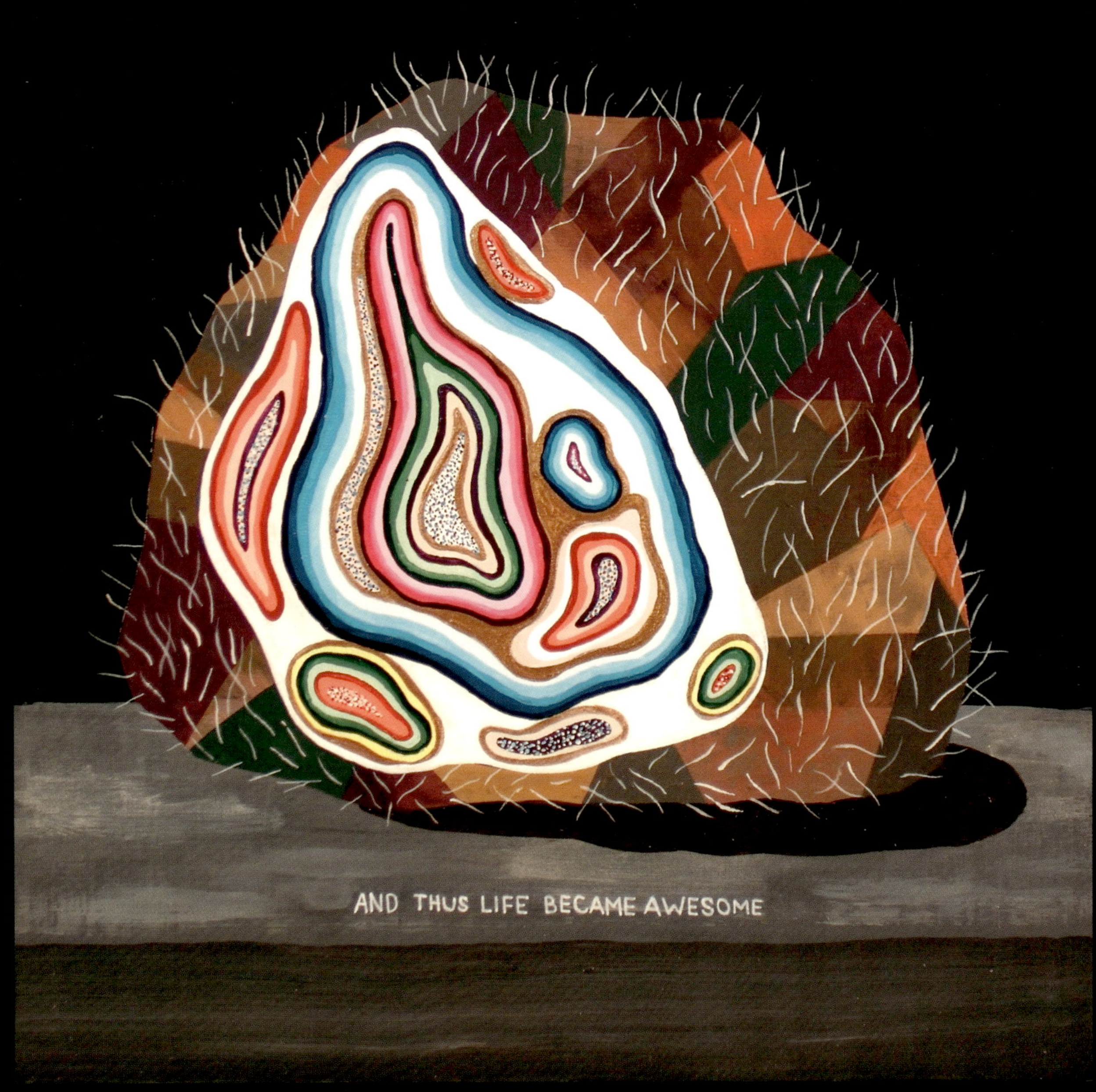

Geenius 2010a

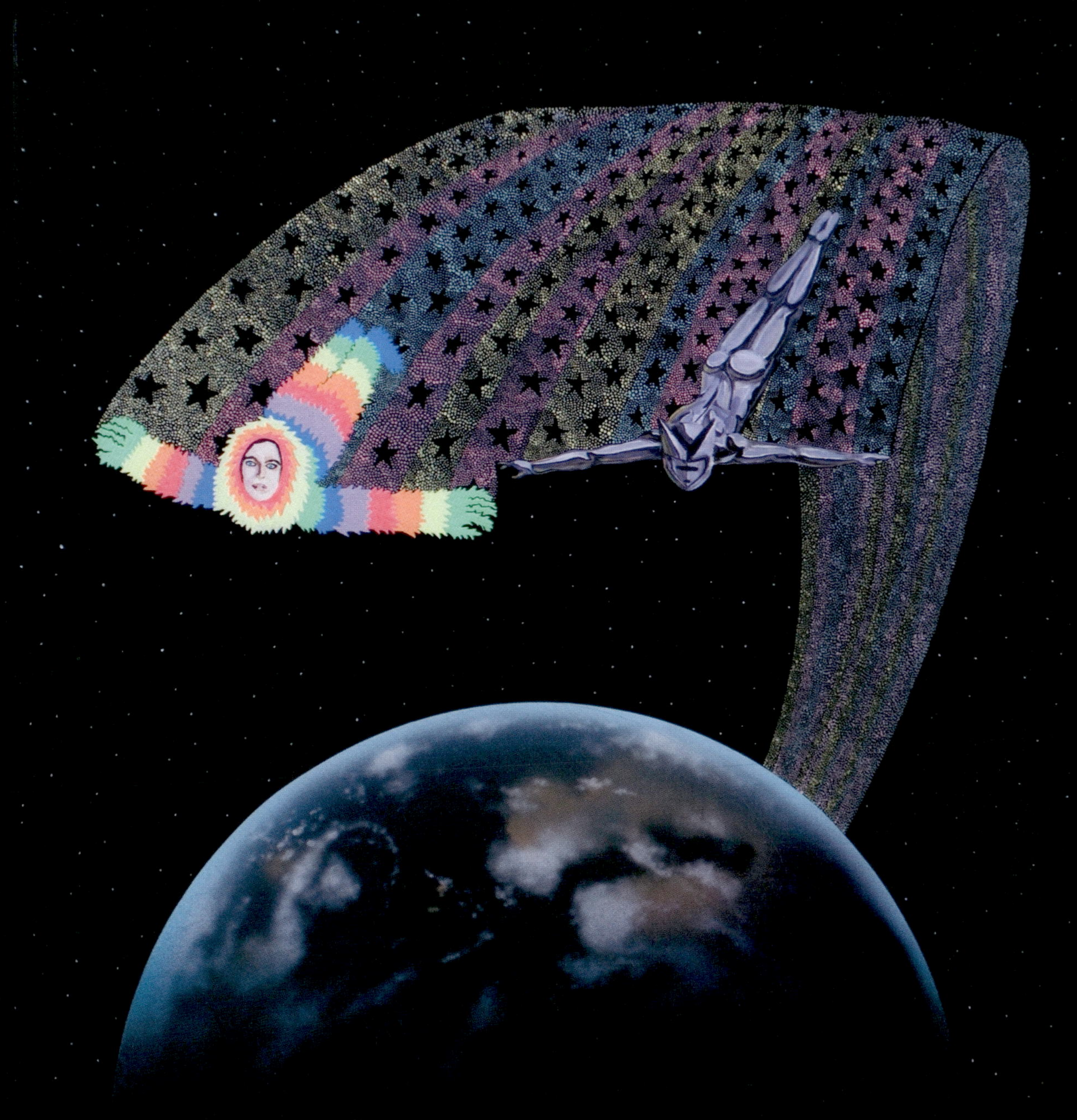
Star Search   2010

DEEP IN THE SHIRT YURT

An interview with Team Macho

by Maggie MacDonald

AGO, Jan 2012

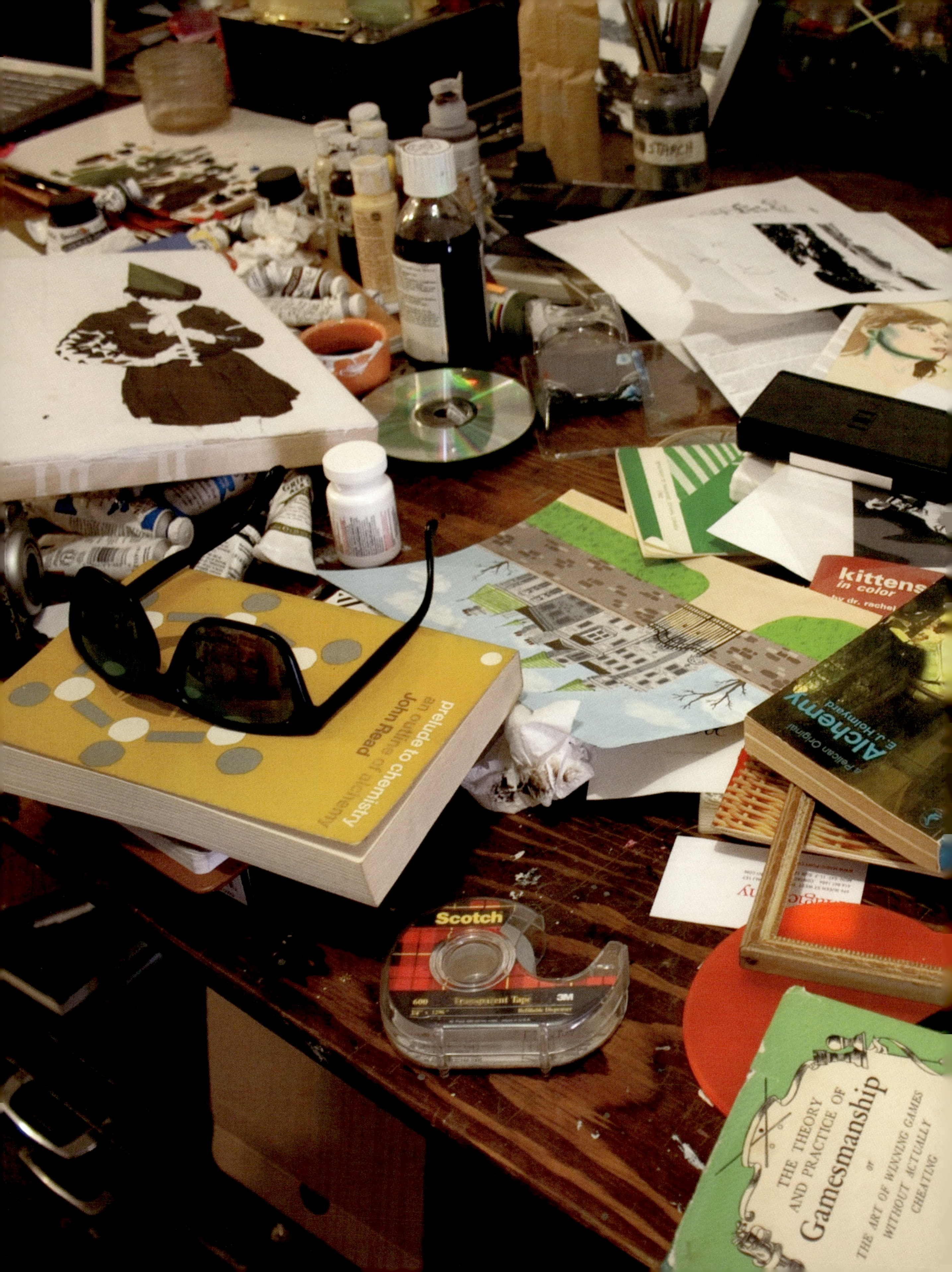
STARCH
prelude to chemistry
an outline of alchemy
John Read
kittens
in color
by dr. rachel
Alchemy
E. J. Holmyard
a Pelican Original
Scotch
600 Transparent Tape 3M
THE THEORY AND PRACTICE OF
Gamesmanship
or
THE ART OF WINNING GAMES
WITHOUT ACTUALLY
CHEATING

DEEP IN THE SHIRT YURT
An Interview with Team Macho

By Maggie MacDonald

I first met Stephen Appleby Barr at a Barcelona Pavilion show at the Rivoli in 2002, though he claims it was a Hidden Cameras show. Stephen was wearing a faded 'Cats' t-shirt and an ink-stained canvas bag with a small sketchbook that he would shamelessly pull out to draw in, mid-conversation, in any social setting. At the time Stephen was a Sheridan College illustration student, spending his school days as a member of a made up fraternity of four with fellow students Chris Buchan, Lauchie Reid and Nicholas Aoki. This fraternity blossomed into the art collective Team Macho, and acquired a fifth member, Jacob Whibley, who left the group in 2011.

We started our interview in the Weston Family Learning Centre Wing of the AGO, where Team Macho had been working all hours to install their new show.

M: To start, I want you to say your name, and where you are from originally.

L: I'm Lauchie Reid, I grew up in Thunder Bay, by way of Vancouver, or is it the other way around? Started in Vancouver, went to Thunder Bay.
C: My name is Chris Buchan, I was born in raised in the garden city, St Catharine's Ontario.
N: My name is Nicholas Aoki, I am from Cold Water Ontario. No adjective for the city of Coldwater.
S: Stephen Appleby Barr, born and raised in Toronto, summered in New Brunswick
L: [Laughs] that sounds real cool.
M: How did you guys all meet? I know you went to Oakville, but I'd like to know how you all met each other.
L: Stephen and I met in our first year, when the kid I was sitting next to, who turned out to be one of the worst people I've ever met,
C: Stephen?
L: No worse than Stephen, Stephen is a shining example compared to this douchebag. We were in our first class, and Stephen correctly answered a question that was asked to the class, and the guy sitting next to me turned around and said, "That guy. We befriend that guy. We take him down." And I was like, "I don't know, he seems like a bit of a douchebag but he's not that bad." So we started hanging around together, kind of begrudgingly. At first we didn't like each other at all, and that continued into our first year in illustration when we met Nick, who was at the time kind of a... he had a crazy hair cut and a really big hoodie, and we thought that was interesting. Stephen and I eventually moved in together, still hating each other, and that didn't fall off until halfway through school when we were like, "I think we actually like each other."

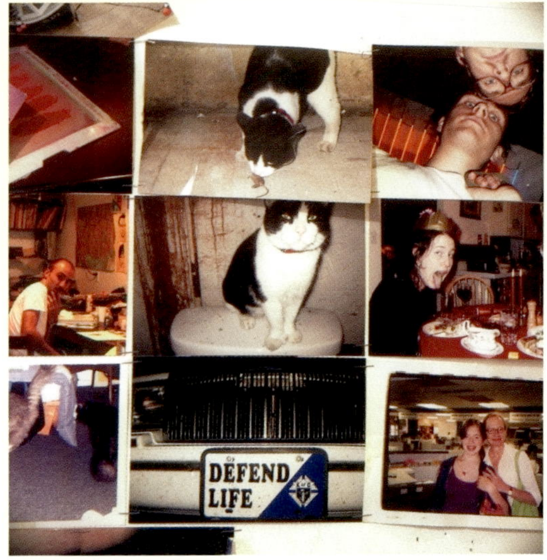

M: And you were all in the same year, in the illustration program, at Oakville?
L: Yeah, Buchan got held back a year. [All four laugh.]
C: Yeah,
L: No, he dropped out of the technical illustration program and then started with us in the interpretive. Then Nick, Stephen and I started hanging out together, and Stephen and I were living together, and then Nick moved in to that place with us. We all thought Buchan was a little bit of a weirdo, kinda really standoffish and strange.
S: Violent.
L: Then he ripped off one of Nick's ideas and we though "what an asshole," then his next project we saw and thought, "this is really good."

M: Were you all living together at that little bungalow?
L: No, Chris never lived with us in Oakville, but Nick and Stephen and I did.

M: At what point did living together become collaboration?
S: That happened in our second year We were already collaborating on critiquing and speaking about what work we were producing-
L: We did our homework together all the time.
S: We were the only people we could count on within the peer pool to speak in any way that wasn't generous back patting... we all sucked, everyone of us, everywhere, but we didn't feel that there was real discussion happening. We found our way into recognizing that discussion within each other and that was the first kind of collaboration we did with each other.

M: And this was 2001?
L: Probably 2002; 2004 was when we graduated, summer of 2002 was when Stephen and I started collaborating on the zines we used to do [about a mummy]. That's probably when we started hanging out with you, right around then.
M: I first met you in 2002. You were living in that Oakville bungalow, that funny place.
L: That serious place, that serious, sad place.
S: Very dark.
L: No furniture in that place.

M: That got me wondering when it became Team Macho. Was that in 2003?
L: 2004 probably, when we graduated we decided to start. Because we were trained in commercial art, we were trained to not collaborate, and go out for ourselves. We decided to start a little union, a firm, a little illustration firm where people could come to get any of the different kinds of illustration we each did. And we added Jacob into the mix because he was a designer and that would mean we could then take on any type of client that we wanted, in order to better serve client-based stuff. But then we found that we had no interest in actually getting clients or trying to get work.
S: It was kind of funny to put ourselves out there for client work when we were changing with every project... you can't build what was known then as an illustration career on that. And that was fine because we ended up connecting with Magic Pony and that was not only acceptable but encouraged.

M: Going back to this idea of a firm, were you drawing on the William Morris idea of a firm, like the one at Bloomsbury?
L: Yes, basically drawing on that idea of a 'house,' a stable,
S: An 'applied arts firm'
L: A union, like Grip Magazine, where Group of Seven started. We realized that the whole idea of going out there and sort of prostrating yourself at people's feet to get a drawing job took the joy out of it, and it just didn't work with what we wanted to do. So we basically hung out for a year and just drew, and we all had shitty jobs and we just worked those and drew in our spare time.
M: You were at a grocery store, Nick?
N: [to Lauchie] You were at Tim Horton's.
L: No, that was before.
N: You were at Gwartzmans.
L: I was at Gwartzmans, the art store.

C: I worked multiple kitchen jobs and odd jobs.
N: [to Chris] And the cleaning supply store, over on--
C: --No, I applied there and I didn't get it.
L: There was the time you had two weeks as a grave robber and it didn't work out.
C: I thought it worked out. I made at least a hundred bucks.
L: Yeah, and you got that cool finger bone, the one we still

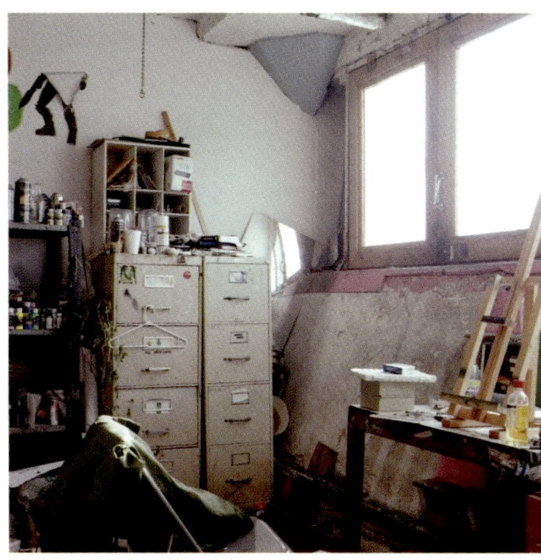

have in the studio. That's pretty cool.

M: At what point did it become official that you would be Team Macho?
C: We were still in school
L: It was just as we were about to graduate
N: No, I think it's probably when we made the move, to Toronto.
L: Yeah, that's when we were halfway through our third year and we were about to graduate, and we went and drew one day together, and we drew on each other's drawings, that was the moment it all just came about. Our drawings were these horrible horrible messes, but they were satisfyingly chaotic, and they had really nice back and forth in them. So we gave those to our drawing professor [Paul Dallas], and said 'we're thinking of making a thing out it.'
S: Was it ever part of the decision to call it Team Macho instead of our fraternity's name?
M: What was your fraternity called?
S: Gammatron.
L: Gammatron. We don't speak it aloud very often.
M: I remember Gammatron. When I first met you guys, you were Gammatron.
L: Gammatron was something that helped get us through

school, and get us through Oakville, because that place was
S: The invisible college. A college within the college. Your own college.
L: It was specific to the school thing.
S: It became a poisonous word.
L: Once we moved to Toronto, we decided to give ourselves a name that was less loaded.

Moving from Oakville to Toronto, and meeting artist and organizer Will Munro, were central to the development of Team Macho.

M: It seems like Team Macho was a rebellion against Oakville, against masculinity, treating it jokingly, "we're a bro team." So you had one foot in Oakville, which is very suburban, everyone is working in cars, having a car--
L: Very bro-ey too.

M: You had an education that was trying to separate you, turn you into competitors. And in Toronto, you had one foot in this queer positive milieu, going to Vazaleen, and working with Will Munro [making posters and flyers for his club nights]. I was wondering about Team Macho as a transition between those worlds.
S: I met you at a Hidden Cameras concert. That was the first queer folk music concert I went to. Then closely after that we went to Will's subway party, which terminated at Remington's. I later got a door job [at one of Will's club nights], and I think Lauchie worked it as well. There are all sorts of Toronto's you can have. The one I grew up in was not the one I returned to after school, that one being the "Queer West" scene, which wasn't even there yet, but was growing rapidly. Everyone was playing with different identities, and taking an identity and completely flipping it on its head, like Ladyfag, or Rage and Paine, and all these people were taking one concept of femininity/masculinity, completely train wrecking it, and coming out the other side with something beautiful and proudly new. And Vazaleen was a hotbed for that kind of attitude, and that was the first thing we got when we came back to Toronto. So we thought it was normal.

M: Who thought of the name 'Team Macho'?
C: I think I did.
N: Yeah, I think you did.
L: We've had this conversation a bunch of times. I know it was me, but Nick swears it was him.
S: I'll also swear it was Nick.
L: No, you used to swear it was me!

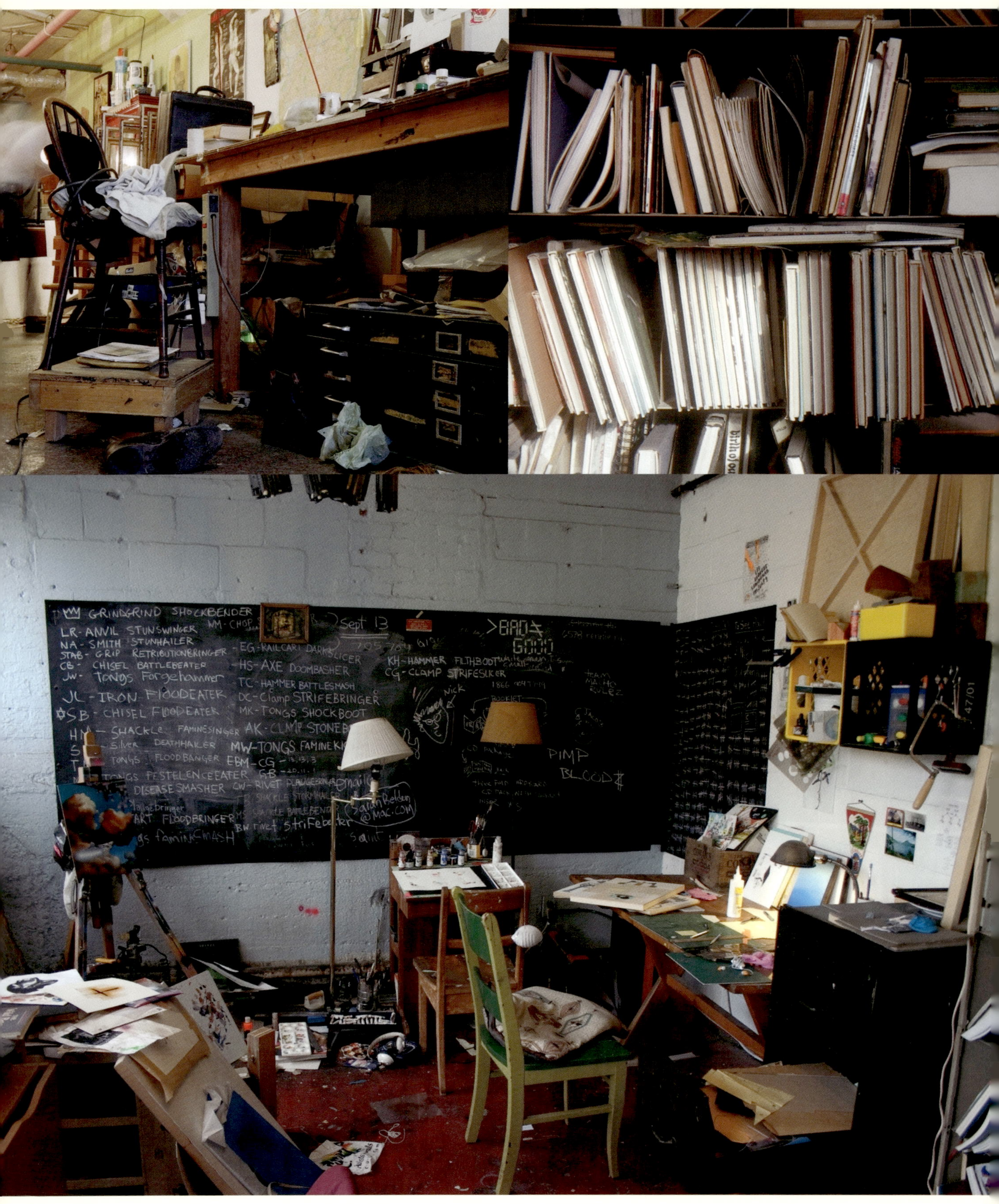

C: Now that I hear that, it might be Nick.
S: It was Nick.
N: If anything it was a Mad-Libs kind of thing.
S: You're the Mad-Libs.
N: There were 60 names we threw around,
L: Yeah, from the first drawings we did, there was also 'Desti-nation Excellencer,'
N: 'The Boyfriends.'
L: But going back to falling in to the queer positive scene, everything in Toronto that was interesting was tied into that scene at the time. It was this huge community, people were doing things. When we got out of Oakville, I was living with Shauna [now his spouse] at the time, and Stephen was going back and forth, and Will got us in at the building.

L: That we managed to get in all became part and parcel
S: It was a beautiful day
L: we started going to shows, it was the exact opposite of what we'd spent the last four years doing.
M: So who still lives together?
N: At this point it's me, Stephen and another artist, Nicholas Di Genova.
M: Is there still a tent?

Ever to my dismay, Stephen has been sleeping in an indoor tent since 2004.

S: The tent is exactly where it was. There's more bottles in it.
M: Oh my god.

I don't know what 'bottles' means, but having toured with male musicians in vans, I imagine the worst.

M: I know I promised I wouldn't bother you about it, but it's an interview, so I just had to ask.
C: He has the same sheets on his bed probably.
N: But you got new pillows.
S: And I got a new bed and put it on top of the old bed.
M: Oh my god.
S: But if you've seen any pictures of Francis Bacon's studio you can't give me shit.
L: But that's the most legendarily rotten place in history!
M: I don't care about him. Now, had you collaborated with any other people before collaborating with each other? Was that in any of your backgrounds?
S: No.

L: No. Like we said, the message at Sheridan was "you are going to be alone... Make sure you have friends here so you can catch up once a year between work..."

M: There is of course a stark contrast between the commercial practice of working alone, and being artists collaborating in a studio. This comes back to the distinction between being an illustrator and an artist, which one of you mentioned in a recent article about your AGO work.
S: I just meant there is a difference between what we do and being "successful" illustrators.
L: I don't know. I won a National Magazine Award. I'd say I'm a professional illustrator. We work twice a week for MacLean's. I'd say that we are illustrators.

(Several groans of protest and interjection are heard around the table)

S: I feel like illustrators work 5 days to 7 days a week.
L: If people produce drawn imagery to accompany text I'd say that they are illustrators. We are indeed that. We do other things to. But we do that.
C: Illustration pays for our studio. It's our bread and butter.
S: I wasn't deriding it as a profession at all.
N: Why don't you just lighten up about it?
S: I'm trying to.
L: Seriously man. You seem like you have a bit of an axe to grind with illustration. It's been pretty good to you.
C: It's starting to sound like you're a little bit anti-tanty.
L: I think you're being a bit anti-tanty right now.
S: Okay.
L: I think someone is getting a little bit too big for his britches over here. We're going to have to get him bigger britches so you can fill them with shit.
S: Or a moo-moo.

S: We find our way into most opportunities in this city in an ass backwards way.
L: Our first jobs came from our first art show.

M: I want to ask about that art show, and how you fell in with Kristin Weckworth, Steve Cober and Magic Pony. How did that come about?
S: We just hung out there a lot, throwing zines at them, and

desperately trying to make them like us because we liked what they did. It came from the zines, "here are some zines and some puppets I made, you have nice stuff that I can't afford" and then Kris would be like, "did you want to trade some things?" So we got some weird Japanese Finish magazines in exchange for our zines. It felt good to be accepted by people who were providing things that we weren't seeing anywhere else in the city. I don't recall how the art show came about.
L: Nick, it was Nick.
S: Oh it was? Nice work.
L: One day, Nick, remember you laid out a drawing and started drawing on it, and then you basically said, "anyone else want to draw on it?" and we did that original, the first group drawing—
C and S: With the carrots!
L: With the carrots across the top, and we did that over the course of the week. Then we went to Magic Pony with a handful of drawings and asked, "would you put this on your wall?" in 2005.

M: And this came about from hanging around the big table at 888 Dupont?
L: Yeah.

M: A little while ago Jacob left the group.

S: I don't want to do this.

M: How do you get through a break up? Collaboration, in my personal view, having been in bands, not an art team-

L: - but it's pretty similar.
M: it's very much like a relationship. It's like a group marriage, except you don't have sex, you have the work that you share and you work out tensions through the art.
L: and we don't have sex.
S: Fleetwood Mac.
L: We're not Fleetwood Mac!

M: Fleetwood Mac is the exception, but there is a reproductive tension, because you have these children together, art is like your kid, your creative process. This is something that I think about quite a lot, having been in quite a few bands, and been through band break ups, and we met in this scene that has

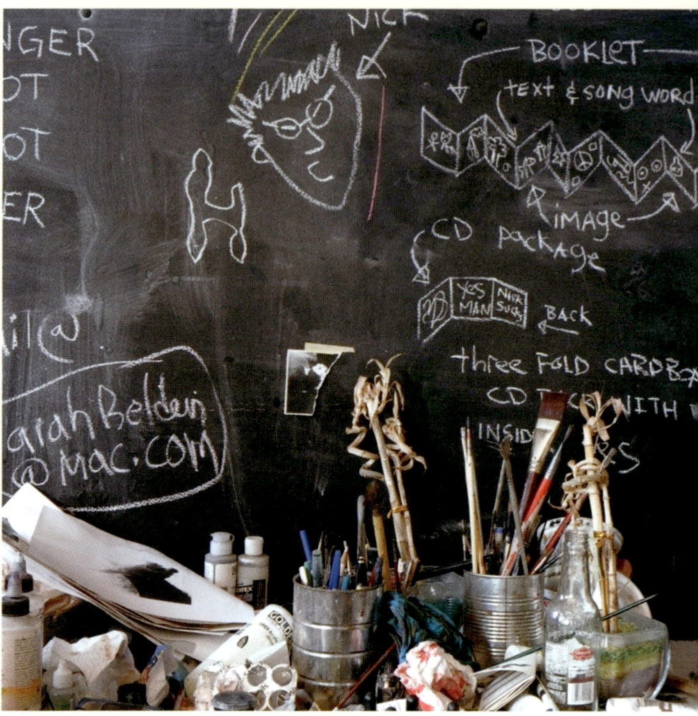

a lot of collaboration. One of the things that's unique about Toronto, compared to a city like New York where the rent is higher, so it's even more competitive, is that we have a lot more collaboration, and collaboration across disciplines. It's totally normal here for someone to have an art collective that works with a film maker, or with a party promoter like Will. I think that's something that is unique and fascinating, but it means that different relationship rules apply. It becomes less like a business relationship and more like a group marriage. How do you navigate, when it's not working out, and there is a departure or a break up? Is it like breaking up with a partner?
S: Kind of, in that you can tell when the relationship changes, when it clicks over into something else, and it's just not 'the thing' anymore. And who's to blame? It's just the way it is, and there is nothing wrong with that. You want to avoid it becoming corrosive, so it's best to be as direct as you can when that happens. Especially when it's more than two people.
L: And focuses shift. The metaphor of a marriage is accurate to a certain point, but it's less emotionally salient than that. In the literal aspect, techniques change, directions take on new meaning for different people. In Jacob's case, he took on a demanding job, in a field that he liked, with a lot of amazing potential and he had his own work that was becoming more of a drive for him, so he saw the sense in leaving before anything got acrimonious or weird.

S: When you look over Team Macho's work, his work is still very much in there, our work was very much a response to his work. That remains.

L: In a large way the fact that we work together can be considered 'the art' of what we do. The drawings and the paintings are the documents of the process of being together They're artifacts, created in the process of being together. To a large part, that's what that self-mythologizing is, we aim to make what can be a hard process more fun, more humorous, more glorified than it tends to literally be.

M: Could there be a Team Macho without 888 Dupont?
N: There could be now, but there would not have been, without that building.
L: We never could have existed without a studio that squalid and crazy to inform our own squalid craziness, but if it shifted out of there now... This installation at the AGO is about how hard it is to get space, how lucky we are to have it.

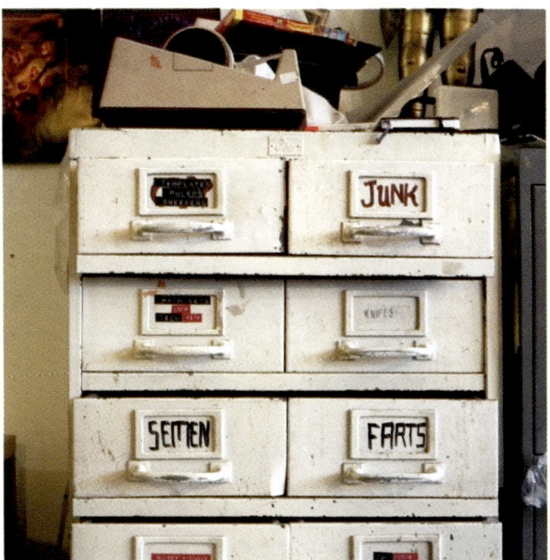

I started off by asking Lauchie Reid, who was the most talkative in the group interview, where he saw the future of the group.

L: We've never been ones to self promote to pursue anyone or hound anyone , convince anyone of our value. Through our hard work people have noticed and our opportunities are certainly becoming more exciting, more auspicious. So if the past is in any way an indication of how things might go, that's great. We are all a little more secure now, a little more stable. I am finally 30, so we are all finally in our thirties... Things have gotten pretty damn exciting, so I have to say I assume things are going to continue on the path and we are going to do our best to rise to any challenge we can.

Stephen Appleby Barr has recently had success as a solo artist. He seemed most surprised the question of what Team Macho's future might look like.
M: What do you see the future of the group as?
S: I have no idea. Which is not to say that I don't see something, or feel like there's something there to do, because there is. That's really the closest thing to an answer I can give, that I know there is something to do, because there is, and that it must happen. That's something to work forward to.
M: You're wide open.
S: Yes, definitely.
M: Your solo practice is quite different from what you do with the group, in terms of colour, its starkness. Do you see that as something that challenges your group work? Is it hard to balance?
S: When I am working on them no, but it's a question of an economy of time, and what can be done and what time is afforded. There have been times when I couldn't participate in Team Macho work because I had a show due. But the participation in Team Macho is excellent for my solo practice because I participate in research and get ideas. And the solo work is about the same themes, or actually, the solo work is about collectives.

M: Like the Royal Society work you did [a series of solo paintings called the Invisible College.]
S: Yes, it's about social tribalisms, within the larger society
there are all these groups that affiliate.
M: Your father was a labour organizer with the Steelwork-
ers Union. How did that affect your understanding? In your
household, the idea of a trade union would have been upheld
as something noble.
S: I didn't really know what that was! Obviously that's a left
leaning thing, [choosing not to preach to your children about
ideology.] They left it open for me to discover. I remember
asking, "What does left wing and right wing mean?" And they
wouldn't tell me. They said, "Yes, what does it mean?"
M: They wanted you to be free to figure that out.
S: Yes, and I am super grateful for that.
M: I had been wondering how growing up the son of a Steel-
workers organizer would have influenced you in working in a
collective, with an underlying solidarity.
S: I guess there were a lot of signs that said 'solidarity' around
the house, and buttons and stuff, but I think Lord of the Rings
has as much of an effect on how I think of the group.
M: Do you see the choice of doing things collectively, rather
than just having a solo practice, as having a larger social
meaning? Or is it just to make good art?
S: Yes and yes. The goal is to make good art and to have an

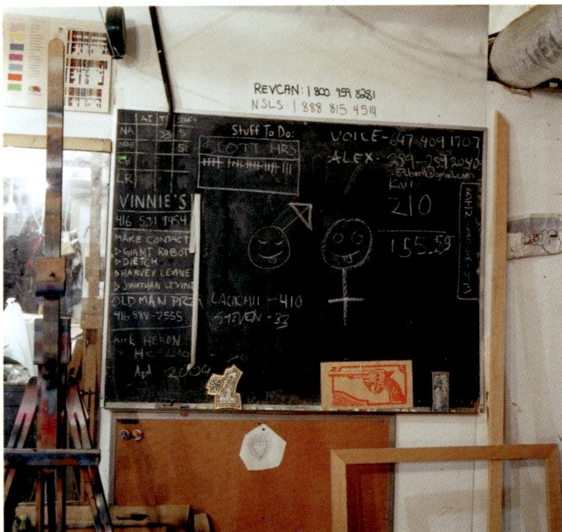

opportunity to do things in an unexpected way.

**Nicholas Aoki was fairly quiet in the group discussion, but
once inside the t-shirt tent, he became philosophical and had
a lot to say, about the purpose of art, and why there aren't any
girls in Team Macho.**

M: How is your own practice going for you, outside of the
work with Team Macho?
N: Not well [laughs].
M: Is it because you don't have enough time?
N: That's definitely part of it. I have a big problem with the
way I approach it
And the problem that I generally have is that if its something
that someone is already doing it, then don't bother because
its something that someone else is already exploring. The other problem that I am having at the moment is that because I
have become so interested in art, the practice of it, that I am
having a hard time figuring out what art does, what it is, why
I should be so interested in it. Why would I choose to do this
over something else? If it's a concept that I have, a series of
paintings or what not, the first question that I have is whether
its something that can be best done in the visual method, if
its not, maybe its best done via dialectical writing.... It's also
due to the fact that I have become really disillusioned with
modern art. I don't like any of it, I think a lot of it is missing
the mark. The role [of the visual] has been taken over by a lot
of new media and they do it much better. So what is it that
this media [drawing and painting] still does that is unique? I
can name a lot of things that the visual image can do much,
and I can think of how art fits into the overall leviathan of
culture; it is the eye of it. It is the only visual representation
of thoughts you that can possibly get, in the straight sense of
it. You can think of sight as being the eye's ability to gage light
but in the brain there's no light going in, there's no image. If
you see something you have to filter it through. You're dealing
with it within the level of thoughts, and those have no shape
or form. That's why the [drawings] are interesting, because at
no point do you look at a drawing, even if it's just a represen-
tational drawing, and think that that is anything other than
a drawing, it's symbolic. For instance a drawing of a statue;
that's not a specific statue, that's just a statue on a field,
whereas in the photograph you know that it is something that
already exists in the world. In the visual image, it's within that
realm of thought, it's in that nonspace, the aether if you will.
M: Getting beyond the realm of the real.
N: And at no point is any image that you compose going to

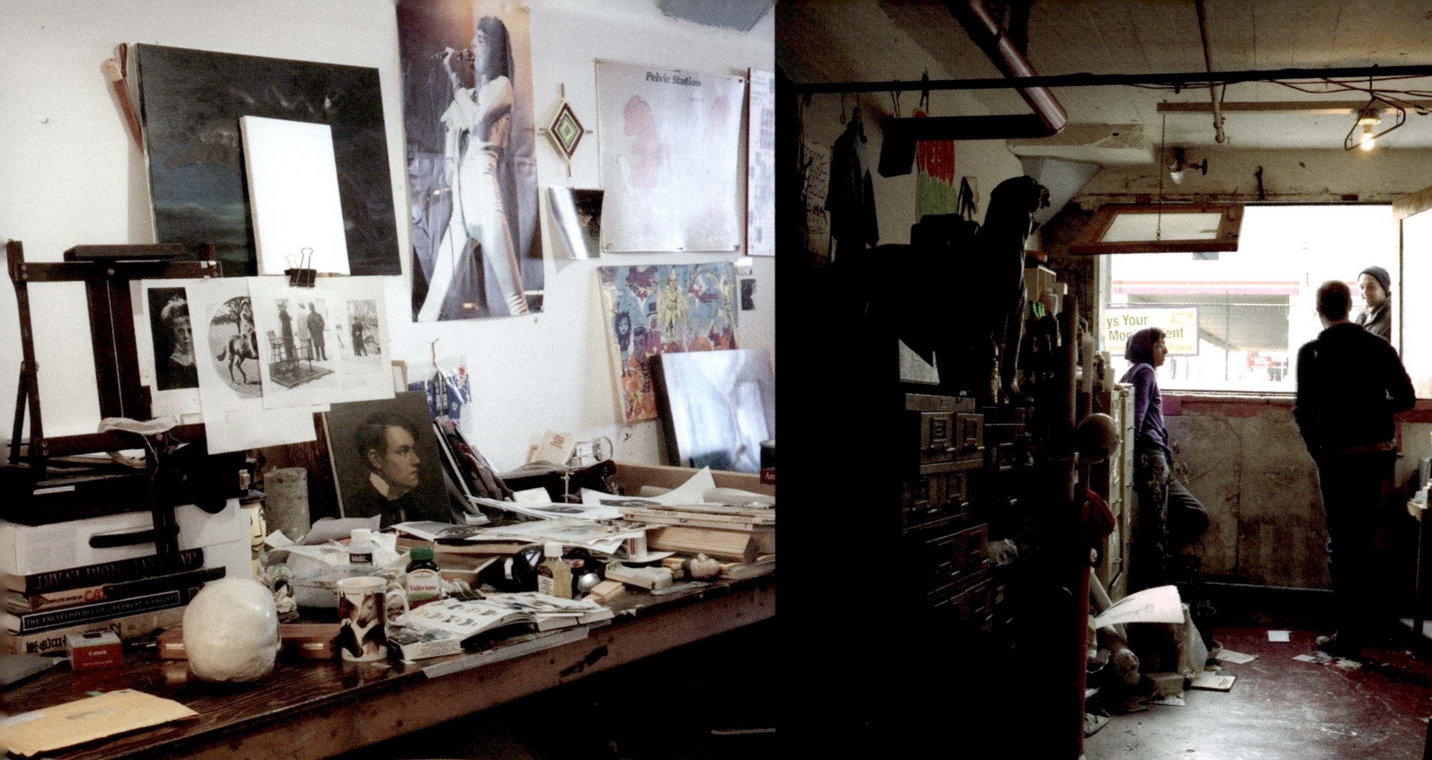

be considered unbelievable, or 'not fact.' It's already in that realm but you choose to believe it. Like if you do a flying cat, you're not like "cat's don't fly." You choose to accept those images. So how do you use that to best advantage, without crossing over to a territory that's best handled by another medium?

M: Your work is accessible. A person without an arts education can have a point of entry, it's not just for people from arts world, in contrast to some conceptual work.
N: If you are going to make art, it needs to be accessible. Art for the art world is ridiculous. Art has never been dictated by a specialized community. It has to be accepted by the general populace first. Generally art works have more effect on someone who is not part of the art world, it can change their life. They can freak out [laughs.]

M: Like Cameron Fry staring at the Seurat painting in Ferris Bueller's Day Off.
N: Absolutely. It can be an introduction to higher culture, not that what we do is higher culture. I think it is important to be accessible. If people aren't connecting with the artwork it doesn't matter if it exists or not. If you are making art for yourself, you don't need to show anybody. Just be ok with having it, and that's fine. If you make art specifically with the pure intent to be inaccessible...then you have missed the point of the visual image. And maybe you should look at the writing, perhaps write a treatise on it. That is something I like about the Group of Seven, they are very up front in their visual imagery, you know right away what its about.

M: Why no girls in Team Macho?
N: Girls could join team macho, if there were girls we knew for as long as we've known each other. But at this point no new people could join because its so bizarre, the weird shorthand we speak with each other, and there would probably be a sexual tension going on there because we are such 'manly men' [laughs.]

M: Where do you see the future of Team Macho going?
N: Ideally or where might it go?
M: When you close your eyes at night and you are having visions, aspirational or plausible, what do you see for the Team?
N: I hope that it might continue on in the same sort of fashion and we don't specialize too much in Team Machoness. My own hope is that we keep getting to do whatever it is that we want with the same sort of artistic anarchy. That would be nice. I hope that's the way it goes. And if people want to support us in doing that then that would be better, if not, I hope that we have enough art to continue on anyways.

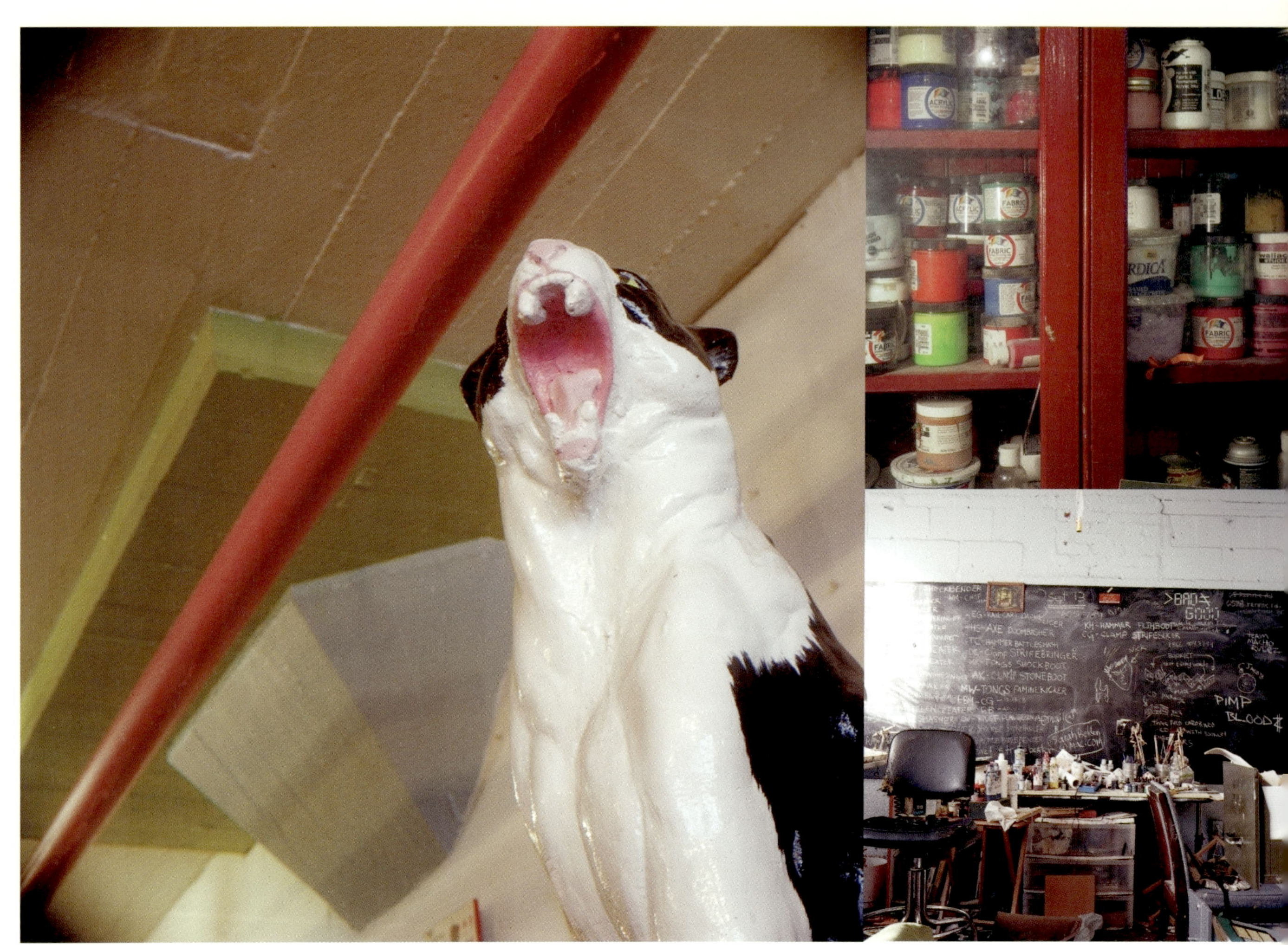

Chris Buchan's life outside of the collective is devoted to working in the community, rather than to a solo practice or teaching art. In 2011 he married his longtime partner, fellow artist Melinda Josie, and lost his mother to cancer. These changes in his personal life have left him introspective, and less attached to any particular outcome. It seemed fitting then, to finish the interview with Chris.

M: How do you feel your personal practice is going?
C: I am getting in tremendous shape...
M: Your technique?
C: Physically. I don't do much artwork outside of the group. I am probably the least active out of the four of us, in art. It doesn't rule my world the way it rules their world. I don't feel the need to constantly be creating. I do other things. I get bored really easily with stuff. Once I get good at something, I want to learn something else, gain a whole new skill set that will be useful. Not just art skills, but also life skills, challenging my body and challenging my mind in different ways.
M: What else are you working on? You are working out, what else are you doing out in the community?
C: I spend a lot of time swimming, and I spend a lot of time at my other job, which is at the YMCA. I am in charge of some aspects of swimming lessons there, lifeguarding, and dealing with families and children and other people who work there. When I started doing it, I really liked it. It's not something I want to stop doing. I am pursuing more work with them all the time. It's become a big part of my life, so I am going to keep it up. I am not going to stop this [Team Macho] stuff either.

M: Where do you see the future of Team Macho?
C: I have two different ideas, two different answers, and that all depends on where we go. One possibility would be us becoming more successful and following the same path [we are on now]. We seem to be just riding slowly up the hill and I think we'll continue that way. And I also think that it could very easily go in the other direction; a few of us split off and have extremely successful painting careers and then other people just kind of move into their lives. Maybe not lose contact, maybe we would still keep it together in a long distance way, but I think one or the other is going to happen and probably nothing in between.

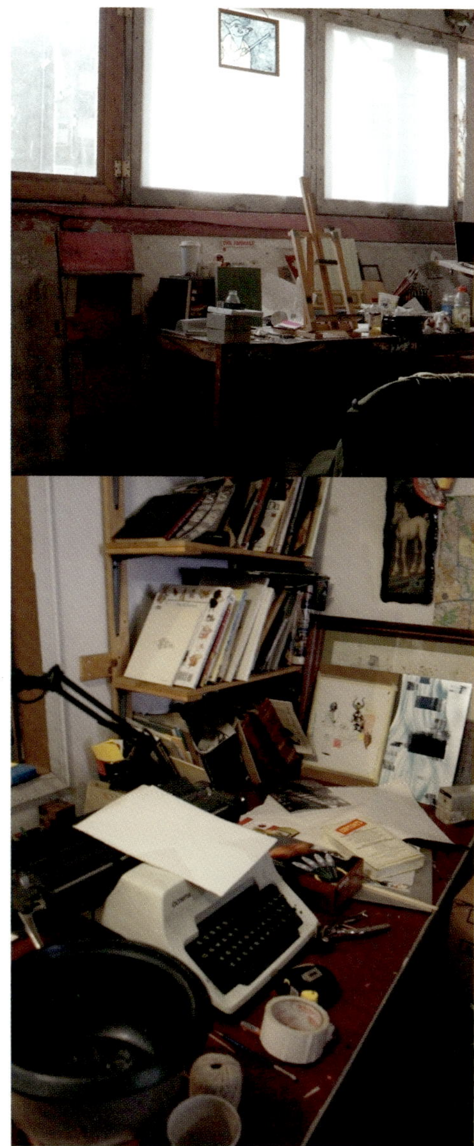

Being Macho
A Working Draft

by

A. James Bradley

appended and edited for publication by

Team Macho*

This could be cooler... "DONKEY PLAYING A SAXOPHONE" for example

BEING MACHO — A. JAMES BRADLEY
grammatically incorrect — should read "An James BRADLEY"   _MORE UP THIS!_

Intro

On the eve of Team Macho's first show at the AGO, I sit in the basement of the gallery watching the creation of their large-scale installation and wonder, how do four art-school kids end up here in this space that also houses Reubens's "Massacre of the Innocents"? How did they get here? During a walking tour of the gallery one of the guys is quick to point out how "really good" a set of paintings by Clarence Gagnon (a relatively unknown French Canadian impressionist) are, citing details about the technical virtuosity involved in creating his landscapes. Forever concerned with the process of art, their jaunts around the gallery are not meant to be leisurely. They may move slowly through the salons but their engagement with the art on the walls is frenetic; they hone their craft by consuming things like the variations in colour-use and consistency of the brushstrokes of the gallery's artists. For Team Macho this is a serious study and they deconstruct paintings in much the same way that a musician separates instruments in a radio mix: peice-by-piece, instrument-by-instrument.

Team Macho is rarely labeled serious. Read about them in any of their previous publications and you will hear about how witty and fun they are, how their work is an amalgam of illustration and painting, how they collectively undermine each other's offerings in a type of ego-destroying game, and how the everyday, when seen through their eyes, somehow becomes extraordinary. We are told this is what it means to be "Macho" in their world, which is all true. But what this description lacks is a description of what Team Macho does. The stylistic brushstrokes in much of their work are a challenge to the area of what constitutes art and how it is made. Their friendly spirit of competition is present in nearly all of their work: they brainstorm with friendly disagreements about most things, including who came up with the name Team Macho.   — _Nick did_

If there were a primer on Team Macho, the first thing it would tell you is that to pigeonhole them as a certain type of art collective is simply to miss the point of their work altogether. In general the consensus from the team is that they are always amazed by interpretations of their work because they don't know how to interpret it themselves. The second thing you should know about Team Macho is that they are working out of Queen St West in Toronto, where they show their art, it may appear that everyone is making art. The streets are filled with everything from ladies on the corner hawking what seems like paint-by-numbers dogs to galleries selling high-priced pieces. But while most of these people call themselves artists, Team Macho make their living as artists. To understand Team Macho, you must understand that their work is their life and their living. They have dedicated themselves to performing the act of mark-making, and their collective goal is to reveal the process of this endeavour, to demystify what it means to live a life dedicated to art, and to display both their mistakes and triumphs in front of a crowd.

Bear Wrestlers!   _Bear Wrestling!!_

This could be cooler...
"DONKEY PLAYING A SAXOPHONE" for example

BEING MACHO — A. JAMES BRADLEY

grammatically incorrect "AN JAMES BRADLEY"
should read

MORE OF THIS!

INSERT FROWNIE FACE FOR EMPHASIS

On the eve of Team Macho's first show at the AGO, I sit in the basement of the gallery watching the creation of their large-scale installation and wonder, how do four art-school kids end up here in this space that also houses Reubens's "Massacre of the Innocents"? How did they get here? During a 888 walking tour of the galleries one of the guys is quick to point out how "fucking good" a set of paintings by Clarence Gagnon (a relatively unknown French Canadian impressionist) are, citing details about the technical 888888888 virtuosity involved in creating his landscapes. Forever concerned with the process of art, their jaunts around the gallery are not meant to be leisurely. They may move slowly through the salons but their engagement with the art on the walls is frenetic; they hone their craft by consuming things like the variations in color-use and consistency of the brushstrokes of the gallery's artists. For Team Macho this is serious study and they deconstruct paintings in much the same way that a musician separates instruments in a radio mix: piece-by-piece and moment-by-moment.

THAT'S WHAT HE SAID

This part should be exactly like this but backwards

↳ replace with hyphen

Team Macho is rarely labeled serious. Read about them in any of their previous publications and you will hear about how witty and fun they are, how their work is an amalgam of illustration and painting; how they collectively undermine each other's offerings in a type of ego-destroying game, and how the everyday, when seen through their eyes, somehow becomes extraordinary. We are told this is what it means to be "Macho" in their world. This is all true. But what this description lacks is a real sense of what Team Macho does. The slapstick brushstrokes in 888 most of their work are a challenge to the idea of what constitutes art and how it is made. Their trademark spirit of competition is present in nearly X all of their work: they brainstorm with friendly disagreements about most things, including who came up with the name Team Macho. — Lauchie — Nick did

If there were a primer on Team Macho, the first thing it would tell you is that to pigeonhole them as a certain type of art collective is simply to miss the point of their work altogether. In general, the consensus from the team is that they are always amazed by interpretations of their work because they don't know how to 8888888 interpret it themselves. The second thing you should know about Team Macho is that they are working artists. Around Queen St West in Toronto, where they show their art, it may appear that everyone is making art. The streets are filled with everything from ladies on the corner hawking 88 what seems like paint-by-number dogs to galleries selling 888888888 high-priced pieces. But while most of these people call themselves artists, Team Macho make their living as artists. To understand Team Macho, you must understand that their work is their life and their living. They have dedicated themselves to performing the act of mark-making, and their collective goal is to reveal the process of this endeavour, to demystify what it means to live a life dedicated to art, and to display both their mistakes and triumphs in front of a crowd.

on the corner of

Like this

— Bear Wrestlers!

Bear Wrestling!!

Often charged with being funny or base, ~~Team Macho does not present only the best of 88 what they make,~~ and, paradoxically, it's by overcoming their collective ego that this approach always produces their best. In general their work is not purely and 888 exercise in aesthetics, although walking around a Team Macho show you will overhear wild interpretation claiming that it is. The Team ill say outright that their work is not meantto be decoded, not intended to flummox or bamboozle their audience; they simply paint and draw, exposing what goes on inside their heads. But the public disagrees.

Team Macho have chosen to walk a differnt path, to live what they call the "Macho" lifestyle, which inevitably means that they are enamoured by the way other people live: things like new frying pans and home fixtures that work are simple pleasures that they have chosen to forge to be able to get to this point in their 88 career. In this part of their universe the word "Macho" is used ironically, inverting the expected notions of what people think they should be and how they should live. To experience this lifestyle one need only pay a visit to their downtown headquarters. Climbing through the basement window of their studio is like falling down the rabbit hole, and after five minutes among the machines one realizes that it is not an act, that Team Macho's secret lies in their everyday belief that art is about process, about form and content, about the ego-less pursuit of the interesting. And it is about sometimes staring at a painting to try to find out what's missing and someone crying aloud: "Lets just put some dicks in it." This is the story of being Macho.

PROCESS AS ~~B~~ART

In her essay Against Interpretation, Susan Sontag writes that "(n)one of us can ever retrieve that innocence before all theory when art knew no need to justify itself, when one did not ask of a work of art what it said because they knew (or thought they knew) what it did." If, as Sontag claims, an interpretation is now inescapable, then we must conclude that the philosophy of Team Macho is based on a type of anti-art. It is an attempt to return to artistic innocence before art had to be a certain way. This is a slippery slope for the gallery-goer, who wants to interpret, who feels that and picture of a baby with "dyke" written across her forehead in big black letters must be a comment on something. But for Team Macho this art is presented without an overt message and they take great pride in the myriad of explanations they have received over the years from the gallery-going public as to what their work means. In that particular piece, one member began the process by painting a charming watercolour of a smiling infant and then passed it on to another to finish. This is when "dyke" got scrawled across her forehead. And then they laughed. In this particular work there are no subtle clues that allude to the baby identifying as gay, which are often missed because of initial outrage. The process that is demonstrated in a painting like this is both an act of creation and destruction: the only intent is to ruin what was already done and in so doing to augment what has been made. In most cases the motivation for such an addition is humour.

Often charged with being funny or base, <u>Team Macho does not present only the best of what they make</u>, and, paradoxically, it's by overcoming their collective ego that this approach always produces their best. In general their work is not purely an 888 exercise in aesthetics, although walking around a Team Macho show you will overhear wild interpretations claiming that it is. The Team will say outright that their work is not meant to be decoded, not intended to flummox or bamboozle their audience; they simply paint and draw, exposing what goes on inside their heads. But the public disagrees.

Team Macho have chosen to walk a different path, to live what they call the "Macho" lifestyle, which inevitably 888888 means that they are enamoured by the way other people live: things like new frying pans and home fixtures that work are simple pleasures that they have chosen to forgo to be able to get to this point in their 88 career. In this part of their universe the word "Macho" is used ironically, inverting the expected notions of what people think they should be and how they should live. To experience this lifestyle one need only pay a visit to their downtown headquarters. Climbing through the basement window of their studio is like falling down the rabbit hole, and after five minutes among the machismo one realizes that it is not an act, that Team Macho's secret lies in their everyday belief that art is about process, about form and content, about the ego-less pursuit of the interesting. And, it is about sometimes 8888888 staring at a painting to try 88 to find out what's missing and someone crying aloud: "Lets just put some dicks in it." This is the story of being Macho.

PROCESS ASBART

In her essay Against Interpretation, Susan Sontag writes that "[n]one of us can ever retrieve that innocence before all theory when art knew no need to justify itself, when one did not ask of a work of art what it said because one knew (or thought one knew) what it did." If, as Sontag claims, 888 interpretation is now inescapable, then we must conclude that the philosophy of Team Macho is based on a type of anti-art. It is an attempt to return to artistic innocence before art had to be a certain way. This is a slippery slope for the gallery goer, who wants to interpret, who feels that any picture of a baby with "Dyke" written across her forehead in big block letters 888 must be a comment on something. But for Team Macho their art is presented without an overt message and they take great pride in 8888 the myriad of explanations they have received over the years from the gallery-going public as to what their work means. In that particular piece, one member began the process by painting a charming 88888888 watercolour of a smiling infant and then passed it on to another to finish. This is when "Dyke" got scrawled across her forehead. And then they laughed. In this particular work there are subtle clues that allude to the baby identifying as gay, which are often missed because of initial outrage. The process that is demonstrated in a painting like this is both an act of creation and destruction; the only intent is to ruin what was already done and in so doing to augment what has been made. In most cases the motivation for such an addition is humour.

Team Macho shies away from posturing. Their work can be both
funny and dark but is is always accessible, and their willingness
to fail in public helps the viewers to make sense of what they are
seeing. In another of my favourite paintings they have embedded
the deliberately ungrammatical text: "dear diary Today I ask my
father where babees com-form This is a drawing of his expination."
It ends up presenting and aesthetic of representation using lines and
text, making the actual picture secondary to the misspelled words
that do not seem to match the doodle-like 8 sketch that stands below
it Team Macho have their own language not unlike the text in the 8
"babees" painting. After years of working in such close proximity 88
they have a shorthand way of talking that borders on the 88888888888
unintelligible. Spending time with them is like being in the
presence of quadruplets who speak their own brand of Pig Latin so as
not to divulge their secrets to their mother. This is how they live,
work and operate--collectively--andtheir make of art reverberates
with thes fact in every piece. Their goal has always been to reveal
the process, to paint in public, and to externalize the 8 grind of
making art. Spending years learning the grammar of the brush and 888
then producing some of the finest paintings around does not mean
that they must always create art using the same methods. Theuy are
constantly trying to unlearn 8 what they know, to push the boundaries
of their work, and to reclaim their innocence and playfulness in
regards to art. FREDDY MERCURY that

"He she has learned what is commonly considered the whole
art of painting, that is, the art of representing any
natural object faithfully, has done little or nothing, 888
as yet only learned the language by which his thoughts are
to be expressed He has done just as much toward being that
which we ought to respect as a great painter, as a man who
has learned how to express himself grammatically and 88
melodiously has toward being a great poet" (Ruskin, On
Painting 40).

Team Macho believes that to be great painters their art must challenge
challenge the idea of how to unlearn what they have been taught, that
the process of making art should not be privileged so as to be
hidden, and that the interpretation of art of this belongs in the
hands of the viewer.

As and example, their current installation, Axis Mundi, has a
large mural backdrop of a forest that has bright pink spots on it
standing ready for analysis. These marks have a special meaning for
the artist, but Team Macho simultaneously harbour excitement waiting
to see what they mean to everyone else. After the process of
transmission and reception concludes they always seem to find 88
humour in how wide the spectrum of interpretation that relates to
their work really is. The mythos that drives them is always
private and, in an ironc twist, their art seems to charm specifically
because their final products are approachable. Making theirprivates
amicable is what Team Macho does.

Team Macho shies away from posturing. Their work can be both funny and dark but it is always accessible, and their willingness to fail in public helps the viewers to make sense of what they are seeing. In another of my favourite paintings they have embedded the deliberately ungrammatical text: "Dear diary Today I ask my father where babees com form This is a drawing of his explnation." It ends up presenting an aesthetic of representation using lines and text, making the actual picture secondary to the misspelled words that do not seem to match the doodle-like sketch that stands below it. Team Macho have their own language not unlike the text in the "babees" painting. After years of working in such close proximity they have a shorthand way of talking that borders on the unintelligible. Spending time with them is like being in the presence of quadruplets who speak their own brand of Pig Latin so as not to divulge their secrets to their mother. This is how they live, work and operate — collectively — and their brand of art reverberates with this fact in every piece. Their goal has always been to reveal the process, to paint in public, and to externalize the grind of making art. Spending years learning the grammar of the brush and then producing some of the finest paintings around does not mean that they must always create art using the same methods. They are constantly trying to unlearn what they know, to push the boundaries of their work, and to reclaim their innocence and playfulness in regards to art. Ruskin writes that

"He who has learned what is commonly considered the whole art of painting, that is, the art of representing any natural object faithfully, has as yet only learned the language by which his thoughts are to be expressed. He has done just as much toward being that which we ought to respect as a great painter, as a man who has learned how to express himself grammatically and melodiously has toward being a great poet" (Ruskin, On Painting 40).

Team Macho believes that to be great painters their art must challenge the idea of how to unlearn what they have been taught, that the process of making art should not be privileged so as to remain hidden, and that the interpretation of all of this belongs in the hands of the viewer.

As an example, their current installation, Axis Mundi, has a large mural backdrop of a forest that has bright pink spots on it standing ready for analysis. These marks have a special meaning for the artists, but Team Macho simultaneously harbour excitement waiting to see what they mean to everyone else. After the process of transmission and reception concludes they always seem to find humour in how wide the spectrum of interpretation that relates to their work really is. The mythos that drives them is always private and, in an ironic twist, their art seems to charm specifically because their final products are approachable. Making their privates amicable is what Team Macho does.

But in this process their artistic intentions are almost always
different from the meaning that the viewer extracts. This is one
of the things that draw people to Team Macho; their art is so
varied and seemingly disparate that publicly it is hard to dispute
and interpretation. In the same essay quoted above, Sontag makes
the statement that "art is seduction, not rape." When read this
statement, half of [illegible] Macho swore that their work was the former
and the other [illegible] swore it was the latter, and they they
laughed, the joke being that it is probably both.

SERIOUS ART

     What Team Macho understands collectively is that seious art
need not be filled with serious content. They often employ [illegible]
traditional painterly techniques to create works of the utmost
beauty and then playfully undermine the [illegible] entire endeavour by
including some subversive act. My favourite example is (The
Acrobats) from a recent show. It is a painting, done in oils on [illegible]
board, of a pyramid of acrobats, presented in painstaking detail
that looks more like a renaissance piece than a contemporary offering.
But, in usual Team Macho style, upon closer inspection the viewer
will notice that the leotards of the acrobats are crothless and that
their acrobatic members are all hanging out. A product of the team
mantra ("lets just put some dicks in it"), this painting appears to
be funny -- but for them it is not a joke. They want to put you in
a critical space in which you are forced to question what [illegible] you are
looking at, and then you [illegible]. Because of moves like [illegible], Team
Macho are often labeled as being jokesters, but they are [illegible] so much
more than that. What they do with their work is create a large
metaphorical gap to allow the viewers to engage with a piece of art
on their own terms." This is why the interpretations [illegible]
[illegible] of their work
are so varied. The edges of their metaphors are [illegible] - often
producing a humorous response because the content borders on the [illegible]
absurd - but their process allows something much more important than
humour. It allows room for interpretation, not solicited, rarely [illegible]
agreed upon, but always possible.

     Team Macho [illegible] different to each viewer
and in this way [illegible] connection to those who
seek out their work, often [illegible] and object and asking
their [illegible] patrons to consider that the painting may in fact be
looking at them. Viewers of the Acrobats engage the painting in the
usual way until they realise what is happening on the canvas and
their embarrassment becomes the new [illegible] dialogue. In this
way the painting is acting on the viewww [illegible] as the viewer's
interpretation [illegible] on the painting

THE MACHO INSTANT

     One final [illegible] thing to consider is that time as we usually
experience it in art is absent in Team Macho's work. The [illegible]
collaborative nature of their art means that each piece and each
contribution has a different axis of time, one in which every addition
marks [illegible] another instant of the narrative. Each work is about that
exact thing at that exact instant; it does not allude to the moment
before or the moment after, but is about right now. The right now [illegible]

But in this process their artistic intentions are almost always different from the meaning that the viewer extracts. This is one of the things that draw people to Team Macho; their art is so varied and seemingly disparate that publicly it is hard to dispute any interpretation. In the same essay quoted above, Sontag makes the statement that "Art is seduction, not rape." When read this statement, half of Team Macho swore that their work was the former and the other [illegible] half swore it was the latter, and then they laughed, the joke being that it is probably both.

SERIOUS ART

What Team Macho understands collectively is that serious art need not be filled with serious content. They often employ [illegible] traditional painterly techniques to create works of the utmost beauty and then playfully undermine the [illegible] entire endeavour by including some subversive act. My favourite example is (The [illegible] Acrobats from a recent show. It is a painting, done in oils on [illegible] board, of a pyramid of acrobats, presented in painstaking detail that looks more like a renaissance piece than a contemporary offering. But, in usual Team Macho style, upon closer inspection the viewer will notice that the leotards of the acrobats are crotchless and that their acrobatic members are all hanging out. A product of the team mantra ("lets just put some dicks in it"), this painting appears to be funny —but for them it is not a joke. They want to put you in a critical space in which you are forced to question what are you are looking at, and then you laugh. Because of moves like this, Team [illegible] Macho are often labeled as being jokesters, but they are [illegible] so much more than that. What they do with their work is create a large metaphorical gap to allow the viewers to engage with a piece of art on their own terms. "This is why the interpretations [illegible], [illegible]. of their work are so varied. The edges of their metaphors are wide — often producing a humorous response because the content borders on the [illegible] absurd — but their process allows something much more important than humour. It allows room for interpretation, not solicited, rarely [illegible] agreed upon, but always possible.

Team Macho paintings mean something different to each viewer and in this way deliver a sense of personal connection to those who seek out their work, often inverting subject and object and asking their [illegible] patrons to consider that the painting may in fact be looking at them. Viewers of The Acrobats engage the painting in the usual way until they realize [illegible] what is happening on the canvas and their embarrassment becomes the new [illegible] dialogue. In this way the painting is acting on the viewer, just as the viewer's interpretation acts on the painting.

THE MACHO INSTANT

One final [illegible] thing to consider is that time as we usually experience it in art is absent in Team Macho's work. The [illegible] collaborative nature of their art means that each piece and each contribution has a different axis of time, one in which every addition marks [illegible] another instant of the narrative. Each work is about that exact thing at that exact instant; it does not allude to the moment before or the moment after, but is about right now. The right now

before or the moment after, but is about right now. The right now
may be about Siamese robots and twenty-three 8888 toed cats, but it 8
is about those things in the moment they were imagined Collectively
they all seem to view this moment a little differently and their
contributions explain this, meaning that each work of art is a
collection of how they each individually see the moment, together
For Team Macho that moment is waht they are trying to show you It
is a way to challenge your expectations of them, including what the
word 8888888 "macho" means in relation to their work It is about
being in their world and about the exposure of the process that make
these four guys and 8888888 everyone who engages in the experience
of their art, Macho.

before or the moment after, but is about right now. The right now may be about Siamese robots and twenty-three 8888 toed cats, but it 8 is about those things in the moment they were imagined. Collectively they all seem to view this moment a little differently and their contributions explain this, meaning that each work of art is a collection of how they each individually see the moment, together. For Team Macho that moment is what they are trying to show you. It 8 is a way to challenge your expectations of them, including what the word "8888888 "macho" means in relation to their work. It is about being in their world and about the exposure of the process that makes these four guys, and 88888888 everyone who engages in the experience of their art, Macho.

NOPE

Yes

WHAT?

Sure

WHO?

MOVE THIS WORD OVER TO THE LEFT SIX SPACES

DEBATABLE

We're so sorry

Charges PENDING!

mostly meghborhood kids and unwilling friends

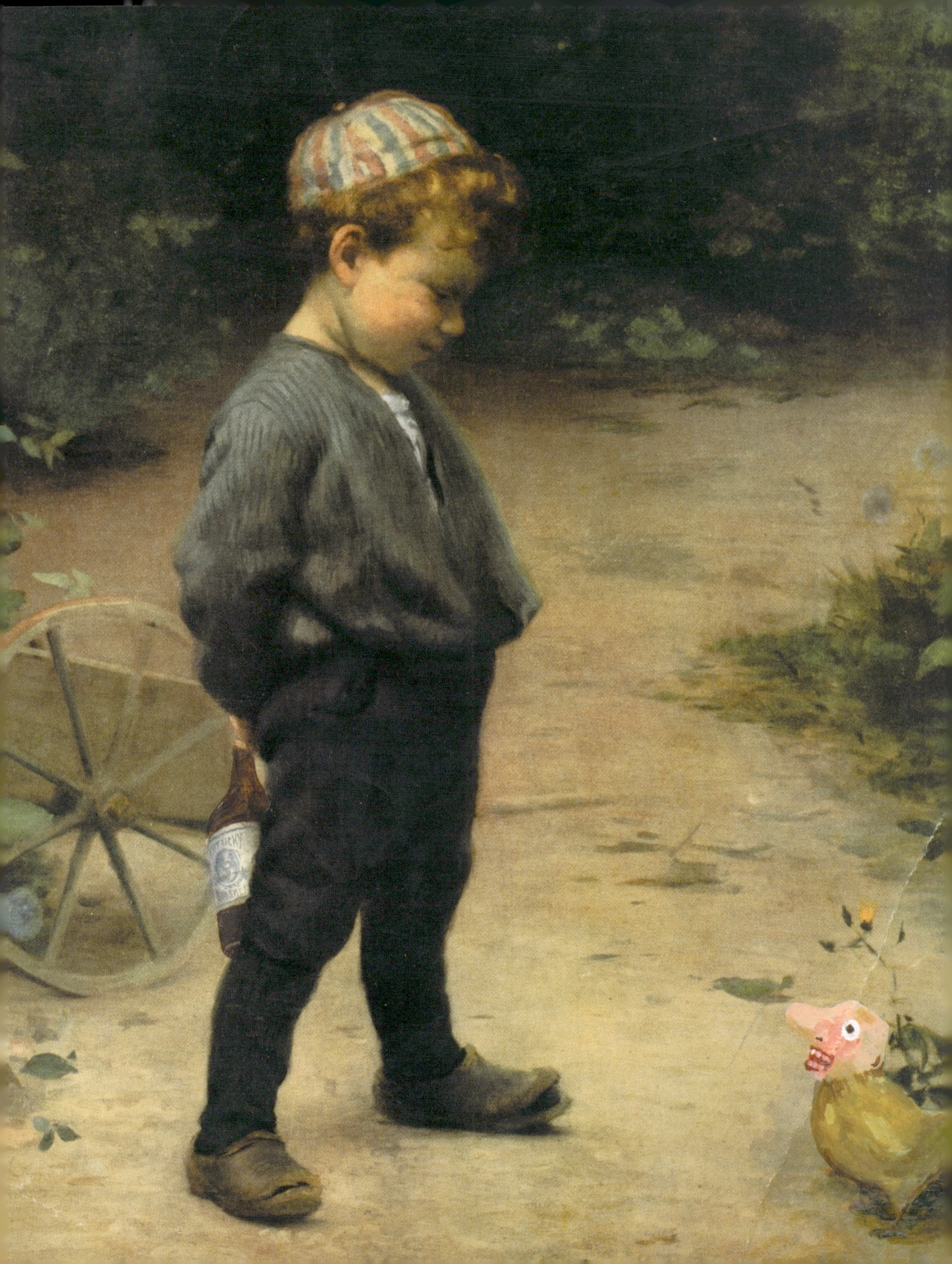

ACKNOWLEDGEMENTS

Team Macho would like to thank:

Jacob Whibley, Each other, Shauna Kushner, Melinda Josie, Steve Cober and Kristin Weckworth,
Ann Marie Peña, A. James Bradley, Maggie MacDonald, Richelle Forsey, Jessica Palmer, Lesley Ashton,
"Fuckin" Johnson, Heather, Tina, Corrie, and everyone at the AGO, Paul Dallas, Paul Tjepkema, Scott
Leeming, Derrick Guerin, Anne Koyama, Jackie Musial, Pedro "Busy P" Winter, Optica, Sid Lee, Giant
Robot and Mark Gilson, and our wonderful and supportive collectors and patrons.

This book is dedicated to the memories of Will Munro, Punchy, Bob Whibley, and Charlene Buchan;
Beautiful animals who we miss dearly.

CONTRIBUTORS

A. James Bradley

A. James Bradley is currently pursuing his PhD in English at the University of Waterloo. He has been known to
carouse from time to time with Team Macho, engaging and usually losing at games of chance like drinking gin
and political debate. He currently holds the coveted Team Macho table tennis championship belt.

Maggie MacDonald

Maggie MacDonald is an award-winning playwright, well-traveled musician, and author of the illustrated novel *Kill The
Robot* (McGilligan, 2005). Maggie's non-fiction writing has appeared in The Globe and Mail, Broken Pencil, THIS Magazine, and Shameless, and her short film *You Can't Wear Suede in the Rain* was screened at the Ottawa Internal Film Festival
in 2011. In 2012, her musical *Paper Laced With Gold* will be staged as part of a Harbourfront Centre HATCH residency;
her first musical *The Rat King*, co-directed with Stephanie Markowitz, was staged in Toronto in 2006, and in New York at
the Lucille Lortel Theatre in 2007.

Ann Marie Peña

Originally from Toronto, Ann Marie Peña runs the Artist in Residence program at the Art Gallery of Ontario.
She worked previously directing large-scale production and participatory projects as Studio Manager for artist
Yinka Shonibare MBE, in London, UK and has taught at the University of the Arts London, where she also obtained
an MA in Visual Arts from Central Saint Martins College of Art and Design.